With a Book in Their Hands

With a Book in Their Hands

CHICANO/A READERS AND
READERSHIPS ACROSS THE CENTURIES

EDITED BY

Manuel M. Martín-Rodríguez

University of New Mexico Press • Albuquerque

Library of Congress Cataloging-in-Publication Data

With a book in their hands : Chicano/a readers and readerships across the centuries / edited by
Manuel M. Martín-Rodríguez.
p. cm.
Includes index.
ISBN 978-0-8263-5476-1 (cloth : alk. paper) — ISBN 978-0-8263-5477-8 (electronic).
1. Mexican American authors—Books and reading. 2. American literature—Mexican
American authors—History and criticism. 3. Mexican Americans—Books and reading.
4. Books and reading—United States. 5. Book collecting—United States. I. Martín-Rodríguez,
Manuel M. editor of compilation.
Z1039.M5W58 2014
028'.9—dc23
2013048361

Cover and interior design by Catherine Leonardo
Composed in Minion Pro 10.25/13.5
Display type is Adobe Garamond Pro and Univers LT Std

For my parents, who instilled in all of us the love of reading.

For Virginia, Diego, and Alberto. They know why.

Contents

Acknowledgments

First of all, I would like to thank all of the contributors for making this book possible and for sharing these amazing stories. I also want to thank Carolina Valero and Lucía de Anda Vázquez for their work on the Chicano/a Readers Oral Project, which has produced the oral interviews included in this volume.

I would like to express my gratitude as well to the two external reviewers for their comments and suggestions that have made this a better book. Thanks to Dr. Durwood Ball (editor of the *New Mexico Historical Review*) and to Michael Knoop (director of News Research and Archives at the *San Antonio Express-News*) for their kind permissions to reproduce materials for which they hold the copyright.

Last, but not least, my thanks to Elise Muriel McHugh, senior acquisitions editor for the University of New Mexico Press, for her faith in and continuous support for this project. The team of editors at the press have also been of great help along the way.

Introduction

Manuel M. Martín-Rodríguez

Chicano/a literature has been the subject of many scholarly publications and debates that have tried to define its nature, main characteristics, and history. Most critics nowadays agree that Chicano/a literary history reaches well into a past that is still being rediscovered, as numerous unknown or forgotten texts are brought to light through the efforts of individuals and several collective recovery projects.[1] Even before this reclamation of the Chicano/a cultural past started, Luis Leal proposed in 1973 an influential periodization of Chicano/a literature that is still useful today, and that will help me structure the brief introduction that follows. Leal distinguished five stages, which he termed the Hispanic Period (lasting until 1821), the Mexican Period (1821–1848), the Transition Period (1848–1910), the Interaction Period (1910–1942), and the Chicano Period (1942 to the present).[2]

During the Hispanic period, the U.S. Southwest was the northernmost colony of the Spanish empire in the Americas. From 1539 to 1821, poems, chronicles, narratives, and plays were written, performed, and printed. Gaspar de Villagrá's 1610 lengthy poem *Historia de la nueva Mexico* (History of the new Mexico) stands out as the earliest published literary text of Chicano/a and U.S. literary history. As is the case with many other texts from the past, Villagrá's *Historia* has been recovered and embraced by critics and readers alike, thus signaling its continued currency for contemporary readerships.[3] This period also gave us Álvar Núñez Cabeza de Vaca's *Relación*

(*Account*, 1542), as well as some of the earliest forms of European theater in the Americas.[4]

After Mexico's independence from Spain in 1821, a brief period of Mexican literature in the Southwest began. Although this phase ended promptly with the signing of the Treaty of Guadalupe Hidalgo in 1848, scholars have been able to identify several printed works from this era, including Lorenzo de Zavala's *Viage a los Estados Unidos de América* (A trip to the United States of America, 1834), and the play *Los Texanos* (ca. 1832). Another significant development is the arrival of the printing press. In New Mexico, for instance, Ramón Abreu imported the first press in 1834. Father Antonio José Martínez bought the press from Abreu, and he began using it to print a newspaper, school books, and religious and political texts.

The Treaty of Guadalupe Hidalgo meant the annexation by the United States of California, New Mexico, Arizona, Nevada, Utah, and parts of Wyoming and Colorado, and the settlement of the Texas border at the Rio Grande. It also signaled the beginning of a Mexican American culture and literature, a more direct antecedent of contemporary Chicano/a literature. Despite inadequacies in scholarization and difficulties in accessing presses and other institutions of the literary establishment, Mexican American authors soon left their mark on the United States. María Amparo Ruiz de Burton, for example, was one of the first to write about the U.S. Civil War in her novel *Who Would Have Thought It?* (1872). She also published a play, *Don Quixote* (1876), based on Miguel de Cervantes's masterpiece, and a political novel denouncing injustices against the native Californios, *The Squatter and the Don* (1885). Literature in Spanish also flourished during this period, and although most of it is found in periodicals, several writers managed to publish their compositions in book form, for instance Eusebio Chacón (*El hijo de la tempestad. Tras la tormenta la calma* [The son of the tempest. Calm after the storm], 1892); Vicente Bernal (*Las primicias* [The first fruits], 1916); Felipe Maximiliano Chacón (*Poesía y prosa* [Poetry and prose], 1924); and the very prolific José Inés García, a bookseller and newspaper publisher who printed no fewer than ten of his books in his own shop in Trinidad, Colorado.

The literature from this period included almost every genre, from lyric poetry to autobiography, and several salient points are worth mentioning. The depiction of customs is one of them, as writers felt the need to preserve in print a way of life that they saw threatened by cultural and political changes. Personal and family history was also common in both creative and autobiographical narratives. Territorial New Mexican governor Miguel A.

Otero, for example, published three lengthy volumes retelling his life experiences from the nineteenth-century "Wild West" period to the days of his governorship, already in the twentieth century.

With the start of the Mexican Revolution in 1910, thousands of Mexican nationals (including many intellectuals) crossed the border to settle in the United States. Their presence revitalized existing Mexican American communities and their cultural life. Some of the newly arrived journalists founded new periodicals (like the successful *La Prensa* in San Antonio), and soon began writing about the United States and the Mexican American way of life. Theater was also quite popular in those years, and playwrights such as Daniel Venegas enjoyed the continued devotion of their audiences.[5] Venegas also penned the novel *Las aventuras de Don Chipote, o cuando los pericos mamen* (*The Adventures of Don Chipote, or When Parrots Breast-Feed*, 1928), one of the earliest examples of Chicano/a proletarian literature.

Closer to the mid-twentieth century, literature began focusing more on the social aspects of the Mexican American experience in villages and neighborhoods throughout the Southwest, hence Leal's suggestion that the Chicano/a period began in 1942, not in the 1960s, when the term was popularized. Mario Suárez's artistry in depicting Mexican American life in sketches for *Arizona Quarterly* is considered a salient example of social realism before the Chicano/a Movement. But José Antonio Villarreal's novel *Pocho* (1959) is the text that signals for many the proper beginning of contemporary Chicano/a literature. *Pocho* focuses on identity issues, with special attention to changes brought about by migration, contact with other ethnic groups, redefinition of gender roles, and the acquisition of nontraditional cultural capital. Although not well received when it was first published, *Pocho* was recovered by Chicano/a professors and scholars after 1970, and it has remained central in discussions of Chicano/a literature since then.

Pocho's momentous status notwithstanding, contemporary Chicano/a literature came of age during the civil rights era, as a myriad of journals, presses, and authors appeared seemingly everywhere and revitalized a literary tradition that for many was barely known at the time. Initially founded as the cultural arm of the farm workers' strike, El Teatro Campesino came to symbolize and define the ethos of mid-1960s Chicano/a literature, including its revolutionary bent, its popular inspiration and destination, and its occasional cultural didacticism. The same tone of urgency and militancy characterized much of the poetry of this period and, to a certain extent, the short stories and novels as well. Rodolfo "Corky" Gonzales's poem *I Am*

Joaquín (1967) offered Chicano/a readers a sustained interrogation of identity through the lens of historical revisionism and a sense of affirmation and hope. Like Gonzales, most Chicano/a writers from this period, regardless of the genre they cultivated, sought to utilize symbols and images considered unique to Chicano/a culture.

The emphasis on popular culture and organic symbolism resulted in a foregrounding of cultural nationalism. The *Plan Espiritual de Aztlán* (Spiritual plan of Aztlán), adopted by the First National Chicano Liberation Youth Conference in 1969 as its manifesto, advocated self-determination and proclaimed Aztlán (the ancestral birthplace of the Mechica) as the Chicano/a homeland. This connection between the ancient past and contemporary political realities was further developed by the indigenist literature cultivated at the time by authors such as Alurista (*Floricanto en Aztlán* [Poetry in Aztlán], 1971) and Luis Valdez (*Pensamiento serpentino* [Serpentine thought], 1973). While Marxist critics claimed that this literature lacked a dialectical sense of history, Alurista defended its value, arguing that Aztlán had served as a unifying metaphor that brought together Chicanos/as from multiple geographic areas and backgrounds.[6]

The late 1960s also witnessed the creation of the first Chicano/a journals and presses, a deliberate attempt to launch Chicano/a institutions that could foster and guarantee the flourishing of this budding literature. Of special significance were the journal *El Grito: A Journal of Contemporary Mexican-American Thought* (established in 1967) and its sponsor, Quinto Sol Press, whose goal was to publish quality Chicano/a literature and scholarship without interference from non-Chicano/a sources. Quinto Sol quickly released a successful anthology (*El espejo/The Mirror*, 1969) and a substantial number of titles, best represented by those works awarded the Quinto Sol Prize: Tomás Rivera's . . . *y no se lo tragó la tierra* (*And the Earth Did Not Devour Him*) (1971), Rudolfo A. Anaya's *Bless Me, Ultima* (1972), and Rolando R. Hinojosa-Smith's *Estampas del Valle y otras obras* (*Sketches of the Valley and Other Works*) (1973).[7] All of these works soon became recognized as part of an incipient canon of Chicano/a literature, a factor aided by Quinto Sol's interest in placing its publications in educational markets.

By the mid-1970s, as the Chicano/a Movement shifted its aim somewhat from the national scene to local struggles, the urgency of the previous decade seemed to give way to more personal approaches to literature. Rather than accentuating those elements that united all Chicanos/as, an exploration of difference (including gender differences) became the cornerstone of this literature. Also, as more Chicano/a authors graduated from university writing (or literature) programs, the previous deliberate inspiration in the folk tradition and simpler poetics now gave way to an emphasis on literary craft that opened new spaces for Chicano/a letters while earning authors like Gary Soto, Lorna Dee Cervantes, and Alberto A. Ríos, among others, some coveted mainstream prizes. At the same time, Chicano/a literature cemented its expansion to international circuits with such milestones as the awarding of the Premio Casa de Las Américas (Casa de Las Américas Prize, one of the most prestigious in Latin America) to Hinojosa-Smith's second novel, *Klail City y sus alrededores* (Klail City and its surroundings) (1976), and the first publications in Mexico and Europe of works by Alejandro Morales, Hinojosa-Smith, Floyd Salas, and others.

The 1970s also witnessed a more visible presence of Chicanas in the literary scene, a trend that would continue to increase in the following two decades. Although it is hard to generalize, Chicana literature may be best characterized by a strong feminist content, a direct tone (often using irony and sarcasm), an interest in debunking myths and images of women perpetuated in earlier literature by men, the cultivation of novel images of women, emphases on gender and sexuality (including queer identities), a nontraditional approach to the body, the recovery of historical and mythical female figures (e.g., Sor Juana Inés de la Cruz, Malintzin Tenepal), and the need to articulate and denounce multiple oppressions. Groundbreaking Chicana authors from this period include Estela Portillo-Trambley, Bernice Zamora, Alma Luz Villanueva, Carmen Tafolla, Lorna Dee Cervantes, Sandra Cisneros, and Ana Castillo.

New presses and journals saw the light during the 1970s and early 1980s as well, many of them with the explicit intention to connect Chicano/a literature with other U.S. Latino/a traditions. The *Revista Chicano-Riqueña* (founded in 1973) suggested that type of alliance between Chicanos/as and Puerto Ricans in its title. *Chiricú* (1976) added the Cuban Americans by taking the first syllable of each group to construct its name. Arte Público Press and the Bilingual Review Press were also established within the decade. Although many other small presses had published Chicano/a literature before that time, these two stand out for their longevity and for the number of books they have released to date.

As for more recent developments in Chicano/a literature, Charles M. Tatum has outlined some themes and trends that are useful to categorize its many diverse manifestations.[8] The first one, "living on the U.S.-Mexico border," accounts for a visible shift from nationalism to border/borderlands identities; Richard Yáñez and Alicia Gaspar de Alba are among the writers selected by Tatum to exemplify this thematic interest, and the most influential text remains Gloria E. Anzaldúa's *Borderlands/La frontera: The New Mestiza* (1987). The migrant experience, a second area of literary interest identified by Tatum, has been explored by authors such as Helena María Viramontes, Francisco Jiménez, and Elva Treviño Hart, among many others. Tatum also notes a thematic interest in depicting life in the barrio and in the Chicano/a family, as seen in works by Luis J. Rodríguez, Miguel Durán, Sandra Cisneros, Arturo Islas, and Alfredo Véa among others.

Detective fiction has gained notable visibility in the past few decades, even if the first Chicano/a mystery novel (Al Martínez's *Jigsaw John*) dates from 1975. Rudolfo A. Anaya, Lucha Corpi, Michael Nava, and Manuel Ramos are among the most prolific practitioners of this genre pioneered by Martínez and Rolando R. Hinojosa-Smith (whose *Partners in Crime* appeared in 1985). In their novels, cultural practices, ethnicity, and sexual exploration are often foregrounded, giving their fiction a distinctive Chicano/a flavor.

In the dramatic arts, the most visible transformations since the heyday of collective creation and Chicano/a theater groups include the successful careers of individual playwrights such as Josefina López, Carlos Morton, and Cherríe Moraga, whose output of full-length plays and shorter pieces has diversified the Chicano/a stage. Performance, at the same time, has made significant inroads with figures like Guillermo Gómez-Peña and Nao Bustamante.

Finally, Chicano/a children's literature has played an ever-increasing role since the 1990s. Census figures from 2011 indicate that 35.1 percent of Latinos/as are under the age of eighteen, which translates into an approximate figure of 17.5 million Latino/a children and young adults in the United States (most of them Chicanos/as), a significant market that many publishers are interested in tapping. But beyond market concerns, it is clear that multiple Chicano/a authors have begun writing for younger readers because of a commitment to provide quality materials that portray Latinos/as and their cultures in an engaging, stereotype-free manner. Writers like Juan Felipe Herrera, Gary Soto, Yuyi Morales, Guadalupe García McCall, Francisco X. Alarcón, Benjamin Alire Sáenz, and Carmen Tafolla, among many others, have transformed this segment of Chicano/a literary production into one of its most vibrant fields. To further promote quality, the Tomás Rivera Mexican

American Children's Book Award has conferred its prizes since 1996, and so has the Pura Belpré Award for Latino/a works for children.

Despite those significant advances in (re)constructing and (re)interpreting the history of Chicano/a literature, critics have paid little or no attention to Chicano/a readers and audiences until recently. Reception and reading theories were popularized in the United States in the 1970s (even though some of the main theorists had been active in Europe before then), but their influence on Chicano/a literary criticism was not immediate. Nonetheless, even a cursory look at what these theories propose may be helpful for contextualizing the work that I will discuss below.

Hans Robert Jauss's main interest has been to establish an aesthetics of reception that would allow for a constant examination and interrogation of how literary histories and canons are constructed. For Jauss, the engine that drives literary history is not the succession of works in chronological order (for example, the different periods in the history of Chicano/a literature that I outlined above) but the reasons for which certain books continue to be of interest to successive generations. Literary history, in that sense, is first and foremost a history of reading.[9]

Wolfgang Iser, in turn, has concentrated on examining what happens during the act of reading, that is, what kind of communication and dialogue is established between the text and the reader. Iser claims that meaning should not be conceived as some sort of hidden content in the text that the reader has to find but, rather, as something that is created in the process of reading. In Iser's view, a literary text provides its readers with the basis to construct the communicative situation, first by sharing certain norms, values, and knowledge with the reader (what he calls "repertoire") and then by establishing acceptable strategies of communication.[10] Several of the essays included in this collection (Irma Flores-Manges's, for example) are excellent illustrations of how this balance between a shared repertoire and satisfactory textual strategies is essential for literary communication to succeed.

In contrast to Iser, Stanley Fish downplays the role of the text in guiding the reading process, advocating almost total independence on the reader's part. But, to avoid giving the impression that reading is entirely subjective, Fish has developed the concept of "interpretive communities," defined as groups of readers who share cultural and linguistic competences.[11] Fish's concept of interpretive communities is quite useful to study readers who share a similar cultural background, as is the case—to a certain extent—with the contributors to this volume.

My own interest in readers and audiences began with my first book, *Rolando Hinojosa y su "cronicón" chicano: Una novela del lector* (Rolando Hinojosa and his Chicano chronicles: A reader's novel) (1993),[12] in which (following Iser) I explore the multiple ways in which Hinojosa's Klail City Death Trip series[13] demands and facilitates the work of an active reader, one who is willing and able to supply missing links, to organize a deliberately disordered text, and to revise his or her own views on the series as new entries contribute additional materials to that remarkable story of life in the Rio Grande valley.

But it was not until 2003 that my own ideas on the reading and reception of Chicano/a literature were fully developed and presented in *Life in Search of Readers: Reading (in) Chicano/a Literature.*[14] This new book was not restricted to the analysis of one particular author and his works but, rather, it presented a general model for approaching the study of Chicano/a literature from an audience's perspective. My main premise was simple but radical, stating that, historically, Chicano/a literature has been defined as much by its readers as by its texts and authors. I claimed that Chicano/a literature cannot be understood as just the sum of creative works written by Chicanos/as. In consequence, I proposed that—in addition to studying what Chicanos/as had written—it was (and it remains) imperative to consider what Chicanos/as have read over the centuries, in order to present a well-rounded picture of the history of Chicano/a letters. Thus, reworking Tomás Rivera's famous definition of Chicano/a literature as "life in search of form,"[15] I proposed foregrounding the processes by which that literature has also been marked by the search for readers and audiences. The five chapters of *Life in Search of Readers* were devoted to theoretical explorations of such topics as the formation of a national readership during the Quinto Sol Generation,[16] metaliterary discourses that focus on characters as readers and as writers, gender and audiences, linguistic and marketing strategies for addressing a multicultural readership, and the question of how to read the recovered texts from the nineteenth and early twentieth centuries. I concluded with a general theory of literary history, focusing on the shape that a reader-oriented history of Chicano/a literature could take.

An additional goal of my book was to contribute to the final debunking of one of the most pernicious myths about Chicanos/as and literature. Not too long ago, Chicanas and Chicanos were (wrongly) seen as a people without a literature,[17] a fallacy promptly exposed by the Chicano/a Movement, first, and later by the recovery projects, as they amassed a wealth of information on texts produced by Chicanas and Chicanos since colonial times. My contention was that a similar effort was needed to document what Chicanas and Chicanos have read over the years and, to that end, a combination of theoretical studies and practical data collection might give the best results. On the former, I have been rather pleased to see numerous scholars embrace some of the ideas I presented in *Life in Search of Readers*, as more and more critical studies are now paying attention to reading and reception issues in multiple ways.[18] For my part, I have elaborated on many of those topics in several journal articles and book chapters in which I have also illustrated some practical uses of my 2003 theoretical conceptualization of reading (in) Chicano/a literature.[19]

As for data collection, it is obvious that a sustained analysis of reading and reception cannot rest solely on speculative insights and thus, shortly after the publication of *Life in Search of Readers*, I launched several research projects aimed at gathering hard evidence that could support and advance our study of Chicanos/as as readers. The present volume is a direct result of those data-gathering efforts, and I will return to its significance and salient points below. But first I want to briefly introduce the various reader-oriented projects under my direction, in order to give *my* readers a better idea of the potential this information has for the study of Chicano/a literature.

The first—and currently most developed—project is the Chicano/a Literature Intertextual Database (CLID). The goal of this project is to explore all creative works published by Chicanos/as in search of mentions of authors, book titles, newspapers, literary characters, and thirty other elements related to reading and print culture. As of September 2013, the CLID includes more than thirty-one thousand entries that allow us to get detailed information about Chicano/a authors *as readers*. We can document, for instance, which writers and titles are cited more often and by whom, changes in intertextual references in different decades, gender differences that have an impact on reading, the reading tastes of a particular Chicano/a author, the presence of writers from a specific (national) tradition in Chicano/a literature, and multiple other aspects related to intertextuality in Chicano/a literature.[20] The database even has pedagogical uses, as I have demonstrated by creating and teaching an upper-division course at my current institution based on CLID materials and insights.

Because the CLID still focuses on Chicano/a *writers* (even if they are studied as readers), I launched a second data-gathering project in which we collect and analyze information about reading from Chicanos/as of any profession or occupation. This is an important strategy to prevent the potentially biased data that would result if we were to explore only the reading habits of those who are already part of the literary world. The Chicano/a Readers Oral Project (CROP) conducts and archives oral interviews that do not utilize a fixed questionnaire but that always inquire about reading habits, personal libraries, and any other aspects related to the Chicano/a reader's experiences. The information assembled from those interviews is usable in multiple ways for research. For example, references to titles and authors in the interviews have allowed me to create a database that is complementary to the CLID; side by side, these two databases permit us to compare literary and popular tastes in reading, among other aspects. Part 2 of this book contains the transcriptions of four of the interviews in the CROP database, to give readers an idea of the potential wealth of information to be collected through such an effort. Because I rely on local interviewers, the CROP has obtained information mostly from Chicano/a readers in California, whose experiences may not be representative of Chicano/a readers elsewhere. For that reason, when I first envisioned this book I issued a nationwide call for submissions of essays that could offer a glimpse about reading in other Chicano/a communities (see below for the call for submissions). The results, some of which are collected in parts 1 and 3 of this book, have greatly enriched the perspectives obtained through the CROP interviews. The "contributors" section at the end of this volume gives further details on the geographical and biographical experiences of these readers.

The information obtained through both the CLID and the CROP immediately suggested an additional area where research was much needed: book ownership and private libraries. Seeing how much value our Chicano/a readers attached to the books they owned and to the experience of growing up in a home with (or without) books was instrumental in the conceptualization of the Chicano/a Private Library Index (CPLI), a repository of private library catalogs both from previously known collections (e.g., those of Josefina Niggli and Miguel A. Otero) and from others that have never been classified. Expanding on Eleanor B. Adams and France V. Scholes's early analyses of colonial New Mexico libraries, as well as on my own catalog and study of New Mexican territorial governor Miguel Antonio Otero's family library, this project intends to produce a map of Chicano/a private book ownership. The project includes individual indexes (by owner) as well as dynamic access to a database of titles and book covers so that informants and contributors may recognize books that may have been part of their personal or family libraries as well. Part 3 of this book contains several examples of the type of research associated with the CPLI, both in (analytical) catalog form and in the shape of a discursive meditation on book inheritance and loans (see, for example, the contribution by A. G. Meléndez).

The present volume, then, is an excellent illustration of the kind of records I am gathering to document Chicano/a reading practices and experiences, combining aspects and methodologies of all of the projects mentioned above. In Part 1, I include twenty brief essays submitted by Chicano/a readers who responded to a call for contributions for this volume that instructed them as follows:

> Possible topics include (but are not limited to): your experience as a reader in general; your first encounter with books; a memorable reading; remembrances of other people (relatives, etc.) reading to you, or vice versa; books that were owned by you and/or your family; experiences in the library; your favorite genre to read; books you would like to read; among others. In general, any other topics related to reading, personal or public libraries, books, periodicals (including comics), and collective readings are welcome. The main idea is to present the richness and complexities of Chicano/a experiences with books and reading, and, in so doing, to counter stereotypes about the Chicano/a population as a group that does not read.

Contributors' responses to this prompt were diverse and passionate. Alma Ester Cortés discusses growing up in a house full of books and later building her own personal library. Argelia Flores tells of her initiation to the world of reading through Mexican comic books and *fotonovelas*, as well as of later readings in English. Carlos Cumpián writes a vivid history of reading across three generations in his family. San Antonio's poet laureate, Carmen Tafolla, reminisces about school days and the introduction of poetry in her life, in Miss Shanklin's (nicknamed by the students "Miss Chancla") third-grade class. Eliud Martínez contributes a detailed autobiographical account of his experiences with books, reading, book acquisition, and people who influenced his readings. Ever Rodríguez shares the bittersweet memory of lack of access to printed material, fragmentary bathroom readings, and an unforgettable encounter with Pedro Calderón de la Barca's *La vida es sueño*.

In Veronica Flores-Paniagua's piece, we learn of the amazing story of saving books from a partly destroyed public library as the eye of a hurricane passed through the author's hometown. Irma Flores-Manges celebrates her interaction with the poetry of Simon Ortiz as it relates to (and strikes a chord with) her own family history. Lucía de Anda Vázquez takes a lyrical look at a bookcase in her apartment, an heirloom that symbolizes the transmission of reading materials across three generations. Not unlike Eliud Martínez, Anthony Macías tells us of a book-filled journey from childhood to the world of scholarship, from reading Edith Hamilton's *Mythology* as an eight-year-old to professional readings later on. Chicana author Margarita Cota-Cárdenas fondly remembers the day in which her father brought home a secondhand set of Charles Dickens's works. In the same vein, Maria Kelson tells the story of falling in love with John Masefield's poem "Sea Fever" when she was in fifth grade. Chicana librarian María Teresa Márquez writes about her accidental encounter with a box full of books, including an algebra set and the much more memorable poetry of Thomas Hardy. Minerva Daniel contributes a moving memory of a family treasure: the book *Lo peor de Texas* (The worst of Texas), which used to belong to her father. Monica Hanna discusses visits to libraries, books in Spanish, stories read to her by her mother, and the Arabic-language books of her father. Shanti A. Sánchez contributes the experience of circumventing a maternal prohibition to read in Spanish, and her ensuing discovery of Latin American literature.

One of the most harrowing pieces in part 1 is that by Shonnon Gutiérrez, who reflects on reading as an escape from domestic violence. Veronica Ortega, in turn, tells the empowering story of her encounter with Chicano/a literature. For Vito de la Cruz, the most significant memory concerns the role that his paternal aunt played in the author's life after his father abandoned him: Nena was the person who introduced him to books and to libraries. The section closes with Beth Hernandez-Jason's recollection of reading Nancy Drew books at the Fresno Public Library as a child, which she contrasts with a more recent rereading of some of the titles in that series.

Several recurring themes permeate the essays in part 1, and thus some mention of them seems pertinent in this introduction. One of those is literacy. What I find most striking in the treatment given to the topic by contributors is the rich cultural context that normally surrounds it, as in the following excerpt from Argelia Flores's contribution:

I cannot remember learning to read English; as a matter of fact I do not remember learning to speak English either, but I do remember learning to read Spanish. At about the age of seven, I began to pick up fotonovelas that my older sisters would leave around the house and also *Memín* and *Kalimán* comic books. By looking at the pictures and then sounding out the letters I began to make out what the words meant. Eventually, I was able to read short stories in the *Alarma* news magazine my grandfather would buy once a week. I believe my first novel in Spanish was *La mentira* by Caridad Bravo Adams. I continue to read whenever possible in Spanish, but I don't read as fast as I would like.

Notice how even such a short passage as this, barely over a hundred words long, manages to touch upon language, literacy, fotonovelas, comic books, other periodicals, family libraries, reading habits, titles, and authors.

Access to books and printed matter is also a prominent topic for our contributors, in great part due to the adverse socioeconomic conditions in which many Chicanas and Chicanos grew up, and still encounter today. Perhaps the most powerful story in this regard is Ever Rodríguez's "Holy Scripture," in which we read the following:

The toilet room was the place where I did most of my reading because there was a natural need for paper there and often that paper had some type of readable text. My family, like many in Mexico, was very poor and could not even afford to buy toilet paper; instead, we would bring in a newspaper or use any kind of paper to wipe our rears clean. . . . My sisters would often scavenge around the house for paper, and then they would cut it into small squares of about five inches until there was a good stack. They would then run a metal wire through the stack to hang the paper from a nail on the bare wall inside the toilet room, and that was our stash. Reading the text on those pieces of paper was often frustrating; I never knew the beginning or the end of anything contained in those cuttings. Sometimes I would flip through the rest of the stack hoping to find pieces to complete my literal puzzle, but I rarely did. My imagination was frequently forced to give those cuttings a transitional congruence from one piece to the next

The narrator's ability to transcend economic hardship and transform material disadvantage into an empowering act of creativity reminds me of the protagonist of Tomás Rivera's . . . *y no se lo tragó la tierra*. Like him, our contributor discovered that fragmentation and chaos can still be countered with the intellect, and that a reader is not someone who consumes stories but one who contributes to producing them, in this particular case to a greater degree than is typically needed.

As the brief summaries above demonstrate, the topic of access to books (or lack of it) is associated with that of finding discarded books in the dump or in the streets. The following excerpt from María Teresa Márquez's "Reading Thomas Hardy" may serve to illustrate the transformative powers of such an encounter:

> My father was on his way home from his job at a lumber company when he found it. . . . It was a cardboard box filled with college textbooks. My father carried the heavy box on his shoulder, along with his lunch box. When he got home, my father explained what he had found and where he had found it. My father surmised that the box had fallen from one of the trains that traveled through the town. . . . My father placed the box on my parents' bed. I immediately started pulling out the textbooks and reading the titles. The only books I remember now from that treasure trove are a book of poetry by Thomas Hardy and a book on algebra. . . . Perhaps reading Thomas Hardy was an unconscious idea that I would be a college student someday. I thank my father for carrying that heavy box and bringing it home.

But parents are not always credited with facilitating access to books and reading. Shanti A. Sánchez's piece deals with her accidental encounter with Gabriel García Márquez's *Cien años de soledad* (*One Hundred Years of Solitude*), a book her father had left on the kitchen table. As she explains, she could not understand a word in the book, because her mother had not allowed her to learn Spanish. She then narrates the story of how she learned Spanish on her own and was eventually able to read García Márquez's masterpiece. Another Chicana reader, Shonnon Gutiérrez, also reflects on reading and family, but this time with an element of abuse and turmoil:

> Reading saved me from the chaos. I always remember my older sister Terrie reading to me. Late at night, when we were supposed to be asleep, she would pull out the flashlight and we would travel far from all the problems at home. She'd read me *The Hobbit*, *The Chronicles of Narnia*,

and *The Illustrated Man*. I had trouble reading all through first and second grades. It was painful when [I was] asked to read out loud in class. I had a bit of a lisp and was sent to speech therapy. Things at home where always hard; lots of abuse. . . . I counted on Terrie to take me away from home every night. . . . [Today] I am an articulate and somewhat intelligent person. I have no formal education, that is, I only went up to the eighth grade. Dad put me to work to support him and there was no time for school, but I had books, magazines, and newspapers, therefore I had knowledge.

Stories similar to these are found in part 2 of this book, which contains the transcriptions of four interviews from the Chicano/a Readers Oral Project. The longest of those conversations features Fernando Vázquez, who discusses childhood readings, bookmobiles, reading Paulo Freire in college, and his passion for books on horses and veterinary topics. In his interview, Cuauhtémoc B. Díaz tells of his readings in Mexico, his love of the English language, and later favorite reads, including U.S. periodicals like *Time* magazine. For Lupe Rodríguez, her most memorable experiences include learning to read with Mexican *novelas*, family reading habits, and reading the Bible as an adult. Last but not least, Helen Fabela Chávez, the widow of the much-revered Chicano leader César E. Chávez, discusses her own reading habits as well as her late husband's constant advice about reading.

Part 3 is entitled "Reading in the Past: Personal Libraries and Reading Histories," and it consists of longer, more academic essays about the topics of book ownership and personal and family interaction with books. This section reaches all the way back to the sixteenth century, in an attempt to trace the history of the book in the Hispanic Southwest. The first piece in this section is by Chicano playwright Carlos Morton, who discusses archival and personal research he undertook to learn more about his maternal grandfather, a journalist and spiritist in Texas; in the process, Morton gives numerous details about family reading habits, along with information on archives and special collections. New Mexican scholar A. Gabriel Meléndez's contribution ("Growing Up: Book Culture in the Land of Scarcity and Want") can be described as a cultural history of northern New Mexico, with an emphasis on the books that his family owned, their significance, and the intellectual paths they opened for him and others.

The last three essays in part 3 are all about private libraries in New Mexico before it became a state in the American union. My contribution to this section is entitled "The Family Library of Miguel A. Otero: An Analysis and Inventory." Original research in the Otero papers (at the University of New Mexico library) allowed me to reconstruct the catalog of territorial governor and author Miguel A. Otero's private library, and my article combines literary analysis (including some general considerations on researching private libraries) with a full catalog of the Otero collection. In "Two Colonial New Mexico Libraries: 1704, 1776," Eleanor B. Adams studies colonial libraries in (Hispanic) New Mexico, including an inventory of the books owned by Governor Diego de Vargas and another of the library of the Custody of New Mexico.[21] Finally, in Eleanor B. Adams and France V. Scholes's "Books in New Mexico, 1598–1680," Inquisition records and other archival sources allow the authors to analyze and catalog personal and church libraries in sixteenth- and seventeenth-century New Mexico.[22]

Not counting books listed as part of New Mexican private libraries, contributors to this volume mention more than 350 titles and authors. The sum of those references serves as an important reference and visual tool to document what (these twenty-six) Chicanos/as have read and, perhaps, to offer readers of *With a Book in Their Hands* suggestions for further readings of their own. After all, unlike the corrido heroes that Américo Paredes examined in his seminal study *With His Pistol in His Hand: A Border Ballad and Its Hero*,[23] the brave Chicanas and Chicanos who contributed to this collection have learned to fight not with pistols but with books in their hands, and it is my sincere hope and conviction that they will inspire others to do as much. *With a Book in Their Hands* was designed not only to contribute to the documentation of Chicano/a reading (for the benefit of a scholarly audience) but also to play an empowering role in public libraries, community centers, discussion groups, and other collective and public venues, as well as for individual readers. In that sense, it is essential to keep in mind that the personal narratives included in this book are first and foremost testimonies of Chicano/a lives, and, as such, they go well beyond any utilitarian value we may derive from them. For many readers, the experiences of these twenty-six Chicano/a contributors will preserve the feeling of a silent conversation with a friend or a distant relative, one that would trigger—perhaps—similar memories.

Enjoy these stories of literary acquisition, then, and please consider sharing your own by submitting them to the Chicano/a Readers Oral Project, either as a digital recording or in writing, to: mmartin-rodriguez@ucmerced.edu.

Notes

1. The most active among these include the Recovering the U.S. Hispanic Literary Heritage project (housed at the University of Houston) and the Pasó por Aquí Series on the Nuevomexicano Literary Heritage of the University of New Mexico Press.

2. Luis Leal, "Mexican-American Literature: A Historical Perspective," *Revista Chicano-Riqueña* 1:1 (1973): 32–44.

3. Of the numerous editions of Villagrá's *Historia*, I would recommend the following two: for the reader interested in a modern Spanish version of the poem and/or an English translation, the best choice is the one published by the University of New Mexico Press in 1992 (edited by Miguel Encinias, Alfred Rodríguez, and Joseph P. Sánchez); for those who would rather read the original text with all of the original printed documents, the only choice is my own edition (Alcalá de Henares, Spain: Instituto Franklin, Universidad de Alcalá, 2010).

4. The earliest, a play written by Marcos Farfán de los Godos and performed on the banks of the Rio Grande in 1598, has not survived.

5. See Nicolás Kanellos, *A History of Hispanic Theatre in the United States: Origins to 1940* (Austin: University of Texas Press, 1990).

6. See Manuel M. Martín-Rodríguez, "Aesthetic Concepts of Latino Literature," in *The Greenwood Encyclopedia of Latino Literature*, ed. Nicolás Kanellos, vol. 1 (Westport, CT: Greenwood Press, 2008), 5–46.

7. Hinojosa-Smith signed most of his later books simply as Rolando Hinojosa. I will refer to him using either of these names throughout this essay.

8. Charles M. Tatum, *Chicano and Chicana Literature: Otra voz del pueblo* (Tucson: University of Arizona Press, 2006).

9. Hans Robert Jauss, *Toward an Aesthetic of Reception* (Minneapolis: University of Minnesota Press, 1989).

10. See Wolfgang Iser, *The Act of Reading: A Theory of Aesthetic Response* (Baltimore: Johns Hopkins University Press, 1978, 1987). Citations refer to the 1987 printing.

11. For more on Fish's theories, see *Is There a Text in This Class? The Authority of Interpretive Communities* (Cambridge, MA: Harvard University Press, 1980).

12. Seville, Spain: Universidad de Sevilla, 1993.

13. Hinojosa has grouped most of his narrative work under the general title Klail City Death Trip series. As of autumn 2013, the series consists of fifteen volumes.

14. Albuquerque: University of New Mexico Press, 2003.

15. Tomás Rivera, *The Complete Works* (Houston, TX: Arte Público Press, 1992), 327.

16. The Quinto Sol Generation is the label that critics have used to refer to writers who came to fame through the efforts of Quinto Sol Press, including Rudolfo A. Anaya, Tomás Rivera, Rolando Hinojosa-Smith, and Estela Portillo-Trambley. For more details, see Francisco A. Lomelí, "Contemporary Chicano Literature, 1959–1990: From Oblivion to Affirmation to the Forefront," in *Handbook of Hispanic Cultures in the United States: Literature and Art*, ed. Francisco A.

Lomelí (Houston, TX: Instituto de Cooperación Iberoamericana / Arte Público Press, 1993), 86–108.

17. Even prominent Chicano writers like Tomás Rivera seemed to have internalized that feeling, as Juan Bruce-Novoa documented: "As Tomás Rivera remarked to me years ago, Chicanos were the first people to have an anthology—*El Espejo/The Mirror*, by Quinto Sol—before they had a literature." In "Canonical and NonCanonical Texts," *Americas Review* 14:3–4 (1986): 122.

18. For examples, see Allison E. Fagan, "In the Margins: Thresholds of Text and Identity in U.S.-Mexico Border Literature" (PhD diss., Loyola University Chicago, 2010); Marissa K. López, *Chicano Nations: The Hemispheric Origins of Mexican American Literature* (New York: New York University Press, 2011); and Christopher T. González, "Hospitable Imaginations: Contemporary Latino/a Literature and the Pursuit of a Readership" (PhD diss., Ohio State University, 2012).

19. See "Recovering Chicano Literary Histories," *PMLA* 120:3 (2005): 796–805; "La otra historia de la literatura chicana," *Anthropos* 217 (October–December 2007): 128–37; "Reading Gaspar de Villagrá (in the Seventeenth Century)," in *Cien años de lealtad: En honor a Luis Leal*, ed. Sara Poot-Herrera, Francisco A. Lomelí, and María Herrera-Sobek, vol. 2 (Mexico City: UC-Mexicanistas, 2007), 1337–46; and "*La Historia de la Nueva Mexico* de Gaspar Pérez de Villagrá: Recepción crítica (con nuevos datos biográficos de su autor)," in *El humanismo español, su proyección en América y Canarias en la época del humanismo*, ed. Antonio Martín Rodríguez and Germán Santana Henríquez (Las Palmas de Gran Canaria, Spain: Universidad de las Palmas de Gran Canaria, 2006), 189–253.

20. Intertextuality refers to the presence of texts within texts in one way or another. Although several main theories and understandings have been proposed and developed by scholars and theoreticians, for the purposes of the CLID we are documenting direct mentions and those indirect references that can be established without any reasonable doubt. In a forthcoming book about intertextuality in Chicano/a literature, I give more details about these findings.

21. This essay is reprinted here by permission from the *New Mexico Historical Review*. I reproduce all the original text except for the lists of books at the end of the original article. Readers interested in that information are encouraged to consult the original publication.

22. This essay is reprinted here by permission from the *New Mexico Historical Review*. I reproduce all the original text except for the lists of books at the end of the original article. Readers interested in that information are encouraged to consult the original publication.

23. Austin: University of Texas Press, 1958.

1

READERS' TESTIMONIES

Personal Biography

A House Full of Books

Alma Ester Cortés

In 1978, I was born to Ernesto Cortés Jr. and Oralia Garza de Cortés. Raised in Texas, I grew up in a middle-class household of two second-generation Mexican American parents. Both my grandfathers immigrated from Mexico as young men vying for the American Dream. Ernest Sr. came from Veracruz to San Antonio where he met María Velia. He and his wife spoke Spanish to each other but not to their children, for fear that their children would appear uneducated. Héctor, my mother's father, came from San Luis Potosí to live in Brownsville, on the southern tip of the Texas border between the United States and Mexico. Héctor and Angélica raised six children, and spoke Spanish and English in their home. My mother, Oralia, was their oldest girl.

I mention my parents and their parents because I feel that they are all essential parts of who I am today as a person and as an educator. Both my parents were the first to graduate from college in their families. After they graduated, their desire for knowledge grew into a desire for social change in order to help those less fortunate than them. My mother went to work for César Chávez and the Farm Workers Union. My father went to work for Saul Alinsky and the Industrial Areas Foundation. Years later, their desire for social change would bring them to San Antonio, Texas, where they would meet. However, my father and mother fell in love with books long before they fell in love with each other. When they began their life together, a collection of books in Spanish and English lined their shelves in subjects ranging from classical poetry, politics, and histories of Russia to the religion of Islam. So when I came along, already an avid reader in the womb, I continued to be one, long after the day I was brought home to our house full of books.

My earliest memory of reading is constructed from family lore, as well as from the inside jacket cover of Maurice Sendak's *Outside Over There*. It is signed "Congratulations Alma! Winner First Place Summer Reading Contest Houston Texas 1982"; signed: Louis Zwick, the librarian. That summer, my mother read to me every day for three months. The book became my whole world for the next few years, because I made the story my own. I transformed myself into Ida protecting the baby from the goblins while Daddy was away. That year I had a new brother, and Daddy was often away on business. This was the first time I remember being able to see myself within the pages of a book. As I learned to read, I took shape in other novels such as Dorothy in *The Wizard of Oz*, young Jean in *Homesick: My Own Story*, creative Anne Frank in her diary. I read and reread countless tales from Grimms' *Fairy Tales* and other folktale compilations my mother gave me. My mother wanted to raise my brother and me with a multicultural education of folklore and fairy tales. I remember many nights that would end with a bedtime story from England (*Mollie Wuppie*), Holland (*The Elves and the Shoemaker*), Mexico (*La Llorona*) or China (*Tikki Tikki Tembo*). She would fill our heads with all these stories and many more that took us far away from our real lives in central Texas.

In middle school I continued to enjoy reading and literature. I became acquainted with characters in books that I still have relationships with today. Yet I also longed to be an adult. I began to form my identity and wanted to shape my life to be like my parents by making a difference in other people's lives. I had a strong sense of justice from watching my parents watch the news. I wanted to give food to the needy, end oppression, change the school systems, and contribute to world peace. My parents educated me and my siblings to be knowledgeable of all that we had and to understand that other children in the world lacked what we had. I understood that this was why my parents worked often and went to many meetings at night. I also knew that my parents had expectations of me to do well in school and continue to read. At the end of every day my dad would ask, "What are you reading now?" And we would converse about the latest library book or a selection from school. My father still asks me this question today.

When I entered high school I encountered a challenge by moving away from my home in Texas, the only home I had ever known. My father was granted a fellowship at Harvard University, in the Kennedy School's Institute of Politics. He requested that my sister and I come with him. I attended public school (for the first time!) at the local high school in Cambridge, Massachusetts. My classmates and I would be taking a joint history and English class which discussed books from a historical and literary perspective. I couldn't believe it, the syllabus listed books I had only heard of: *The Republic*, *A Tale of Two Cities*, *Les Misérables*, etc. Our goal as students was to discover which of the books and historical times they represented were the best version of a "just society." This was the class I had been waiting for. In this class, I was able to connect my love of literature with my sense for thinking about social change.

For the remainder of high school I found my everyday joy was the English class. I felt I always had teachers that could understand me, either through class discussion or through the encouragement I had to write about what I had read. I understood how to analyze characters and pick apart a novel, I had been doing it all my life. I had been waiting to learn the terms that I was now taught in this class: theme, alliteration, motif, etc.

As my senior year of high school approached I knew that I wanted to study English, and I definitely wanted to go to college on the east coast, where I could continue my enlightening experience in Cambridge. Most of all, I wanted to step out of the shadows of my parents and their greatness and come into my own.

When I began teaching, I knew it was something that would change how I viewed the world forever, but I never knew how much. My first day of my first year teaching school, I was so sure that I wouldn't know what to do. Yet, almost instinctually I found a way to relate to every child and help them adjust to school. During the course of the entire year, in the park, in the block area, dramatic play, home center, each child found their place in my heart. Yet the ones I felt closest to were the ones that I could capture during story time. This I felt was my strength, a tradition I had inherited from my mother, and the way I related to my father. These children who brought in their own books to read over and over again were "my children" for those five, ten, or fifteen minutes. It wasn't about having an audience; it was about creating a world inside a world, inside a world. It was a way I helped make them feel special and part of a community of learners.

When I began teaching I began to remember all of the stories my mother had read to me and my brother. My mother and I formed a new relationship in which she guided me through nursery rhymes, songs, projects, and activities to encourage reading and language. My mother had a gift for reading stories and then telling them in her own words. As a child we formed our relationships around the literature that we read together. Now my mother, a librarian, and I, a teacher, found a way to relate to each other again through story, song, and the pages of books. I found it fitting that the profession I chose was so similar to the one that she chose.

Now I am in my fifth year of teaching and my mother and I continue this relationship of storytelling and sharing. I still consult her when I am unsure of a book title, song, or finger play that I would like to use in my class. Yet, for the most part I now have my own repertoire of books and songs to use. Like my mother before me, I have a library of adult books, and then there is my children's literature library. I am constantly adding to my children's literature library through various trips to bookstores and conversations with other educators and librarians. I now have not only my own house full of books, but also a classroom. Still, every year I take out Maurice Sendak's *Outside Over There* and I watch as the children's eyes fill with wonder and curiosity, just as I did when I was their age. Perhaps this book will someday become another child's first and fondest memory of reading like it was for me.

Learning to Read

Argelia Flores

I came to the United States at the age of three, in the early 1960s. We settled in a small rural community in the central San Joaquin Valley in which my mother and I continue to reside.

I cannot remember learning to read English; as a matter of fact, I do not remember learning to speak English either, but I do remember learning to read Spanish. At about the age of seven, I began to pick up fotonovelas that my older sisters would leave around the house, and also *Memín* and *Kalimán* comic books. By looking at the pictures and then sounding out the letters I began to make out what the words meant. Eventually, I was able to read short stories in the *Alarma* news magazine my grandfather would buy once a week. I believe my first novel in Spanish was *La mentira* by Caridad Bravo Adams. I continue to read whenever possible in Spanish, but I don't read as fast as I would like.

Eventually, I also began reading in English, and that opened many new adventures. I enjoy a diverse selection of books, and have read a few works twice, if not three times. Not because of school, just because the stories being told were that captivating.

I also believe that my stubborn streak has kept me from not giving up on hard reads. It took me, off and on, about three years to read *Doctor Zhivago* by Boris Pasternak. I believe I started it at the age of thirteen. But I remember the emotions today that I felt as the story unfolded before my eyes and imagination.

Another of my favorites is Alexandre Dumas's *The Count of Monte Cristo*. I could go on with listing many of my favorites, but I believe a list is not what you want. I will add, though, that my reading taste is varied: Stephen King, Jonathan Kellerman, Rowling, Poe, Hillerman, Jane Austen, Hemingway, García Márquez, and Sue Grafton are but a few favorite authors.

I also want to share how my mother is now enjoying reading. I always knew that my mom had only attended school through second grade in Mexico. I knew she could read, but I also understood that she read at a level she wasn't happy at. She did always comment about how she wished she had been able to stay in school. But at the age of ten she was sent off to work to help with the family finances.

My mom, in the last five years, has become a better reader through her Bible study. She now has a better understanding of punctuation, and her comprehension of how to read allows her to have a richer experience while reading her assignments. I enjoy seeing her with her Bible, study guide, highlighter, and notepad, sitting at the kitchen table "studying."

Most recently, I had the most wonderful experience: one of my nephews recommended a book to me! I just about burst into tears because, in the past few years, when I have suggested that he read during school breaks, I would get the same response: "I am on vacation, why would I want to read a book?" He currently is on winter break and is reading the second book in the trilogy he has recommended to me. I cannot find the words to describe the joy and pride I feel that this nephew is beginning to enjoy reading, and he did it on his own.

I believe books are gateways to many adventures, and there are so many waiting for me to turn the page!

Learned to Read
at My Momma's Knee

Carlos Cumpián

My parents had the type of marriage that most Americans usually don't have anymore. Specifically, they were a couple with wide educational differences, who got together and stayed together to raise seven children. I was the first of seven, born to a nineteen-year-old mother with a ninth-grade education and a twenty-two-year-old father who held the rank of first lieutenant in the U.S. Army and a baccalaureate in political science from Bowling Green State University, Ohio.

While my father was quite verbal and literate, it was my mother's joyful reading of fairy tales that launched my lifelong love of reading. Because my mom read to me, I was prepared to get on that yellow school bus to find out if other kindergarten kids also knew the stories I had heard. While the first day of school is typically traumatic for the child separating from their parent, I didn't have that experience. I wanted new stories told to me besides the ones *Captain Kangaroo* offered weekday mornings, and that Catholic priests and Walt Disney's *Wonderful World of Color* offered on weekends.

My parents had left Texas and rented a white wooden house just outside sunny San Jose, California. This was decades before the Silicon Valley explosion leveled the nut and fruit orchards. They called the owners of the rented house "the Ponders." I later learned to ponder was to think deeply about something. Did the landlords ponder their rows of nectarines and walnuts?

On that fertile piece of land, I began to ponder the weight of words. For example, across the narrow road was a multigenerational Japanese American family, growing a few acres of strawberries. Occasionally, I waved from my school bus window as they looked up at the bus's arrival and departure in the early morning coolness. Once an elder in a hat pointed like an A, and normally stooped over her red and green clusters, looked up and said "Oh-hi-oh!" I pondered that, until I returned from school to ask my mother what she meant. My mom said, "Your daddy might know, he visited Japan during the Korean War." He told me it was part of a good-morning greeting in Japanese, *Ohayou gozaimasu*. I had no idea where Japan was, only that Godzilla attacked it.

A year before boarding the school bus, we poked our heads inside the landlord's barn. My mom found the courage to climb a ladder to a storage loft. When she came down, she held a cardboard box filled with a few cobwebbed books and curling newspapers.

These abandoned books were to become my first children's books— *Mother Goose* and Hans Christian Andersen's fairy tales. My mom had a natural flair for the dramatic. So, when she would read aloud to us, the stories came alive. She knew how to sing out a phrase or put her hand over her mouth to make muffled voices of a distant giant approaching. She would raise the lilt of her voice at the sight of a question. She would deepen her voice when a man was supposed to have spoken. Some of the fairy stories were accompanied with black-and-white line etchings. Others had full-color illustrations. The visuals and creative edge my mother gave the narrator and character's voices added depth and texture to the stories.

I, too, wanted to read to imitate what my mom could do. I would study the squiggles of ink on the sepia-colored pages and follow her thin fingers across the pages. She may have stumbled on certain words in their pronunciation, but we didn't criticize her as some of the Anglo teachers did upon hearing her northern Mexican accent. We asked her to repeat the stories over and over.

Later, she said she didn't have the time to read to us anymore: "Too many babies!" But she would tell us stories and jokes she learned as a child. Some were Aesop fable–style stories about a super-lazy man who would rather be buried alive than have to work, or about some Anglo man who attended a Mexican party and didn't speak Spanish, committing a series of comical mistakes. The Anglo was told by a trickster to smile and say "más chocolate" when he wanted to say "muchas gracias." She also instilled in us a fear of being alone near the arroyos and ríos when she combed her black hair in front of her face and gave voice to the river spirit crying woman, La Llorona.

After five kids, my father moved us back to Texas, to be close to his parents. Soon I became aware that my paternal grandparents were also very fond of reading. My abuelo, Miguel Cumpián, picked up *Time* and *Life* magazines on his deliveries to Carrizo Springs, Crystal City, Uvalde, Big Wells, and Asherton for Texaco Oil. There were also neat stacks of red and goldenrod *National Geographic*s in his front room. I recall my abuelo's khaki-covered legs stretched out next to a lamp, as he pored over his magazines.

My abuela Maria loved her Bible. She would read a few pages each night and then lecture us on the various lessons buried within. My grandfather wouldn't share his reading, except on rare occasion to call over my grandmother to show her some outlandish costume or brown naked person dancing. This might earn my grandpa a laugh or a mild scolding from her.

My father Ramiro had also been a reader of weekly news magazines, as well as an occasional newspaper. Once, my mom discovered an entirely different magazine peeking out from under my father's driver's seat—*Playboy*. My mother lectured him about not looking at other females, clothed, half-clothed, or airbrushed nude. I thought I heard him say, "OK." I became curious.

Weeks later, the lecture was forgotten at the drive-in theater. Certain racy scenes unfolded, and my mom told us to cover our eyes. She also chided my dad. In the dark, she grabbed for a magazine to block out topless Brigitte Bardot's *And God Created Woman* blonde beauty on the Texas big screen. Without looking at the magazine's cover, she held it over my brother's and my eyes, until the offending scene passed. She then let the contraband fall in the back seat, where we quickly got our hands on another example of banned literature. Seeds of curiosity were planted about what worlds, lessons, and possibly exotic bodies might be orbiting, just pages away. Yes, reading was eye opening.

The true tipping point of what made me an insatiable reader was the weekly ritual of going to the highway convenience store to load up on comic books. Within six months, my father saw my weekly quarter's worth of comics grow to a stack that rivaled my grandfather's years of *National Geographic*s. À la Jackie Gleason's Ralph Kramden character on *The Honeymooners*, he shouted, "Juana, your son just flushed another twenty-five cents down the toilet!" I learned to leave my comics in the closet.

OK. I spent long hot junior high summers in south Texas reading and trading tons of DC comics, a mass of Marvel comics, and the *Turok: Son of*

Stone Dell series, where Kiowas battled dinosaurs. There was the outlandish humor of Alfred E. Newman's *Mad* magazine and the cheap knockoffs *Sick* and *Cracked*. I entered the eye- and ear-popping world of *Hot Rod Cartoons* and *Drag Cartoons*. And from the pen of legendary Texan artist Gilbert Shelton came *Wonder Wart-Hog* magazines. I even went through a Goth period of sorts with *Monsters of Filmland* and *Creepy* magazines. And even though I had never seen snow in real life, I found Jack London's novels *White Fang* and *Call of the Wild* irresistible.

But being considered a true "reader" didn't happen until we moved to Chicago from south Texas. I discovered poetry. It was poetry that took me into the depths of literature. Because I looked older than my age in high school, I hung out with juniors, seniors, and college freshmen. The real action was with guys and gals who could drive and smoked both legal and illegal substances. The first form of poetry I really found exciting was that of the Beats. This included Lawrence Ferlinghetti's City Lights pocket book *Coney Island of the Mind*, Gregory Corso's *The Happy Birthday of Death*, Allen Ginsberg's *Howl*, and Big Table's Andrei Codrescu's *License to Carry a Gun*. Chicano poetry wouldn't become a part of my life until I heard Rodolfo "Corky" Gonzales's epic *Yo Soy Joaquín* in 1973. However, I had read American Indian poetry in *Akwesasne Notes* and in underground newspapers since 1970.

With a desire to understand that powerful vortex called love, I read Lebanese American poet and artist Khalil Gibran's *The Prophet*. My new Chicago friends were hybrid working-class biker hippies unafraid of the mockery that bull-neck jocks and gang-minded greasers of the time heaped at guys who today are called nerds and emos. We didn't flaunt that we had poetry in our jean jackets. Turned out, girls loved poetry. So we didn't shy away from holding occasional church basement poetry readings, open to anyone willing to share or listen.

After six of my friends, including a girlfriend, died suddenly during my high school years, I was moved spiritually to begin seeking answers to the age-old inquires: Why are we here? What's my purpose in life? Is there a God? Besides turning to poetry, I read the *Tao Te Ching*, the *Bhagavad Gita*, *The Tibetan Book of the Dead*, philosophical works by Alan Watts, Buddhist sutras, the Bible, and Gnostic works. To this day, I am still figuring out what these books contain. Maybe if my mom read them to me, I would understand them.

La Mees Chancla

Carmen Tafolla

Miss Shanklin taught third grade, wore high-style high heels, had big calloused feet, and kept a quiet boring classroom. We called her "La Mees Chancla" because the most exciting task of the day was when one lucky boy was picked to "wait on her" with a ritual that involved *chanclas*.

"This will teach you something useful you can do when you grow up," she said. The girls absorbed it all, envious. There was nothing useful *we* could learn. The boy would be allowed to open the highest holy place, the teacher's closet, and remove from there carefully her fuzzy bedroom slippers. Then he would bring them to the floor beside her chair, remove her pointed shiny heels, and slip the slippers on. As he carried the heels to the teacher's closet and closed the door, he would be thanked and return to his seat. Then, at morning recess, he would reverse the process, and transform chancla-clunky calloused feet to stiff and stylish shiny heels. Lunch, afternoon recess, and end of day, he would repeat the ritual in its entirety. Tomorrow a new page would be knighted and kneel at her feet. All of us *mexicanitos* would look on in envy.

By the end of fall, the girls just looked on casually, trying not to notice we would never take part here. We sighed, watched the clock, and did who-knows-what all year long. Except for two things, I remember nothing else from that classroom. One was the week she brought three big thick dictionaries into the classroom and taught us how to look up words using the alphabet's sequence on each letter of the word.

Our class of forty waited in three lines. But even when we got our turn, the pages were musty, pictureless, and cluttered with long lists of disconnected words. We would search, copy down the meaning, and return to the back of the line till our next turn to look up an assigned word from our list. I liked the precision of the search, but overall was unimpressed, my turn in line too far away to care.

But then one day, Mees Chancla shuffled in her pink slippers to the board to write neatly the short paragraph that always started our day, three to four simple sentences we would copy onto our tablets with four blanks where we would match and insert the appropriate vocabulary words of the day. In large capitals she scrawled the title of the paragraph, POETRY. I'm not sure I knew what the word meant exactly, but four sentences later, I was filling in vocabulary items, one of which I'm sure was "rhyme." We were allowed to color an illustration below the paragraph, and on mine, I drew a large-eyed cat, a shapeless brown bat with a black derby, and a voice bubble that said, "I had a cat who saw a bat that wore a hat, and that was that." I was in love.

I don't know where I found the poetry to read, but I would never spend another week of my life without poetry. Our school had no library, our classroom had no bookshelf we were privy to, and the only poems I heard at home were a few long recitations in Spanish with funny words that my elderly aunt had taught me years ago:

Rín, Rín, Ranacuajo,
salió esta mañana,
muy tierno muy majo.
No salgas hijito,
le dice Mamá
pero él hace un gesto
y orondo se va.
Con pantalón corto,
corbata a la moda,
sombrero encintado
y chupando de boda.

About thirty verses later, as I recall it, he gets eaten by a cat and then there's a cute moral to the story, also unraveled in rhyme. I had no idea what *majo* meant, and I was in college before I figured out that the *chupando* phrase meant he was chewing on a fine cigar passed out at some *boda*, but the fascination of the form was enough to entrance me into memorizing it. The whole thing, for nothing else would be acceptable.

Still, knowing that this thing had a name, poetry, encouraged me to go searching through books. My mother paid fifty cents a week to get me a set of Childcraft books, where the first volume, free, was *Childhood Rhymes and Verses*. I still have it. It still entrances me. This is where I learned of Gitcheegumee and Father William. This is where I finally had an exposure to the literature of books. Strange as that sounds, books had been a rarity in my life. My family, pre-Childcraft, had three books in the hall closet, one of which was the Bible (in Spanish, of course). The remaining two consisted of a church hymnal, and something I assumed was about medicine and doctoring: *La Santa Doctrina*. My elementary school, one of the poorest in the already poorest neighborhood in San Antonio, and the last to have a fence put up around its playground, had no school library till long after I was gone. And the west side Mexican barrio of San Antonio, where I lived, had long been ignored by the Anglo City Council. Chugholes in streets weren't fixed, police didn't answer calls to come here, and city libraries were definitely not built here. Those monies were spent on the wealthier and more prestigious sides of town.

But when I was ten, the city finally built a tiny library only two miles from my house. My mother and I made the long walk once a week. I roamed the stacks, grabbing books that caught my fancy. At the checkout desk, however, I was usually turned down by a volume or two. The first week, I found out that no more than five could be checked out at a time. The second week, a book on the History and Lore of Cats that I'd been salivating over was taken off my stack of five because it was not classified as "Juvenile Literature." The third week it was a reference book on poetry that had fascinated me and been taken off the stack. Still, there were five new books in my hands every week, and reading library books became my favorite sport.

When I was twelve, I started seventh grade in the big world of junior high school. Yes! It had a library! By the time I was in high school, I would take the bus regularly to the main library downtown. My choice of colleges was largely decided by a letter I received from one college stating that construction was progressing rapidly and that "the Blumberg Memorial Library is rising to its ultimate massive splendor." I have never fully rid myself of the image of a massive Parthenon rising fully built from the bowels of the earth, some God-given miracle of a classic edifice bursting forth complete and shining, and pushing aside clods of surprised dirt.

Today, I have my own collection of poetry volumes at home, I receive poetry journals in the mail, I read poetry on the Internet and in the newspaper. There is no shortage of books in any room of my house. I read before I go to sleep. I read on the plane. I read while standing in line. I read the labels on shampoo bottles, in English and French, and the ingredients on soup cans; I read the out-of-region newspapers crinkled up around items that have been shipped. I even read dictionaries, and have a row of forty or fifty in different languages, sitting on my hallway shelf. I think about Miss Shanklin's class sometimes, when I see them. And I whisper a peaceful "thank you."

No, I've never worked in a shoe store or even wanted to. I've never "waited on" anyone other than my family or guests in my own home, and instead I've spent a lifetime examining, exposing, and writing about institutionalized racism. I've never felt the need to cram my calloused feet into pointy heels or to hide my chanclas from anyone. But I thank her for that one paragraph, for sharing the word *poetry* on that one day, for letting us read that wonderful and now-anonymous poem on the chalkboard. And, despite a lifetime of reading English, I still defer to the richness and the wonder of my own native language, Tex-Mex, and call her, in my own memory, "La Mees Chancla."

On Reading
Books in My Life

Eliud Martínez

In memory of Donald L. Weismann (1914–2007)

When my *tía* took me to be enrolled in first grade in January 1941, I spoke only Spanish, no English. My aunt took me because, like some *mexicanos* at the time, she had an American seventh-grade education and could speak English. My mother never learned to read and write, in Spanish or English, and my father was always looking for work in the 1940s when Mexicans had a difficult time finding work.

My earliest memory of books dates from the time I was five years old. We lived down the hill from an elementary school. Sitting daily on the porch of a dilapidated house that we rented for six dollars a month, I would look up and listen to children's voices and laughter. I longed to be among the elementary school children. I wanted to share in their jubilation when they had recess or lunch, and at the end of the school day. I wondered why they would toss those strange rectangular objects up into the air. What are they? They are *libros*, my mother said. And she told me, as I have said in my novel, *Voice-Haunted Journey*: next year you will go to school, *el año pasará*.

My mother was right, the time passed quickly. In that year when I was five years old, before I was enrolled in first grade, before I could read, I was weaned visually on comic books—about Tarzan, Superman, Batman and Robin, and some woman and a man of the jungle, both skimpily dressed.

One of my dearest friends, Billy Joe Walker, and I used to trade comic books.

From these comic book characters I learned to draw the human figure, the muscles of the arms, chest, and legs. Later, in high school, I studied physiology in order to learn anatomy. Before I learned to read, I learned to draw from comic books. Had I not been a visual artist, I might have majored in medicine because of my love of human anatomy. Eventually, reading and my love of books took precedence over everything else.

From first grade, I remember the small classroom, the pencil sharpener next to the window facing south, the street below the hill on which the small two-room 1-A and 1-B building was located, and inside the classrooms were old wooden desks with inkwells. Vividly I remember the alphabet running left to right above the *blackboard*—not long ago we began to call them *chalkboards*—printed in upper- and lowercase letters. I loved learning the alphabet, sounding the letters and the varied sounds that they made singly and in combinations. It was the beginning of reading.

Later, for second grade and up, children went to school in the larger adjacent building whose granite stone exterior resembled the exterior of the capitol building in Austin, Texas. In the larger building I remember long halls and noisy steam heaters in wintertime. I took art classes every year until I finished high school. From Bickler Elementary I remember the smells that came from art classes—the wax from color crayons, the smells of watercolors, glue, paper, and other smells.

These are nostalgic memories. In retrospect, the windows, the seasons, and the mingled smells of machine oil, pencil wood shavings, and lead whenever I sharpened my pencil—all invited daydreaming. Dreams of travel opened up the child's imagination and curiosity. I see, again, in retrospect that I was born with curiosity about all that is knowable and unknown, about distant and foreign places and peoples.

Since childhood I have been alive with all my senses—to smells, sounds, touch, taste, and sight. Books and reading would take me to faraway places and introduce me to peoples of the world. Around 1960 I became memory haunted. I began to write about childhood memories and about my family.

Today, at nearly seventy-five years of age, I am a professor emeritus of creative writing and comparative literature. I have taught Chicano studies and Latin American studies courses, for which I did a great deal of reading in historiography. I am a novelist, an essayist, a scholar, a dreamer, and a surrealist artist. I have traveled abroad in many European countries—having read the authors from those countries and knowing their artists and thinkers from reading, from books. I have lived and traveled in Mexico and in this country too. I have also read books by our countries' major authors.

Once I learned to read I became a voracious reader and to this day, I still am. In first grade we read and memorized Mother Goose nursery rhymes— Hickory dickory dock, the mouse ran up the clock, among others—and we read Jack and Jill books that taught us how to read. Books repeated words and phrases that we used in daily speech, used alliteration and imparted knowledge of reading incrementally. This was the beginning of a superb mainstream education, long before the social movements of the 1950s and 1960s.

I cannot emphasize how important it was to read ALOUD in first grade, to hear our voices sound the words in what was then a foreign language to many of us. And to have teachers help us to enunciate the words: in the old days being corrected was acceptable, and some wonderful, *old-fashioned* (in a positive, superlative sense) teachers helped us when we were learning English, tactfully, helpfully and—CORRECTLY—to learn. I remember asking when I wanted to go to the bathroom, "Can I go to the bizcuse?"

One day, during the first semester of my first year in elementary school, it seems like I woke up and I could write English and speak two languages, *español* and English. My teachers invited me to help other students with their reading and writing assignments. I was skipped half a grade, a semester, because I could do all the assignments easily. I remember being taken out of the first semester of second grade, 2-A, after only two weeks and placed in 2-B. What does all this have to do with reading and books? This has everything to do with reading and books in my life.

This essay provides me with the opportunity to express indebtedness, to express the deepest and most sincere gratitude to the admirable teachers that made reading and learning joyful, and to my parents, who were also my teachers—my father, who went only to third grade and had a superb teacher at a small village one-room school in Mexico, and to my mother, who never allowed my father to take us out of school to follow the crops when we were boys, when our family was very poor and my father could not find work. My mother and my father knew the value of books and reading.

Yes, I am deeply grateful to all the teachers and my parents for instilling in me an appreciation of learning, knowledge, and culture. I guess that I was born with a propensity to travel, to be—as the child in one of Charles Baudelaire's poems says—always anywhere except where I am. Intuitively, I loved languages. Without enlightened teachers, who knows what would have happened to my love of reading, books, travel, and languages.

Today, I read in four languages—English, Spanish, French, and Italian. I have read Russian and German authors in English and Spanish translations. I have often wondered what if my teachers had punished me for speaking Spanish? What would have happened to my education?

In Austin, Texas, the town where I grew up, barrio Chicanos attended Zavala Elementary School, where they were punished for speaking Spanish. The teachers would wash out their mouths with soap and water and make them write on the board a hundred times: "I will not speak Spanish at school." They became angry adolescents by the time they converged on Allan Junior High School, rightly so. They hated *gabachos*. Many were brighter than I, some were creative and talented, but their anger got them into trouble. During the years of the Chicano movement, reading motivated some of them to become *pinto* poets, among them Raúl Salinas and Ricardo Sánchez. In my case, elementary school teachers would call me *novio* and señor Martínez when I was a child.

In 1943, when I was in third grade, Bickler Elementary was closed to make way for the coming of the I-35, for luxury hotels and motels, and eating places along the great highway. We were transferred to Palm School, where I remember that in third grade English class we learned to diagram sentences. We learned the names of sentences—declarative, interrogative, exclamatory, and imperative sentences. We learned the parts of speech, defined them, and used them in sentences. I loved the English language. I have always loved words. In college I would read *Webster's Dictionary*.

I have always loved reading. From fourth grade on I remember that we would go from class to class. We had different teachers for different subjects—English, math, social studies, science, and next to English my favorite class was spelling and penmanship. The teachers were specialists in their subjects. From year to year they taught their subjects joyfully and incrementally. For me, that made for an excellent education. Little details of my love of learning come back. I remember the smell of the first $1—one dollar—Esterbrook fountain pen that I purchased. I loved spelling and learning to write in cursive.

In fourth grade, I used to check out four books from the school library on Friday and read them over the weekend. I would return them on Monday morning. When my mother died in 1989, she left behind a trunk of memorabilia. Among the memorabilia were our report cards, mine, my sister's, and my brothers'. We were all A students with perfect attendance records. My mother was an incredible collector of written documents. Even though she never learned to read, she had an incredible memory for written documents, and she could find any document that she wanted in the trunk.

As I have said, my mother and father have significantly influenced the direction of my life. In connection with my mother, I have a sad memory of her having to memorize all the medicines that she was taking in her old age. I remember opening a cupboard and seeing her medicines arranged in a very orderly manner. She would arrange them by size and color of the pills after one of us had read to her the instructions for taking the medicines. After she died, I often wondered why we did not teach her to read and write, instead of just translating for her.

Of lasting importance for all the days of my life, when I was eight years old my father began to teach me to read and write Spanish from *La Prensa*, a Spanish-language newspaper in San Antonio. Consequently, my father influenced the direction of my teaching and scholarly career. Without knowledge of Spanish, I would never have studied in Mexico. My father and I used to read *La Prensa* on a regular basis. From the age of eight, whenever I added to my English vocabulary I would also expand my spoken and written Spanish vocabulary. During my childhood my father used to bring home bilingual grammar books to help me develop my knowledge of two languages. "Más valen dos idiomas que uno," he used to say. He loved knowing, before he died in 1996, one day past the age of ninety-five, that he had been a professor's great teacher. He loved when I called him "maestro."

Knowing Spanish and English made the French language easier to learn, to read, write, and speak. In the eleventh grade I took one year of French with an excellent teacher, Ms. Éloïse Roach. The first novel that I read in French was by Albert Camus, *L'étranger* (*The Stranger*). I remember the first sentence of the novel, "Hier, Maman est morte" (Yesterday, Mother died). I greatly identified with the statement in the introduction about the main character, Meursault: "Meursault ne sait pas jouer le rôle" (Meursault did not know how to play the game). It was for me a rather prophetic statement, because many years later in 1963 I became a disillusioned dropout graduate student, because I could not play the game. Living in Chicago and New York City during the 1960s and knowing three languages enabled me to learn Italian on my own. I dreamed then of going to Europe.

I wish to acknowledge at this point the major academic influence in my life. After military service from 1953 to 1956, I went back to the University of

Texas under the GI Bill, as an art student. By 1956 my mind was hungry for intellectual stimulation, but I still aspired to be a commercial artist. Fate had other plans for me. In the fall of 1956 I enrolled in Dr. Donald L. Weismann's art history class, and my life and interests changed after that. Between 1956 and 1960, I took all of Weismann's classes on modern art history. Don was for me *el gran maestro*. We became friends, and our friendship lasted for more than fifty years; he died on March 19, 2007. The first class that I took in fall 1956 with Weismann—later professor emeritus in the arts—was an art history class on modern painting. He was forty-one and I was twenty-one. The class focused on the major movements of the nineteenth century in France and internationally, going from Jacques-Louis David in France and Francisco de Goya in Spain to the avant-garde movements of the twentieth century. It was the first international and cosmopolitan class that I had ever taken. I still have our textbook for the class, John Canaday's *Mainstreams of Modern Art*, and all the notes that I took in his classes.

Don's classes opened my eyes to a world of higher learning and fine arts about which I had no previous knowledge. I was a studio art major with an interest in commercial art. In the 1950s, however, the professors in the art department were encouraging students toward abstract and nonobjective art. I was perplexed, and they could not explain modern art to me. Don could, and in his classes he made it understandable.

No theoretical paradigms or references to literary works of art as *texts* tainted his frequent allusions to parallels in the visual arts and literature. Don's approach to each artist's body of work included systematic, thoughtful, insightful commentaries. His interpretations were knowledgeable and per-suasive, never dogmatic, consistently sympathetic, characterized by generos-ity of spirit and a warm sense of humor. His lectures were well organized and down-to-earth, in a word, intelligible. He welcomed questions and invited student participation.

Don's lectures covered artists' biographies, history and society, nation and culture; they touched on artistic periods and movements shared by other arts—literature, music, and drama—and he stressed the influence of earlier artists and traditions on later ones. His undergraduate courses in art history were much more. Superb in quality, the classes were an outstanding prepa-ration for graduate work, independent reading and scholarly research, and for teaching comparative literature.

For each class, Don Weismann provided extensive bibliographies. In his many classes Don always emphasized the connections between art and life.

Reading his bibliographies occupied me for many pleasurable years. For the benefit of his students he would choose from the available books the best, the most enlightened, and the most reasonably written. Don omitted the works of pedantic scholars. As a professor I followed this practice.

Each day in class he would write on the board the names of authors and books that he was reading at the time, authors who were lucid thinkers, impressive and insightful interpreters of works of art and cultural history. This is how Weismann introduced me to Bernard Berenson, José Ortega y Gasset, and many others. Because of his classes I developed an interest in reading artists' and writers' biographies, social and intellectual history, and philosophy. His classes opened up my mind to all kinds of learning, and from Don I learned about the arts of painting, sculpture, poetry, the novel, film, and music. From him I learned about comparative literature before I knew such a thing existed. In his classes my mind became receptive to all kinds of learning. From him I learned about international painting—in Spain, France, Italy, Germany, Holland, England, and the United States. From his classes and bibliographies I learned about the writing and rewriting of history, about reinterpreting the past—in a word, about historiography.

I was infinitely curious and inquisitive. My independent reading became even more voracious and *the objective of my reading*, which later became the goal of teaching, was *to learn* and to understand. I remember the day when I visited Weismann in his office. I was twenty-one or twenty-two years old, awed and delighted by knowledge and learning. All knowledge seemed very systematic and to fit into a pattern, I said to him. If one had the pattern, new knowledge could be inserted into it. Very politely Don suggested the impossibility of acquiring all knowledge. I know that to be true. However, since taking his classes, in the words of Francis Bacon and echoed by Alfonso Reyes, I have made all realms of knowledge my domain. From then on reading and writing became inextricably linked, but I did not know when I was his student that I would become a writer. Weismann's classes provided me with an excellent preparation for the rest of my life.

When I graduated from the University of Texas at Austin in 1959 I was awarded two consecutive ED Farmer International Scholarships by the Institute of Latin American Studies at the University of Texas at Austin for study in Mexico. Reading and speaking in the Spanish language (and having learned French in high school) enabled me to receive a superlative education at the Universidad Nacional Autónoma de México in Mexico City. I took classes from the most outstanding professors of the time at UNAM—Miguel León-Portilla, Justino Fernández, and Francisco de la Maza—and I read the most amazing books then being published in the late 1950s and in early 1960 by my Mexican professors, other authors, thinkers, poets, and scholars. Books were priced reasonably in the old days when the dollar was worth twelve and a half pesos. The habit of buying books began in Mexico. I bought some books in available collections. I read for the joy of reading, to learn and to understand Mexican thought, culture, and arts.

In Mexico, I read Miguel León-Portilla's *La filosofía náhuatl* and Octavio Paz's *El laberinto de la soledad* in their second 1959 editions. In Mexico, I also read Justino Fernández's *Coatlicue* and *Arte moderno y contemporáneo de México*, and countless books about Mexican colonial history. Among them, Robert Ricard's book, *La conquête spirituelle du Méxique*, fell serendipitously in my hands. In 1975, three years after my joint appointment at the University of California, Riverside, in Mexican American studies (later, Chicano studies) and Latin American studies, I designed and taught a course based on Ricard's book in English translation, *The Spiritual Conquest of Mexico*. For this course I also used the English translation of León-Portilla's book, *Aztec Thought and Culture*.

In Mexico, too, far from home and my place of birth, I became memory haunted. Reading led to writing, and ever since about 1960, reading and writing became inseparable. In the years to come I would not be able to pass by used book stores without walking in, and in the days when books were reasonably priced I would buy countless books at a time.

The intellectual life, cultural and otherwise, of Mexico City in 1959 and 1960, and in Chicago in 1963 and 1964, further opened my eyes to reading, books, and films. In 1964 I moved from Chicago to New York City, where I met my wife Elisse. A year before, when I was living in Chicago, two years after returning from Mexico, a book by William James fell serendipitously into my hands. In Chicago, I also reread Edgar Allan Poe and, in 1963, I saw Fellini's 8 ½. I also read Arthur Schopenhauer's *World as Will and Idea* and more of Ortega y Gasset. By 1980, my personal library contained numerous books by and about Poe, film, and other arts.

Elisse and I married in 1965. After living and traveling for nearly a year in Europe with my wife in 1966 and 1967, we were back in New York from 1967 to 1969. Before I met Elisse, I remember buying books at the Strand Book Store down in Greenwich Village, not too far from Washington Square. Sometimes I would go without eating to buy books. From these years in New

York I also remember how few mexicanos lived there and how hard it was to buy Mexican tortillas and *chiles serranos* or jalapeño peppers. My mother used to mail me fifty cents worth of serrano chilies, and the postage was between six and seven dollars. After we married, Elisse used to laugh about how jubilant I became each time I received them.

My wife Elisse and I lived in Spain for six months, where I acquired the complete nine-volume works of Ortega y Gasset and the three-volume works of Johann Wolfgang von Goethe, in Spanish, plus many other books. After Spain, we traveled through Europe for about four and a half months. In Rome, regrettably, the books were stolen from our Volkswagen automobile in the parking lot near the hotel were we stayed. Fortunately, we were insured and the insurance money enabled us to continue into northern Germany, Belgium, and Holland. Then back to France and home.

We returned to New York City, where our first daughter, Laura, was born in 1968. Thanks to Elisse, I went back to graduate school in 1969 at Ohio University, Athens. I am greatly indebted to her for persuading me to continue with graduate studies. Because of my voracious reading, at Ohio University I was invited into the PhD program in English and comparative literature. The program was ideal. It was international and cosmopolitan, and embraced many national literatures and genres. The professors were immensely sympathetic to my voracious interests. By then, I had read many of the authors on the PhD reading list, but I had little background in literary criticism, history, and interpretation, in which I immersed myself during long hours at the university library.

Weismann's classes had prepared me for comparative literature—for the study of influences, movements and periods, genre studies, literary history, and the comparative study of the arts. My minors were art history and film studies. The long hours in the library were joyful. I learned to pull fifteen or twenty books on the same subject and to read and glean information and knowledge from them. I will always be grateful to my professors at Ohio University, among them David Heaton, Rainer Schulte (head of comparative literature), Antonio Serna-Maytorena, and Dean McWilliams.

I often think of books and the importance of reading in life. In my young manhood I was always reading, and I used to walk around with beautifully written passages in my head from books that had made a deep impression on me. I used to haunt the bookstores. At the Strand Bookstore in New York I bought many books during the 1960s for a dollar fifty—Malcolm Lowry, *Under the Volcano*; Eugene O'Neill, *Long Day's Journey into Night*. I read biographies of William James and Arthur Schopenhauer. I read plays and short stories by Tennessee Williams, and much more.

Years before, as an adolescent in the 1940s, I had read all the fairy tale books in the Austin Public Library, by the Brothers Grimm, and by Hans Christian Andersen. I haunted the stacks of the library and discovered history books on Europe in the nineteenth century, especially on France. I was reading for the sake of reading, nonutilitarian at the time. Then, as an art student at the University of Texas in the 1950s, I thought I would become a commercial artist. My dream was to do cover illustrations for the *Saturday Evening Post* or *Collier's* magazine. Norman Rockwell was my model. As I have said, taking Weismann's classes changed the direction of my life.

Many years after, I became a professor of Chicano studies and Latin American studies at the University of California, Riverside, in 1972. As a professor, I would make frequent trips to Mexico and haunt the bookstores on Avenida Madero and around the *zócalo*, and I would come home with boxes of books. Also, I would haunt Shakespeare & Co. Books in Berkeley, California, in the seventies and eighties. On annual trips to the MLA convention in New York City, there too, I would buy many books each time I visited, at the Strand Book Store. My multivolume personal library tells the story of my reading life and my life as a traveler and dreamer. It tells the story of books that fell serendipitously into my hands.

I look back now to the beginning in Pflugerville, Texas, where I was born, to childhood in the country where my propensities as a daydreamer began. Once more I can see in retrospect that my propensities led me to reading, to travel, and to languages. After expressing indebtedness to all the people of whom I have written, I also wish to thank the countless students who have taken my classes.

Unlike my mother and father, who did not have the opportunity to go to school, even though we were poor I had the privilege of books and a university education. I found that teaching at the university provided me with an ideal opportunity to learn continuously, endlessly, joyously, and to share with hundreds and hundreds of students during more than thirty-five years the immense value of curiosity and intellectual inquiry, and the joys of learning for its own sake, through reading.

Like Weismann shared with his students, I learned that by sharing with my students the books that I was reading and learning from, I was in fact learning. Importantly, I learned from my intellectually curious and inquisitive students. My reading and writing have served my persistent efforts to promote knowledge of the connections between Latin American and Mexican cultural and intellectual history with Chicano studies, literature, and the arts. Over the years also, my interest in international historiography has grown tremendously. Interpreting and reinterpreting the historical past led me to develop an interest in many other cultural groups from many countries of the world. My efforts have been directed to placing Americans of Mexican ancestry and their contributions to history and the arts in the context of other Americans and peoples of the world.

My firm belief is that we Americans of Mexican ancestry—*mexicanos en los Estados Unidos*—are the beneficiaries of the social movements that began in the 1950s, and that one must never underestimate the value of reading and a good education. *Con la lectura y la buena educación, ¡sí se puede!* Reading and a good education can enable us to be citizens of the world without turning our backs on our cultural heritage, intellectual history, language, and traditions. We now know that Mexico has a vast and admirable intellectual history in the humanities, social sciences, and all the arts. From reading I have learned, in addition, that the highest achievements of world civilizations belong to us all.

Holy Scripture

Ever Rodríguez

Rarely do we stop to ponder upon the mindless activities we do daily such as walking, eating, talking, reading, and all that become second nature and which we do almost mechanically. Very seldom do we remember how we learned and when we mastered such basic skills. Most of us do not recall taking our first steps alone, babbling our first words, first eating an entire meal with a spoon, or reading our first complete word ever.

Learning to read was a painful task for me. I remember crying several times over my reading assignments while my mother preached at me, telling me how she did not want me to be like my ignorant father, who had never learned to read or write. Her preaching eventually paid off, and little by little a miracle happened to me as I gained the ability to put letters together, first into nonsensical syllables, then into complete words. Eventually those words gave way to actual sentences communicating a string of discernible thought. In retrospect, learning to read was quite an accomplishment for me, considering that I was constantly uprooted by my family's job migrations and that I had neither mentors nor support outside of school.

Unfortunately, the miracle of reading never happened to my father. My grandmother once told us that when my father was sent to school as a youngster back in Mexico, he had a great deal of difficulty learning to read and write. One day the teacher told my grandma that her son was not good for school: I teach him the lesson, read to him, ask him to repeat; and when I ask him to try to read for me from the same text, he looks at the text and repeats eternally: "tantas-natas, tantas-natas, tantas-natas." The teacher also complained that while the rest of the children had advanced from drawing circles and dashes to writing actual letters, my father would continue drawing the same circles and dashes—"puras bolitas y palitos," as she said. My grandmother was furious at first, and she even tried to enforce the harsh old system of blood instruction—"las letras con sangre entran," as she used to say. Eventually she also gave up on my father, and the issue made a natural transition from anger to irony until it finally banked on humor. My grandmother now simply laughs every time she recounts the story about my father's *tantas-natas*. She blames her aunt Angeles for influencing the kid with such terms, which referred to the nonsense and gossip traded by the women in the small town where they grew up. Since the teacher did not know what to do with my father and since there was so much work around the house, my grandmother decided that my father was better off working instead of wasting time mastering his *tantas-natas*.

But the first words I ever read were from *El Libro Vaquero*, a pulp fiction, Western comic still available today in Mexico. Reading does not usually come easy for most people; something has to trigger the interest, and for me the colorful drawings did it. The cheap Western displays such sexy drawings that it recently stirred up arguments in the Colorado public libraries that carry this publication for their Spanish-speaking patrons. But for me, the sexy drawings became secondary when all of a sudden I realized that I had acquired the ability to put words together and that I was able to read entire sentences. I felt proud and special particularly because I knew that my father—the adult with all the power and authority in my home—had not succeeded at reading. The first words I ever read were "Me vuelves loco," part of the corny dialogue of a romantic couple in *El Libro Vaquero*. The phrase turned out to be true for me as well in my romance with reading. I began to read anything that crossed my way: cheesy pulp fiction that my older siblings brought home, stories in textbooks and old magazines or newspapers that I found along the way. One day, as I walked back from school, a whirlwind came by, covering me with dust, leaves, and all kinds of light trash. A piece of newspaper got stuck in my armpit as I tried to cover my eyes from the dust. I grabbed the piece of paper and began to read the text it contained. The incomplete picture showed awesome sand dunes, and the story told of a nomad who traveled to and fro in the Moroccan desert. I did not get the full article, but the little I read made me realize that reading could transport me into faraway places and distant worlds, allowing me to live other people's lives. My passion for reading was boosted that day; sadly, however, we had no books to read at home.

The toilet room was the place where I did most of my reading because there was a natural need for paper there and often that paper had some type of readable text. My family, like many in Mexico, was very poor and could not even afford to buy toilet paper; instead, we would bring in a newspaper or use any kind of paper to wipe our rears clean. There is a popular Mexican verse which alludes to wiping an ass clean with any kind of paper, and one will often find this verse scribbled on the walls of public restrooms in Mexico:

Cuando vayas para el baño
no te olvides del papel,
no importa que sea un diario
el culo no sabe leer.

This means:

When you go to the restroom
don't forget to bring paper,
it doesn't matter if it's newspaper
the ass doesn't know how to read

My sisters would often scavenge around the house for paper, and then they would cut it into small squares of about five inches until there was a good stack. They would then run a metal wire through the stack to hang the paper from a nail on the bare wall inside the toilet room, and that was our stash. Reading the text on those pieces of paper was often frustrating; I never knew the beginning or the end of anything contained in those cuttings. Sometimes I would flip through the rest of the stack hoping to find pieces to complete my literal puzzle, but I rarely did. My imagination was frequently forced to give those cuttings a transitional congruence from one piece to the next. Eventually some members of my family began to complain about how long I stayed in the restroom. My father warned me, and he asked me not to read too much while I was in there. I complained to my mother, asking her menacingly if she really wanted me to learn how to read or not. I told her how unfair this was, especially since my father took just as long in the restroom and he did not even read. My mother was supportive but she asked me not to hold the restroom hostage, and asked me to try to read outside.

Sometimes my sister would get paper without text from wrappings or old, unused notebooks and then I would be out of the restroom quickly because there was nothing interesting to hold me in there. But it was during those textless times when I began to notice a major lack of reading material in our house. I was the youngest in my household, my father was illiterate and my mother could barely read or write, my older siblings worked all day and they only brought their cheesy pulp fiction home infrequently. The only book in the entire house was a voluminous old Bible which nobody was supposed to read because it was sacred—or so my mother told me when I attempted to open it once in her presence. Back then, in pre–Vatican II Catholicism, the priests were the only ones who were supposed to read the Bible and interpret it for the flock. But I had become a curious brat, and I took a peek at it when my mother was not around. The book might as well have been written in tongues, because I could hardly understand any of what I read in there. I figured I would need to work at it with a dictionary, word by word. I understood why nobody even attempted to touch that old book, and I let it continue to be the untouchable Holy Scripture that it was. I also thought that the pages of the Holy Scripture were so thin that this book would not even make good paper for the restroom. The pages would simply break in the hand.

One summer something interesting happened to me. Someone had brought into our home the first half of an incomplete book and had placed it in the bathroom as toilet paper. When I saw it I started reading it and then seized what was left of it, bringing it in and out of the toilet room with me every time. The book did not have covers or any other information identifying it, and the only other information besides the text were the numbers on pages that went up to forty-seven. The book rescued me from my reading vacuum, and it also saved me from the occasional lack of wiping paper. I ripped only a few pages from the ones I had already read, but for the most part I tried to keep it intact because I really liked the story and I knew I would start reading it again when I finished it. I had been reading the book for about a week and a half when my mother told me and my younger sister that we were going to go for a couple of weeks to visit my grandmother who lived in the province. This was a great opportunity for me to have fun as my grandma had a couple of horses, and cousins around my age lived near her. Knowing that I would not have time to read, I hid the book behind an old, dusty cabinet in the toilet room, thinking that this was a piece of furniture nobody ever used or moved. The next day my mother put me and my sister on the bus, and we left. I had a really good time with my grandma and my cousins, but I was also looking forward to returning home to continue reading the book I had hid.

When I returned home I said hello to everyone, put my belongings away, and then went straight to the toilet room in search of my book. To my surprise, the restroom was neatly organized, the cabinet dusted, and my precious chunk of book gone. I stormed out of there and asked my mother and sisters what had happened in the toilet room. My mother told me that she had cleaned up and reorganized the room while we were out because it was such an ugly mess. I asked her if she had found my piece of book and she told me she had left it in the restroom for everybody to use. I didn't have to ask any more details; I knew what that meant for any piece of paper left in that room. It is an awful feeling to start reading something, really like it, and then be unable to continue reading. I kept telling my mother in anger that I was reading that book, that I had not finished reading it and that I wanted it back. Each time she looked at me in awe and said she was sorry but nobody could do anything about it. "You should have told me and then I would have saved it, or you should have taken the book with you," she said. I was furious and did not talk to anyone else for the rest of the day. As my older siblings came back from their jobs, they each laughed when they found out my reason for being upset.

Time went by without anything interesting to read in the toilet room. I also felt demoted by having to go back to reading those small squares of paper that my sister cut from wherever she could. I confess that when I found out that my book was gone forever I thought about getting my mother's Holy Scripture, ripping off the covers, and putting it in the restroom to suffer the same fate that my book had. But I knew that this would imply severe physical punishment; and besides, the Bible's pages were so thin that not even my father would have liked them to wipe his rear. I thought maliciously how sweet it would be to tell my mother that her Bible was not even good to wipe somebody's butt, and that even my father would complain about her useless book. Now every time I come across a badly written book I tell myself that at least the paper may be good for wiping somebody's butt.

Several years later, while working on a bachelor's degree in Spanish literature, I took a class about the Spanish literary period called El Siglo de Oro. The book *La vida es sueño* by Calderón de la Barca was one of the readings required for the class. I remember that while reading the book, some of the names of the characters sounded very familiar to me, yet I was sure that I had never read that book before. But suddenly I understood that this was the very same book I had begun reading in the restroom when I was a child. I was overwhelmed with joy when I realized what I had in my hands. Here it was finally, a copy of the book that had enchanted me long ago with only a few pages. I devoured the text and finished reading it the same day. It was not only a pleasurable read, for the book is a masterpiece, but it was also a time lived again with my childhood and with all the memories of how I began my love affair with reading. I remembered my mother's Holy Scripture, and how sacred that book was for her even when she had not read its contents. I realized that people treasure books for various reasons. I also realized that *La vida es sueño* had just become my Holy Scripture for what was said in the text, as well as for the reminiscence it brought me of my tender years and my beginnings as a reader.

Storm's Impact
One for the Books

Veronica Flores-Paniagua

As it is with anyone who has coastal interests, I watch weather news closely whenever a storm is in the Gulf of Mexico during hurricane season. With Hurricane Dolly in July 2008, I worried about my mother's house and the family who still live in my hometown, Corpus Christi. But that worry was mixed with delight—delight in a memory of long ago.

It was 1970, and Hurricane Celia made a beeline for the Texas coast, ultimately raking the Corpus Christi area on August 3rd. I was four years old and every bit a mama's girl. Everywhere she went, I went. When Celia struck, I remember standing next to her, peering out of a crack between the boards over our windows, watching in amazement as the porch on the house next door crumbled. It was no match for Celia's winds. Our house, on the city's West Side, miraculously sustained only minor damage, save for the broken plate-glass window in the dining room that a flying rock shattered when it hit the one spot that wasn't covered. The house on the other side of our home had been converted into a small public library and it, like our neighbor's home, was heavily damaged.

I have absolutely no recollection of ever going to this particular library to check out books. Given my mother's love of books, I have to believe we went frequently, but the memory may just be one that's lost to the years.

One glorious memory not lost, however, is what happened in the calm of Celia's eye. (It may have been the calm after the storm, but in my mind, I've always remembered it this way.) Blue skies emerged, a light breeze blew, and, but for the damaged houses and downed trees and power lines, it would have been a beautiful summer day. Radio alerts warned residents to stay sheltered and that a citywide curfew meant we might be subject to criminal prosecution if we were to venture outside.

I may have been only four, but I grasped the gravity of the situation. Still, my mother did something uncharacteristically bold. My mother was the shy sort, not one given to looking at people directly. But when she perceived an injustice, her head popped up and she stood strong. So, too, she did on this day.

Celia's winds took their toll on the library's roof, causing it to collapse and let the rain in. My mother figured that the books inside, having been soaked, would be destroyed along with the rest of the library. So she took the matter—and a wheelbarrow—into her hands.

During the eye's brief stillness, I walked alongside her as she rolled the wheelbarrow next door. I vaguely recall entering the building, though I don't remember using a door. A broken window, perhaps? Shelves were knocked over, books were scattered on the wet floor. Working quickly, we scooped up as many as we could get into the wheelbarrow and made a speedy exit. In legal terms, we were looting. But in her view then, as surely now, the crime would have been greater had those books not been rescued. She later regretted not having gone back for more.

We took enough to fill a small bookcase, and the titles ranged broadly. A few took days to dry, while others were only slightly damp and otherwise unscathed. Most distinct in my memory are *Gulliver's Travels*, *The Robe*, various editions of a children's encyclopedia, and a science textbook with a brown cover and the symbol of an atom on its spine.

Most children my age in my parents' lower-working-class neighborhood didn't know such riches. I treasured those books. I couldn't yet read them but recognized their value because I understood the risk my mother had taken to get them.

That adventure would form the foundation of my own love of books. And the memory is inescapable. I conjure it whenever we enter hurricane season every year, whenever a storm threatens the Texas Gulf Coast, and, now, with my own young children, I get to relive it every time they ask me to read a book.

As it turned out, Celia's winds did, indeed, do quite a number on the building. The roof, only partially collapsed when we'd gone in, completely caved in. Demolition crews later hauled away what was left, books and all. Except the ones on our bookshelf. They survived. And they were loved.

Note

© 2008, *San Antonio Express-News*, reprinted with permission.

Gift of Poetry,
Gift of Reading

Irma Flores-Manges

The most memorable and meaningful readings I have attended featured Acoma poet Simon Ortiz. I first heard him read his poetry at the Inter-American Book Fair in San Antonio, Texas, in 2001. I had read poetry in high school and in college, but I never connected to that style of literature. Poetry was too confusing. In the discussions, whether in class or with my friends, I just never got the point of reading poetry. I felt alienated from this type of literature. I had started to write and felt that I needed to try listening again. I decided to drive from Austin to San Antonio to hear Ortiz read. I heard he was a dynamic and inspiring poet. Listening to him read his work gave me a new appreciation of poetry because it was beautifully lyrical and told a story. It was easy to connect to his feelings. I could see in my mind's eye the people and places he writes about. Ortiz's poetry speaks to the senses, especially the heart/soul. After his reading, I realized the experience had opened up the world of poetry for me, which had always been elusive. I now knew that the poetry I had been exposed to for so long was not one I could relate to because it did not speak to the experiences in my life. I read all of Ortiz's work and proceeded to read Native American poets and Chicano poets. I felt a connection to poetry that I had been searching for. The poetry spoke to my heart and soul.

I related to specific poetry of Ortiz's having to do with his family. In the poem "A Story of How a Wall Stands," I felt and saw his dad moving his hands and making the mud in his palm. He showed his son how the mud would help stabilize the wall to endure the test of time. In "Yuusthiwa," I saw the elder walking down the road not wanting a ride but just walking. Yuusthiwa lived a long life by appreciating life, taking care of himself, and being friendly. My Tío Lencho was like him because he walked everywhere so he could meet people and for his health. I could see my family in Ortiz's family poems. In "My Mother, My Sisters" the reader glimpses how his sisters make their pots and the careful way his mother paints her pots with a yucca brush. This brought back memories of my abuelas, tías, and my mom working on their quilting very meticulously and sharing stories with each other. Potters and quilters are artists to be respected for their work. All of these poems show the respect and love of a son for his parents and their way of life.

While I was reading and listening to Ortiz's poetry, it evoked in me memories of how I felt about my mom and my dad and the gifts of reading and education they gave me. Reading was my mother's gift to me. Reading and books have always been an important part of my life. My mother is ninety-three now, and she reads three to four books a week. She is completely bilingual and reads in Spanish and English. My mother is an incredible woman. She was born in 1919. She went to school in the 1920s and 1930s, graduating from high school in 1938. She played softball, volleyball, and tennis. My mom and my abuelos worked the fields. When she was six years old, Tía Panchita, my Abuelito Güero's sister, asked Abuelita Sara if my mother could come live with her. She had no children. Abuelita Sara told Tía Panchita to ask my mom. Tía told my mom she would buy her new clothes and shoes. She told her she would have a room of her own. My mom said yes, and she went to live with Tía Panchita and Tío Chencho. Tía Panchita was a midwife and healer. She was a very independent woman, whom I knew and loved all my life. My memory of her was that she was a loving and liberal person who encouraged her family to try different experiences to grow intellectually, spiritually, and emotionally. Tía paid for my mom to get everything to be successful in school in the 1920s and 1930s. Mom did very well in school and made everyone proud. In high school, she was given a ride to school in the morning but in the afternoon she had to walk for an hour and a half to get home. She and her friends had to walk through ranchland, or along the highway, because they lived in a small town with about a hundred people. It took a lot of strength of character to continue on with school when all her six brothers and sisters did not graduate, except for her younger sister. It took a lot for my tíos to let her continue going to school and not make her work in the fields. My abuelos loved my mom enough to let her go to have a better life. Life was really hard for them, but they made it. I am so proud of my mother Andrea Rodríguez, Abuelito Güero, Abuelita Sara Rodríguez, Tía Panchita, and Tío Chencho Cárdenas. Mom even started correspondence class for accounting. She read only what she could find in the little town or school books. She realized, though, how important a good education is in order to succeed in life.

My mom married my dad and moved to San Antonio. My sister and I were born there. I can remember always having books to read and colors to paint. My parents read to me and my sister when we were small. My father, Miguel Flores, died when I was eight, and we moved back to Laredo to be with family. My mother was all of a sudden a single mom. She wanted to have family support, not for the money, just having them there to help raise us. We had about twenty family members in a four-block radius. This was really nice and comforting. We never felt alone. Tía Panchita and Tío Chencho lived next door to us. They were still as helpful and encouraging, but now to a younger generation, me and my sister. They were always there for me. They may not have had much but they would always buy whatever I needed, even if it was a book. To buy a book for me on their fixed income was a true gift because most other people would think it was frivolous. They viewed it as helping my education. I loved them so much.

I went to a Catholic school in San Antonio. My mother saved money so I could continue my schooling at Our Lady of Guadalupe School in Laredo, run by Ursuline nuns. The nuns taught all the kids with patience and compassion. They expected us to do our best because they wanted us to believe in ourselves and succeed. Sister Genevieve, Sister Ignatius, Sister Gerard, Sister Gabriel, Sister Timothy, and my friend for over fifty years, Sister Helen Archibald from Boston, were an inspiration for me to do my best always. Sister Helen has been someone who always remembers me in her prayers and with cards at least six times a year. She encouraged me to read and know that I could do what I wanted in life no matter what it was. She has always believed in me. There have always been stories all over the world about nuns mistreating children in school and punishing them for speaking their own language. The Ursuline nuns who taught me never punished us for speaking Spanish. They always tried to help us live up to our potential. These nuns respected our culture and our right to speak Spanish. We were taught to be proud of who we were and respect our culture. We were taught to respect other cultures and religions, which at the time was extraordinary. Ecumenism was just starting in the 60s and 70s. They embraced the idea and took us to different churches and synagogues in town to acquaint us with other religious ideas. We were taught to respect other points of view and beliefs. I don't know if it was because Laredo is a border town and 98 percent of the kids in school were Mexican and Mexican American, but we were never made to feel inferior or punished harshly by the nuns. They encouraged us to read all we could because that was the basis of our succeeding in all other subjects. They would tell us just read, read anything you can.

My high school English teacher, Sister Gerard, exposed me to all types of literature: Dickens, Tolstoy, Keats, Shelley, Cervantes, and others. I wrote twenty-page papers on Faulkner, Shakespeare, and the Arthurian legends. I was taught how to think critically about what I was reading. I had an easier time in college because of her training. It was difficult, but well worth the effort. I thank all the nuns who taught me for the patience and love they shared with me. They cared about how I learned and prepared me for college life. I don't think I would have considered college if my mother and the nuns had not encouraged me and prepared me so well. I was one of the few people in my family to go to college, and get a BA in anthropology and a master's degree in library science.

At home, my tíos and abuelos could not read or write well, but they told great stories out on the porch at night or in a cozy kitchen. All the family stories, gossip, ghost and spirit stories, and *remedios* made life interesting and fun. We knew about everyone in the family and all the old *cuentos*. My abuelos and tíos liked to have books so they could look at the pictures. All of us kids would take turns reading them a story or making something up to go along with the pictures in the book. It was a chance for us to spend time with our elders and have fun telling them stories from books. This was our way of thanking them for all the stories they told us about our culture and family. During this time, there were no Chicano writers to look up to, so the elders kept the culture alive with the oral tradition. Writing down what we heard was important so we would not forget our family stories/cuentos for future generations.

My mom considered it important to buy us encyclopedias and dictionaries from traveling salesmen so my sister and I could do our homework. I took Latin in high school. She bought me flash cards and everything to help me succeed. There was an old used bookstore downtown, and mom would take me there to buy books. She joined kids' book clubs. We received books every two weeks. She was always reading. She would take me to the public library every Saturday and wait until I was done looking for books. We went to Nuevo Laredo, Mexico, to go to the bookstores and shopping. I bought books there so I could practice my Spanish reading. My mom is incredible. I don't know how I can ever thank her for all she has done for me and continues to do for me. She did all she could to keep me reading. She even saved enough money all those years to give me money to go to college for my BA without my having to work. She wanted me to concentrate on my studies. Her saving that money was phenomenal because she did not work. She stayed home to take care of me and my sister. She saved all her money from the little she got from my father's veteran's checks. I will always be grateful and love her more than she can imagine for that gift of my education and love of reading. She sacrificed a lot for me. She has lived with me and my children for the past twenty years. I am a single mom, and she is helping to raise another generation of readers with her grandchildren and great grandchildren. The kids love to watch her read and listen to her scary stories and stories about growing up in the '30s and '40s. They ask about La Llorona, Chupacabra, El Cu Cui, and other stories I tell them that I have heard from her. I now bring her books to read three to four times a week. I am a librarian, and I love my job.

I have shared my appreciation of Ortiz's work with my mother. She enjoys reading and discussing his short stories because she can relate to them. Seeing how much she enjoys his work brought back a vivid memory of the second reading by Simon Ortiz that made an impression on me: "To Exculpate Sorrow." This reading encouraged me to ask my mom a question about her life that I had always wondered about. The essay was reflective of Ortiz's gift as a writer. His intimate knowledge of the oral tradition brings a story to life for the listener. The essay was rich in feeling that left the audience breathless as he read his essay in the bookstore. The audience just sat and listened to every word with bated breath. Everything in the room was so still you could have heard a pin drop. The feeling in the room was electric with raw emotion. The audience was moved as the essay came alive with every word Ortiz read. The raw emotion in the essay came from his essence heart/soul. His description of how his father felt when his brother left him and his sister was heartbreaking because they felt abandoned. His father still felt this way after many years. The sorrow his uncle felt after his brother died touched my heart. I could feel the sheer agony of not being there for his little brother. Ortiz's sorrow and abandonment at the age of six was heartfelt, being left by a parent to wait knowing they are not coming back even though they promised they would. There was a feeling of resignation and sorrow in the essay. I have never felt that much sorrow, so for me the essay was a new experience. I realized that a gifted writer can convey emotion to the reader/listener that is real. The writer can cause the reader/listener to ponder those feelings and think about how this relates to their own lives. Ortiz asks who will mourn the indigenous people and cultures. I think that the best way to honor the past is for healing to start to take place. The government needs to acknowledge the mistreatment of the indigenous people and other people of color in this country. The wrongs need to be corrected by validating indigenous people to themselves and the world. The government needs to quit pretending the indigenous people have vanished because they are still here. They demand to be acknowledged. THEY WILL NOT GO AWAY OR BE INVISIBLE ANYMORE!!!!!!!

After the reading, everyone was quiet. Days later, the experience from the reading was still very powerful and thought provoking as my friends and I discussed our reactions. We felt drained after the reading. The essay brought up several questions for each of us to discuss: What emotions did the essay bring up for me with my own memories? What do I do to others to make them feel abandoned? How can I change how I treat people? What does abandonment mean in my life? How would I define abandonment? How has abandonment affected my life, or has it? How do I get involved in social justice issues? We have to look within ourselves for answers. This was a very powerful essay and reading by an exceptionally talented and gifted author who connects with his audiences on many different levels. Attending his readings has opened up a new world of not just poetry but issues for me to deal with in my life. If I had not gone to the original reading, I think poetry would have been lost to me. It was synchronicity that led me to San Antonio that weekend. This reading brought up a question about my mom. I read the essay to her, and she was thoughtful after I finished. I asked her, did you ever feel abandoned by my abuelos? You did not live with them? Did you feel they gave you away? She thought about it for a while, and she said no. "I was loved very much by Tía and Tío. I was always visiting my brothers and sisters. I felt I was lucky because I could go to school and not work in the fields." I have always wondered if my mother felt sorrow because she was not raised by her parents. Now I know the answer, and reading the essay made it easy to ask her; it opened the subject up for me.

The stories are synchronistic because my mother's gift of reading led me to Ortiz's gift of poetry. Love of reading encouraged me always to appreciate all types of literature. Poetry was the one venue I needed to relate to, and Ortiz's poetry did that for me. Ortiz's poetry led me back to my mom and family with the memories evoked by reading/listening to him. I would not have tried to look into a different type of literature without the initial love of reading. The memories from Ortiz's poetry and essay helped me clarify some important family questions with my mother. My mother and I discussed them after reading his work. It shows how important it is to be able to connect to the written word by hearing it read. The influence of both these people in my life makes me want to read more about different perspectives on life and other cultures. I should question what I read and explore the issues. I enjoy reading biographies or biographical essays of the author I am interested in, to see how their life is reflected in their work. I love to read. I never go anywhere without a book. Reading is important for all of us to know where we came from and who we are. Reading helps us to understand others, which should help us get along better in this world we live in. I don't know what I would do if I could not read. My children, grandchildren, nieces, and nephews consider it a treat to go to a bookstore to get a book to read. I would encourage people, if you can hear an author read their work, do it. The dimension added by listening to someone read their work and watching hand gestures and facial expressions is priceless. It may open your senses to a new type of literature that did not appeal to you before you heard the author read their work. With a stereoscopic view, both stories could stand alone, but the combination of the two provides a richer view of my life experiences with reading.

The Bookcase

Lucía de Anda Vázquez

I polish the bookcase and admire its rich dark color and the grain of the wood. I notice for the first time the trail of scratches on its surface. The trail brings to mind drunk ants, they are the scribbling loops and curves of someone new to writing. As I fill it top to bottom with books, I appreciate the depth and varied heights of its shelves. It is sturdy, and I laugh at myself for thinking, "They don't make things like they used to." I am happier than I have been in a long time.

The bookcase is being filled with a portion of my personal canon, and many other books that I look forward to reading. Works by Latina authors fill the two top shelves. In shelf three there are books by other women of color, Maya Angelou, Amy Tan. In the bottom will go what fits the "other": self-help, fiction, and women's issues books. This has become the Women's bookcase; its place of honor is in the living room. There are six other bookshelves in my new two-bedroom apartment. Realizing this makes me laugh out loud. I congratulate myself on letting go of the full sets of my "lady" private eye books: Janet Evanovich, Sue Grafton, and Diane Mott Davidson, along with the eight other boxes of books I left behind.

This bookcase stood, unnoticed, in the hallway of our family home for years. It was purchased by my maternal grandmother, Mama Quica, from a Japanese family before they were taken away to an internment camp. Although she never had the opportunity to attend school, Mama Quica, widowed at age thirty-five with eight children, appreciated the importance of reading.

Growing up, we lived in a very small (population two thousand), dusty, dried-out town in central California. One hot summer day, after my allotment of "women's work" was done, I was very bored. Washing and hanging loads of sheets, towels, T-shirts, and *chones* on yards of clothesline is therapeutic but not very entertaining. My sister, Marty (baptized Maria de Martha), tired of me bugging, suggested I read something from the bookshelf. What bookshelf? Where? Turns out, it was filled with books. Some books in Spanish, which I could not understand, some *Reader's Digest* condensed books, and two shelves of boy books. The mystery series of the Hardy Boys, to be exact. Apparently, one of my brothers (I have five) had bought them to encourage the younger brothers to read. Lucky for me, I was just at that age when I had an interest in boys. That Joe Hardy sounded pretty darn cute. I spent a lot of time and had many adventures with those Hardy boys. I always wondered why there were no girls involved. To this day, I find smart men very attractive and devour female detective novels. The bookcase saved me that summer and created a reading monster.

Two of the bookshelves in our new apartment are in my daughter's room. She packed her set of Harry Potter, some pony books, and a few favorite children's books. There is a small bookcase that sits in the corner of the dining area, next to the toy box and small table and chairs I keep for small visitors. Along with the children's books and puzzles, I have taken to buying and adding books to the shelf without telling her. Books that I know she's read more than once, and books she hasn't read by some of her favorite authors. Last week, *Esperanza Rising* and *The Color of My Words* disappeared from this bookcase, and found a home in hers. It's a game we play; I'm creating a monster.

We have moved to this new town so I can go to graduate school and read many more books. I feel an urgent need to learn more about Latina writers. When I read Latina fiction, sometimes I laugh, sometimes I cry, and, always, I am validated. They make me proud. I want to know what aspects of their writing interested my daughter enough to make her into a reader, and continue to make her read the same book, again and again. We are happier than we have been in a long time.

Pocho Librolandia; or, Yes We Do Read Too

Anthony Macías

I t's my earliest memory of an intense, captivating literary experience—reading Edith Hamilton's *Mythology: Timeless Tales of Gods and Heroes*. When I was eight-and-a-half years old my mom gave me a used paperback copy so that I could draw the illustrations by Steele Savage. Instead, I read the entire 315-page book. I remember enjoying *The Lion, the Witch, and the Wardrobe* and riding my bicycle to the local public library, solo. As a boy in the late 1970s, I used to consume *Mad* magazine, through which I plunged deeper into American popular culture via subversive satire. I also grew up on *The Amazing Spider Man*, *The Uncanny X-Men*, and the other Marvel superheroes long before these comic books became television cartoons and Hollywood feature films. By 1980, at the age of eleven, I entered adolescence reading underground comix like *The Fabulous Furry Freak Brothers* as well as the adult illustrated fantasy–science fiction magazine *Heavy Metal*.

In high school, graphic novels like Frank Miller's *Ronin* and *Dark Knight* fascinated me, as did fantasy novels like Piers Anthony's Incarnations of Immortality series and Michael Moorcock's Elric series. But my favorite literary genre, science fiction, truly stoked my imagination, from Aldous Huxley's *Brave New World* to Frank Herbert's *Dune*, Philip K. Dick's *Do Androids Dream of Electric Sheep?*, Gene Wolfe's The Book of the New Sun series, Simon Hawke's TimeWars series, and William Gibson's *Neuromancer*. I recall to this day reading in wonder H. G. Wells's *The Island of Dr. Moreau*;

Edgar Allan Poe's "The Raven," "Annabel Lee," and "The Tell-Tale Heart"; and Edgar Rice Burroughs's *Tarzan* and John Carter of Mars novels. In high school English classes I remember reading short stories like "Flowers for Algernon" and "The Most Dangerous Game," plays like *Death of a Salesman*, novellas like *The Pearl* and *The Old Man and the Sea*, and novels like *The Great Gatsby* and *My Ántonia*. In addition, I voraciously devoured "pleasure reading" books such as John Irving's *The World According to Garp* and Stephen King's short stories and early novels.

During my freshman year at UC Berkeley, Cherríe Moraga introduced me to Chicano/a literature and poetry in Chicano Studies 1A/1B, an ethnic studies alternative to the standard English and composition first-year requirement. In her class I discovered the writings of Ana Castillo, Gary Soto, Gloria Anzaldúa, Alurista, Carlos Fuentes, Arturo Islas, Ron Arias, Jimmy Santiago Baca, Rudolfo Anaya, and Lorna Dee Cervantes. In English classes I read poets like Keats, Coleridge, T.S. Eliot, e. e. cummings, Langston Hughes, and Amiri Baraka, as well as novelists like Thomas Pynchon, Ishmael Reed, Amy Tan, Leslie Marmon Silko, and Toni Morrison. At Cal, during the height of the Allan Bloom–era culture/canon wars, I read everything from Herodotus's *The Persian Wars* to *The Iliad* and *The Odyssey*, *Othello*, Fielding's *Joseph Andrews*, Conrad's *Heart of Darkness*, *The Autobiography of Malcolm X*, *The Communist Manifesto*, *Things Fall Apart*, Frantz Fanon's *The Wretched of the Earth*, Richard Wright's *Black Boy* and *Native Son*, and Michael Herr's *Dispatches*. Although I read Kerouac's *On the Road*, I preferred Ginsberg's "Howl." For a seminar with the cultural historian Lawrence Levine, I read *Slaves of the Depression*, *How to Win Friends and Influence People*, and *The Grapes of Wrath*.

I gained an entirely new appreciation for and developed an entirely new relationship to books in graduate school, first for one year at UCLA in the history PhD program, then for four and a half years at the University of Michigan, Ann Arbor, in the American Culture Program. In grad school I read one book per week per seminar, plus journal articles, in courses that included eighteenth-, nineteenth-, and twentieth-century U.S. historiography, Latino historiography, Chicanos and Latinos in film, Latinos and language, Latina literature, Latino popular culture, gender and transnationalism, the sociology of racism, the 1950s and the 1980s, the culture industries, and disciplinary and research methods. Reading and synthesizing scores of books while studying for my oral field exams sharpened my facility, as did learning how to write book reviews. Researching my dissertation and my first book led me to new kinds of reading, as I sifted through personal papers, news clippings, and ephemera, and pored over oral history transcripts in special collections and other archives. Between my coursework, fieldwork, and secondary research, I have read encyclopedias, bibliographic indexes, and biographical, musical, and etymological dictionaries, as well as published writings by the likes of E. P. Thompson, Ira Berlin, Richard White, Sandra Cisneros, José Antonio Burciaga, Martín Espada, Stuart Hall, Dick Hebdige, Raymond Williams, Michael Omi and Howard Winant, Janice Radway, Richard Drinnon, Reginald Horsman, Richard Slotkin, Néstor García Canclini, Jesús Martín-Barbero, Carlos Monsiváis, George Chauncey, bell hooks, Carey McWilliams, Richard Dyer, Chon Noriega, Mary Romero, Sterling Stuckey, and Jack Forbes.

Over the years, I mastered the art of reading old periodicals on bulky microfilm machines, scrolling, staring, and squinting for hours until my eyes burned. I began my long association with major research-university libraries at the Berkeley campus's Main Library. Deep in the bowels of the stacks of the flagship library of the University of California system, I roamed the cramped corridors and rode the service elevators, lost in the labyrinth of bound journals, hardcover monographs, and oversize tomes and folios, first as an undergraduate researcher, then as a campus facilities maintenance worker. Eventually, as an independent contractor document retriever, I ended up visiting almost every library at UC Berkeley, UCLA, and the University of Michigan. Once I embarked upon the PhD program voyage, I rarely found spare time for pleasure reading, save for Neal Stephenson's *Snow Crash* and Jean Auel's *Earth's Children* series.

Teaching Chicano Studies and Ethnic Studies courses has enabled me to assign the work of Ricardo Flores Magón, Aimé Césaire, Rodolfo "Corky" Gonzales, Juan Felipe Herrera, Tomás Ybarra-Frausto, Patricia Zavella, Denise Segura, Beatriz Pesquera, Mario García, Al Camarillo, Vicki Ruiz, David Gutiérrez, George Sánchez, Olga Nájera-Ramírez, Yolanda Broyles-González, Rosa Linda Fregoso, Mary Pardo, Catherine Ramírez, Michelle Habell-Pallán, Robin Kelley, George Lipsitz, Douglas Monroy, Margaret Rose, David Roediger, George Frederickson, and Edmund Morgan, among many, many others. In my capacity as educator and mentor I help my students become critical thinkers, confident writers, and close readers, as I train the text message/Twitter/Tumblr/Instagram/Facebook generation to rigorously analyze a variety of texts. Of course, the main text I have read and reread (and written and rewritten) is my own book, ten-plus years in the making, since its origins as a doctoral dissertation. Finally holding my book in my hands for the first time proved a slightly surreal moment, signaling my arrival at a major milestone in my long journey as a scholar. In addition, my professional experience as an author has shown me some of the behind-the-scenes inner workings of publishing and printing, as has my close study of the reference guide *The Chicago Manual of Style.*

My wife, Connie, and I have tried to pass on a love of books to our two kids by always reading them bedtime stories, from the African sage Aesop's fables to classical myths (the hunter goddess Artemis unexpectedly became a fiercely independent female role model for my daughter, Paloma, at age eight); from modern retellings of fairy tales like "Little Red Riding Hood," "Cinderella," "The Three Little Pigs," and "Rapunzel" to shelves full of children's books (my son, Anand, at age three, unexpectedly started "reading" the father-son sing-song *Hush Little Alien* to me from memory). These naptime and nighttime narratives include fun rhymes and near tongue-twisters by Dr. Seuss as well as favorites like *Goodnight Moon, Little Gorilla, One Hungry Monster, The Tale of Custard the Dragon, The Doubtful Guest, Way Out in the Desert, Telephone, The Spider and the Fly, Whoever You Are, Raven, Frida, My Name Is Georgia, Diego, In My Family, The Mystery of the Shark and the Poi, The Upside Down Boy, The Old Man and His Door, Prietita and the Ghost Woman, Merlin and the Dragons, Richard Wright and the Library Card,* and *The Girl Who Loved Wild Horses.* Their books, along with their subscriptions to children's magazines, help to counterbalance their multimedia reality of cable TV, videos, DVDs, DSL desktops, laptops, iPads, iPods, and cell phones. In elementary school, my children have read the Mexican American oral history *Esperanza Rising,* books on African American historical figures, the Harry Potter and Percy Jackson series, loans from the library, and purchases from book fairs, not to mention books bought at independent and chain bookstores (and at *segundas*) and borrowed from local libraries. Nevertheless, we still need to deprogram them not only from the industrial institutionalization of public education but also from the mainstream junk culture of consumerism, materialism, and mediocrity.

The book format itself has gone gadget, with the seemingly *Star Trek*–inspired pads like Kindle and other e-reader devices, and gone digital DIY with the rise of amateur online self-publishing. But hey, Chicanos have long been putting their own work out there, from community newspapers and journals to small, grassroots *floricanto* chapbooks, Xeroxed punk fanzines, Kitchen Table Press, and Los Bros. Hernandez's inaugural *Love and Rockets* comic book. May spoken, printed, and scanned words help set all of us all the way free. May we empower ourselves in this twenty-first century brave new world order of continued militarization, globalization, deregulation, and multinational corporate flexible capitalist Wall Street, banking, and real estate speculation. May our poets, professors, and publishers keep telling our diverse, compelling stories, histories, herstories, and queerstories; rural, urban, and suburban stories; Emma Tenayuca, Josefina Fierro, and Dolores Huerta stories; Franklin Boulevard, Florin Road, and Folsom Prison stories; the stories we tell ourselves, in Spanish, *caló*, Spanglish, and/or, for *los pochos*, English.

From my privileged position as a tenured UC professor, I enjoy the freedom to read and teach a continuum of books, to peer review new articles and books, to explore limitless research topics, and to visit the stacks, archives, and used bookstores of the world. All my decades of disciplined, sustained study, my childhood and teenage years of absorbing alternative, pulp publications, and my ongoing outlet of personal poetry, have confirmed my bookworm's love of the beauty, dignity, and power of the written word. Books are indeed magical portals to ancient eons and distant stars. Books reveal vistas to broader horizons, open minds to other possibilities, lives, and realities. Books expand our knowledge of small societies and grand civilizations, of humanity's everyday dramas and crowning achievements, of its cruelty and violence, its splendor and spirituality, and its humbling, recent habitation on this blue planet.

In the end, we can never recover the volumen lost in antiquity, the rare parchment scrolls burned in the library of Alexandria, the heretical Gnostic gospels excluded from the Old Testament, the birch bark Maya codices burned by the Spanish bishop of Yucatán, or the countless Native, Black, and Chicano poems silenced before they could be put to paper. Yet, human beings have always painted on cave walls, created petroglyphs, pictographs, cuneiform, and hieroglyphics (Greek for "sacred carving"). We have all inherited the legacy of Egyptian papyrus rolls, the palimpsest of Archimedes, the pillars of Ashoka, the Diamond Sutra, and the Book of Kells. As a species, we are hardwired to wander and ponder, rhyme in rhythm, compose epic poems and corridos, create tragic and comic plays, publish dissident political pamphlets, broadsides, *planes*, and manifestos, and scribble inspired ideas on scraps of paper. We are driven to story-tell through technology—from intaglio etching, Gutenberg's press, and incunabula typographic technique to banging on typewriters and writing computer code. Ultimately, this inner drive of articulation and self-expression bodes well for our survival, as poetry and prose will forever cast spells with written incantations, satirical observations, and theoretical explanations for the ages.

Un juego de libros añejos

Margarita Cota-Cárdenas

Cuando yo tenía unos trece–catorce años, mi padre entró al "porche" viejo que después remodelaron a mi recámara, cargando una caja de cartón. Fui la mayor de los seis hijos de mis padres, quienes por muchos años manejaban un "campo laboral" para trabajadores, a veces familias, agrícolas en el Valle San Joaquín de California. A esa edad, ya vivíamos en Newman, y como he contado en mis escritos previos, nuestro padre no quiso que sus hijos trabajaran en los "files". Insistió que debíamos "educarnos" o ir a la escuela, y eso fue lo que cada uno de nosotros hicimos a nuestra manera particular. Cuando me preguntan de cómo me interesé o empecé a escribir, siempre empiezo explicando que aprendí a leer en español primero, y se debía a los "comics" o "funnybooks" mexicanos que los adultos traían a casa.

Mis días de adicta a los "monitos" empezaron con el *Pepín* de Mexicali, libritos que allá en mi recuerdo los empecé a leer como mi primer contacto con "literatura". Así, caminé el camino de lecturas que me imagino caminaron igual muchas otras chicanitas: de los monitos a *Vanidades*, las revistas de cultura popular como *Confidencias* o algo así. Los periódicos que más impacto me causaron eran los "tabloids" mexicanos, con sus titulares como POLICIA MATA A SU MUJER POR AMOR, MUERTES DE CAMPESINOS EN CAMION VOLCADO, cosas así escandalizantes y por el estilo. Siempre estos "tabloides" llevaban algunas fotos chocantes, imágenes directas y horribles con sus muertos sangrientos, el preso haciendo una cara seriota, etc.

Con cariño recuerdo días bochornosos en el campo laboral de mis tíos, en las horas libres de mi prima. Ella ayudaba a cocinar y trabajaba algunas veces en la cocina del campo; yo no. En una de las recámaras sencillas de la parte de la "barraca" donde también vivían mis tíos, mi prima y su hermanito, nos acostumbramos un par de veranos a leer "comic books" y esas revistas mexicanas. Hacíamos fiesta: rebanadas de limón con sal en un plato entre nosotras, en el suelo o acostadas, leíamos, nos contábamos y reíamos, chupe y chupe los limones con sal. Literal y literariamente, fueron memorias "agri-dulces". Hablábamos español primero, y sólo llegamos a aprender el inglés, a fuerza y "por inmersión total" en la escuela primaria del pueblito fronterizo.

De verdad, en la primaria y en la secundaria no recuerdo haberme entusiasmado con ningún libro "literario" ni en inglés ni en "castellano". Llevé las clases recetadas de español, inglés, le di un poco al alemán con lecciones después de clases, con un maestro quien se voluntarizó a tratar de enseñarme a hablar alemán. Escribí, sí, para el periódico en la "high school", y me saqué buenas notas en inglés y español como en las otras clases; pero no recuerdo más que un sólo encuentro de mayor impacto en mi vida como lectora de "libros", verdaderos libros de literatura. Y ese encuentro fue debido a mi padre, quien entró en mi cuarto con una caja de libros viejos, cubierta verde, páginas amarillentas y deshaciéndose las orillas, todo polvoriento.

"¿Qué es, Papá?" me levanté yo de mi sofá/cama. Hija mayor, empecé ese día mi inclinación hacia la literatura y la verdadera lectura de libros, de toda índole. No aprendí a cocinar excepto por lo que había visto en la cocina de mi familia (cocinadora testigo). No me ponían a limpiar ni casa, aunque después me tocó cuidar a hermanitos nuevos después del divorcio de mis padres, debido a que mi madre ya no tenía "prima, una muchacha o señora" que le ayudara en casa como antes. Mis padres simplemente trabajaban de día a noche, y por otra parte he descrito algunas memorias gratas y otras distintas. Nos pasó lo que a muchos chicanitos cuyos padres chicanos se divorciaron o separaron: aprendimos a vivir en un mundo más "americano" que el añorado conjunto de familiares, fiestas, encuentros juveniles, al estilo de la frontera mexicana-americana. Terminamos siendo bilingües, y nuestras lecturas cambiaron. Yo empecé ese día lejano con la literatura, con un juego añejo de libros que me entregó esa tarde, mi padre, como regalo sencillo.

"Es un juego completo de un escritor americano, un Dickens... Lo encontré en 'la segunda' esta mañana... El dueño me dijo que era un escritor muy famoso, no sé de dónde". Así diciendo, mi padre me pone la caja en el suelo, y sale, yo brincando para ver qué era lo que traía la caja.

Me despertó una curiosidad con los libros, y me acuerdo haber ido a la pequeña biblioteca del pueblito norteño donde para entonces vivíamos, para ver qué otros libros me recomendaban. Leí el *Quijote* en inglés, Mark Twain, y me picó la vena irónica de estos escritores. Recuerdo muy bien un librito de poesía que me compré, de Edna St. Vincent Millay, como estos versos: 'Tis not love's going that hurts my days, / but that it went in little ways".

Así y a través de los años, con berrinches y patadas, frustraciones, pecados y triunfos pequeños, fui conociendo en la universidad la literatura española, inglesa, americana, muestras de escritores mundiales desde sus orígenes en traducción, etc. Y me llenó un gusto de querer leer, leer más ensayos, cuentos, novelas, y aprendí a saborear el lenguaje de cada uno, los giros, los chistes sutiles abiertos, tragedias, inspiraciones sin fin a ver cómo sentían, veían, decían. Estudié literatura en francés, inclusive italiano, como parte de mis estudios más "avanzados".

Después, como estudiante de estudios graduados, mis sueños literarios se fueron llenando con escritores en español, autores mexicanos, desde Balbuena a Sor Juana a los escritores de la Revolución hasta los ya mencionados por muchos de nosotros, Yáñez, Fuentes, Rulfo; los latinoamericanos como José María Arguedas, libros desde *Doña Bárbara* a *Los ríos profundos* a *La vorágine*; saboreaba las escritoras del postmodernismo, Delmira, Storni a mi lado, casi todas lecturas nocturnas. Después conocí y me despertó el anhelo de escribir yo misma, al conocer las escritoras y los escritores chicanos. ¡Qué gusto, qué lenguaje, qué mundo y realidad tan nuestra veía allí! A la luz del día, seguía el continuum de mis ciclos: trabajo oficinista; clases, hijos, familia, amores, equívocos, muchos amores.

¿Mi padre? Le gustaban las novelas de Zane Grey; en español, no sé qué leería en su madurez aparte de periódicos, tal vez. Mi madre no leía novelas, que yo sepa, pero sí llegó a conocer la Biblia—en los dos idiomas, claro. Lo que sabía y se oía en la conversación de Mamá eran los dichos y refranes, salpicando de vez en cuando alguna tradición oral. Creo que ella hablaba así porque vino de Nuevo México; así hablaban mi bisabuela, quien la crió, y mis tías de allá también. Mis hijos todos leen, escriben poesía y relatos, aquí y allí, como lo hacen algunos de mis hermanos y hermanas. Leen y le han dado a todo: estudios de religión y filosofía; novelas populares, y así la cadena de lecturas, uno inclusive ha leído sobre historia de la lengua. Hoy mismo me contó mi hija menor, maestra también (pero de danza, no literatura), que estaba luchando con un librote: Tolstoy en inglés. ¿Por qué leen los chicanos en inglés? Porque la mayor parte de nuestra literatura en este mundo se escribe y se vende en inglés. Es mi impresión personal.

Por varios años empecé a leerme puras novelas románticas, las llamadas "trash novels", solamente para contrarrestar el efecto psíquico de tanta literatura y lectura requerida por mi propia carrera. Ya las dejé, y ahora pues ya sabes lo que me ocupa, nada nuevo pero solamente en otra dirección: hijos, escritura de a jalones muy de vez en cuando, estudiar cómo se escriben guiones, cuidar a nietos, etc. Entre mi familia, mis "payasadas" literarias (en español y bilingües) no acogerán mucha admiración. Es mi impresión.

Mi madre me amonestó que cuidara bien de mi matrimonio. "¿Por qué te preocupas, mamá?" le preguntaba; ella me respondió: "porque tu marido *es tu RESPETO!*" Pobre mamá, no supo que mi respeto lo empecé a conjuntar, con el polvito en las manos, de la lectura de unos libros verdes añejos, las obras completas de Charles Dickens, verdadero observador de la condición humana, en los años 50s.

A Set of Old Books

Margarita Cota-Cárdenas

When I was about thirteen–fourteen years of age, my father entered the old porch which later was remodeled into my bedroom, carrying a used cardboard box. I was the eldest of my parents' six children; they had for some years run a "labor camp" for farm workers, sometimes entire families, in the San Joaquin Valley in California. By that age, we already lived in Newman, and as I've recounted in my previous writings, our dad was opposed to his children working in the "files" or fields. He insisted that we had to "educate ourselves" or go to school, and that was what each of us did in our own particular way. When I'm asked how I became interested in or began to write, I always begin explaining that I learned to read in Spanish first, and it was owing to the Mexican comics, or "funnybooks," that the adults would bring home.

My days as an addict of the *monitos*, or comics, began with the *Pepín* from Mexicali, little books that back in my memory I began to read as my first contact with "literature." Thus, I traveled the path of readings that I imagine was taken the same way by other Chicanitas: from the monitos to *Vanidades*, the magazines of popular culture such as *Confidencias* or some such. The newspapers that caused the most impact on me were the Mexican tabloids, with their headlines like POLICEMAN KILLS HIS WOMAN FOR LOVE, DEATHS OF FARM WORKERS IN OVERTURNED TRUCK, scandalous things like that. Those tabloids always carried some shocking photos, direct and horrible images with their bloody corpses, the prisoner making a serious face, etc.

With tenderness I recall lazy sluggish days in my uncles' labor camp, during my cousin Gloria's free hours. She helped cook and worked from time to time in the camp kitchen; I didn't. In one of the simple bedrooms in the part of the barracks where my uncles, my cousin, and her little brother also lived, she and I became accustomed a couple of summers to reading comic books and those Mexican magazines. We made it a fiesta: slices of lemon with salt on a plate between us, lying on the floor or on the beds, we would read, gossip about it, and laugh, sucking and sucking lemons with salt. Literal and literarily, they became "bitter-sweet" memories. We learned to speak Spanish first, and only began to learn English by force and total immersion in the primary school of that little border town.

In truth, neither in grammar school nor in high school do I remember having become enthusiastic with any "literary" book, not in English nor in "castellano." I took the prescribed classes of Spanish, English; I even gave a whack at German with lessons after my school day was over, with a teacher who volunteered to try to teach me to speak German. I did write, for the high school newspaper, and I got good grades in English and Spanish as I did in my other classes; but I don't recall more than one real encounter of major impact in my life as a reader of "Books," true books of literature. And that encounter was owing to my father, who came into my room with a box of old books with green covers, yellowed pages with frayed edges, all covered in dust.

"What is it Papá?" getting up from my sofa bed. The eldest, I began that day my inclination toward literature and the voracious reading of books, of all kinds. I never learned to cook except for what I had observed in my family's kitchen ("a witness/cook"). They didn't make me clean house, although later on I began to help with new baby brothers after my parents' divorce because my mother no longer had "a cousin, a muchacha, or señora" to help her at home as she'd had before. My parents simply worked from morning to night, and I've described elsewhere some sweet memories and some not. It occurred as with many other Chicanitos whose parents were divorced or separated; we began to live in a more "Americano" reality, different from the nostalgic yearned-for world of family, fiestas, youthful get-togethers, in the style of the Mexican American *frontera*. We ended up being bilingual, and our readings changed. I began that long-ago day my life with literature, with an ancient set of books that my father handed to me, one afternoon, as a simple gift.

"It's a complete *juego* of books by an American writer, some guy named Dickens. . . . I found it in the segunda used store this morning. . . . The owner told me it was a very famous writer, I don't know from where." Saying this, my father sets the box on the floor for me and leaves, I jumping to see what it was the box carried.

It awakened a curiosity in me for books, and I remember having gone to the small library in that little northern *pueblito* where we lived by then, to see what other books they would recommend to me. I read *Don Quixote* in English, Mark Twain, and the ironic vein of those writers piqued my interest. I remember very well one small book of poetry that I bought by Edna St. Vincent Millay, such as these lines: 'Tis not love's going hurts my days / but that it went in little ways."

Thus and through the years, balking and kicking, frustrations, sins and small triumphs, I began knowing in the university about Spanish, English, American literature, samples of world writers from their origins and in translation, etc. And I was filled with the pleasure of wanting to read, read more essays, short stories, novels, and I learned to savor the language of each one, the turns, the subtle and open jokes, tragedies, endless inspirations to see how they felt, saw, and spoke. I studied French literature, even Italian, as part of my more "advanced" studies.

Later, as a graduate student, my literary dreams began overflowing with writers in Spanish, Mexican authors, from Balbuena to Sor Juana and the writers of the Mexican Revolution, up to the often mentioned by so many of us Yáñez, Fuentes, Rulfo; the Latin Americans such as José María Arguedas; books from *Doña Bárbara* to *Los ríos profundos* to *La vorágine*; I savored the postmodernist writers, Delmira, Storni at my side, almost always nocturnal readings. Later I came to know and it awakened in me the yearning to write myself, upon knowing the Chicana and Chicano writers. What gusto, what lenguaje, what a world and reality that was there, and our very own! By the light of day, I followed the continuum of my cycles: office worker, classes, children, family, love affairs, errors, many loves.

My father? He liked the novels of Zane Grey; in Spanish, I don't know what he might have read in his maturity other than newspapers, perhaps. My mother didn't read novels, that I know of, but she did get to know the Bible—in both languages, of course. What she did know and you'd hear in Mamá's conversation were the sayings and *dichos*, peppered here and there with some oral tradition or story. I think that she talked like that because she was from Nuevo México; that's how my great-grandmother who had raised her also talked, and my aunts from over there also. My children all read, write poetry and short stories, here and there, as do some of my brothers and sisters. They read and have tried some literary everything: studies of religion and philosophy, popular novels, and thus goes the chain of readings; one even has studied history of the language. Just today my youngest daughter, also a teacher (but of dance, not literature), told me that she was struggling with a huge book: Tolstoy in English. Why do Chicanos read in English? Because the majority of our literature in our world is written and sold in English. That's my personal impression.

For many years I began to read only romance novels, the so-called trash novels, simply to counteract the psychic effect of so much required literature and reading due to my own career. I've left off with them, and now, well, you know what occupies me, nothing new but only in another direction: children, creative writing by fits every so often, studying how to write screenplays/scripts, babysitting grandchildren, etc. Among my relatives and extended family, my literary "clowning around" (in Spanish and bilingual) is not going to capture much admiration. It's my impression.

My mother would warn me to watch out and take care of my marriage. "Why do you worry about it, Mamá?" I would ask; she answered me once: "Because your husband *is your RESPETO!*" Poor Mamá, she didn't know that I had begun to gather up my respect, with dust on my hands, with the reading of some green-covered vintage books, the complete works of Charles Dickens, a true *observador* of the human condition, in the 1950s.

Note

Submitted in both English and Spanish by the author.

Sea Fever

Maria Kelson

Never allowed to watch *The Simpsons*—Bart was too snide—never allowed to watch *Donna Reed* reruns on Nickelodeon—she wasn't a good role model for the "new woman," vacuuming in her pearls—as a child, I chafed at the restrictions that made an almost airtight ring around my engagement with pop culture. The library and local bookstore were two precious areas where I could engage the words and works of human minds and hearts without proscription. Early encounters with poetry that really shook me and stayed with me—poems that pounded their own resonance onto the blank drumhead of my growing soul, ten or eleven years old—came from hours of uninterrupted browsing at Goodenough Books, the independent bookstore that lasted more than twenty years in my hometown of Livermore, California.

The same woman who, when I was a teen, permitted me just one rousing hour of Led Zeppelin per week, my mother always gave me free rein in Goodenough. My first memory of a poem really taking the top of my head off, making my whole body answer "yes," was John Masefield's "Sea Fever." I think I must've been in fourth or fifth grade, a very daydream-intensive age.

I must go down to the sea again, to the lonely sea and the sky,
And all I ask is a tall ship and a star to steer her by;
And the wheel's kick and the wind's song and the white sail's shaking,
And a grey mist on the sea's face, and a grey dawn breaking.

I'd found it in Nancy Larrick's magical anthology, *Piping Down the Valleys Wild*, then available in a Dell Yearling paperback edition (I remember recognizing the galloping horse silhouette on their book spines—irresistible branding for preteen girls!). We lived the perfect distance from the Pacific for the ocean to become a panacea of all mystery and desire for me. The drive over the coast range hills and out to the San Francisco shoreline, probably an hour and a half, was just long enough to qualify as a parental "hassle," which meant it wasn't something we could do just any old time. On the other hand, it was close enough that, along with the Winchester Mystery House (stairs that go nowhere! a haunted frog pond!) and Big Basin Redwoods State Park, it became a place we might go on a special Saturday, when the grown-ups felt well paid and expansive. All totaled, I'd probably been taken to the beach about five times, maybe twice by the time I met Masefield's poem.

But I loved being in natural areas, and daydreaming about natural areas. As a suburban kid raised on "critter shows" (no viewing restrictions for them) and hikes with my dad in Sycamore Grove and Sunol Parks, I learned nature as an adventure to be met. Distinct from a lawn, distinct from a hedge, the wild nature of my childhood meant physical movement (hiking) or visualized movement (TV or reading) away from society's outward forms of order—straight rows of houses—toward a different order, more complex, pliant before the elements, more dynamic.

And here comes "Sea Fever," affirming that a place exists—yes, this poem knew it!—a place neither too close nor too far away, where the elemental earth becomes enough to feed the whole of a person all the adventure, passion, and contact with wildness they'd ever need to feel alive, vital, sharp as the whetted knife of a Pacific wind.

> I must go down to the seas again, for the call of the running tide
> Is a wild call and a clear call that may not be denied;
> All I ask is a windy day with the white clouds flying,
> And the flung spray and the blown spume, and the seagulls crying.

The "grey mist on the sea's face" in the first stanza brings the sea mist to our faces, and the sensation recurs, more intensely, here in this second stanza's "flung spray" and "blown spume." Here is a nature that strikes back! You reach out for contact, and it makes a grab for you. The tide pool trolling I'd done on those rare beach visits confirmed the ocean's limitless power to answer and answer. Reaching down to gingerly feel an urchin's spines, I might get dappled in salt spray if I didn't watch for the next incoming wave; wading into rocky pools, the water moved, pulse by pulse, incrementally higher up my calves.

"Sea Fever" became a companion that went with me onto the playgrounds at Smith Elementary and into my kitchen on Elvira Street. "I accompany you in your grief" is one translation of a traditional Spanish phrase of condolence, which reflects the idea that grief and all its emotions should not be tackled alone—withstanding wrenching feeling is something best done with companions. John Masefield's poem, a pearl nested in Nancy Larrick's collection, shelved in the children's section of Goodenough Books, taught me that a poem can accompany you through wrenching desire . . . for experience, for freedom, for the breathing earth, itself.

Reading Thomas Hardy

María Teresa Márquez

My father was on his way home from his job at a lumber company when he found it. His usual route was to walk along the railroad tracks that divided the city along economic and social lines. My family, along with many other Mexican American families, lived on the wrong side of the tracks, in "el barrio del Diablo," one of the roughest parts of El Paso that had no paved streets or sidewalks. The street lights that did not have shattered bulbs were few. The police, when they had to, entered at their own peril. Drugs, drinking, shootings, gangs, and murder were common. In one incident on a late summer afternoon, Estella, a neighbor pregnant with her fifth child, was being beaten by her drunken husband, Carlos. Her brother, who came to her rescue, killed Carlos on the spot with a rifle. I still remember seeing the man lying on his back in the backyard of his home with his guts spilling out like white snakes and body heat escaping from the hole in his stomach. But I digress.

On that afternoon when my father found it changed my life. It was a cardboard box filled with college textbooks. My father carried the heavy box on his shoulder, along with his lunch box. When he got home, my father explained what he had found and where he had found it. My father surmised that the box had fallen from one of the trains that traveled through the town. We did have a local college, Texas Western, a four-year school that, at the time, had just one doctoral program and it was in geology. The idea that the box had come from a local college student did not enter our minds. Texas

Western was not a place that we had aspirations of seeing in the present or future. Neither did we think anyone in our neighborhood was a student at Texas Western.

My father placed the box on my parents' bed. I immediately started pulling out the textbooks and reading the titles. The only books I remember now from that treasure trove are a book of poetry by Thomas Hardy and a book on algebra. I do not remember the titles. I read the poetry on several occasions, pretending I understood what I was reading. The algebra text, of course, was way above the level of arithmetic I was learning at Zavala Elementary School. The poetry was different from the type of reading I did under my parents' bed where I could escape from my brothers and sisters. Along with the books I borrowed from one of the branch libraries that was about three or four miles from my house, I read my mother's Mexican detective magazines printed in sepia color, that showed graphic pictures of dead people, her knitting and crocheting magazines, and the romance magazines, in English, that she subscribed to. I honestly believed the stories in those magazines were true romances of real people. The book of poetry by Thomas Hardy, however, changed my life, opening new insights into literature. Perhaps reading Thomas Hardy was an unconscious idea that I would be a college student someday. I thank my father for carrying that heavy box and bringing it home.

They Say That
Mejicanos Don't Read

Minerva Daniel

I look around my home and my heart lifts as I look at all my books. Books and magazines can be found in every room. Some have been read, others yet to be read, and a few are always in the process. My favorite book is a little translated Western paperback in Spanish called *Lo peor de Texas* (The worst of Texas) by Lou Carrigan. The paperback is yellowed with age showing here and there where the reader folded corners to mark their spot and spilled a drink—perhaps coffee—on the first few pages. This book once belonged to my father. And when he passed away, it was the only belonging of his that I wanted. Every time I look at it, I remember my father, who left his legacy of love of reading to all his children. I remember accompanying him to the local library to check out books. I would go to the children's area, which had its own section in the library, and my father would go to one solitary rack of Spanish paperbacks to check out any new books, many times rechecking out the old. I now understand that given the nature of the times, we were fortunate that our small town library even had a few books in Spanish. Growing up in that small rural town, I was a constant fixture at the library, along with my father.

They say that Mejicanos don't read. Another myth, another stereotype; for I am witness through my published writings that we not only read, but we write as well. I am witness of my father's enduring legacy that was his only gift to give. A gift of himself. His gift of modeling the love of reading.

In the Stacks

Monica Hanna

My childhood church was the Baldwin Hills branch of the Los Angeles Public Library. Growing up, my mother took me and my sister to this library religiously. As soon as I got past the turnstile, a new public realm opened before me. When I was very young, I ran my hand along the spines of the colorful children's books in the short bookcases. I brought stacks of those books to the short glazed wood tables specially set up for the youngest readers on the brightly colored rug in the children's section. At that age, the library seemed immense. There were so many books, and I could check out *any* that I wanted, even if only two at a time, until our return visit the following week.

The library was one of the few places where I could pick up anything I wanted as a child. But my mother was determined that we have consistent access to reading materials. My mother always emphasized the value of literacy and education. Despite the fact that she had been unable to continue her education in Mexico past middle school, she was able to continue to educate herself, teach herself English, and eventually earn her GED in the United States based upon her love of letters. She knew that literacy would be the key to our educational opportunities.

My maternal grandmother was the oldest child in her family, and her parents thought it best for her not to attend school. Instead, she stayed home and helped her mother take care of her younger siblings. She never learned to read or write. Perhaps her parents wondered why a girl would need to learn about the world of letters if her destiny was to get married and take care of children. Female literacy could be deemed suspicious. The young woman who eventually became my grandmother's sister-in-law was the youngest in her family, so her parents did send her to school since she didn't need to help as much at home; her literacy turned into a side business, as she got paid for surreptitiously writing love letters to the boyfriends of her unlettered girlfriends.

My maternal grandfather was an avid reader and taught all of his daughters and sons to read. More than anything, he set an example for them as a lifelong letters lover. My mother watched as he devoured newspapers and Louis L'Amour Westerns and wanted to gain entry into this separate world that enveloped him. She learned to read sitting on his lap, reading stories of kidnappings and violence in the *prensa amarilla*. When she started school, this love of reading extended to poetry, which she read and recited with fervor. When she moved to Los Angeles from Guanajuato, she expanded on the basic English she learned in middle school by picking up a book called *Inglés sin maestro* and went through it as quickly as any of her other books. Before long, she was working through books she picked up in her adopted country about as fast as the Spanish books she read as a child.

Story time was an important element of my young life and shaped my relationship with my mother since then. Even before I learned how to read, the very act of reading with my mother was magical. As a toddler, I usually asked for the same Dr. Seuss story every night. Once, though, I was apparently looking for some variety; I pointed to one of my father's Arabic-language books when my mother asked me which story I'd like to hear. Though she couldn't read Arabic, she picked up the book, started flipping its pages, and began telling a story of her own invention. What difference would this make to a two- or three-year-old who couldn't verify the words on her own? But in the middle of her story, I stopped her and gave her my pronouncement: "You're wrong." She asked what I meant, and I pointed out that my father's books didn't work the way she was reading; she was flipping the pages to read from left to right, while I knew that my father read his books with the different-looking letters from right to left.

Even before I learned to read, I knew that books were sacred; they had to be handled correctly and on their own terms. But at the same time I loved their physicality, their different shapes and sizes, their weight. Books weren't just for reading; they were good for so many forms of play. My sister and I sometimes made forts out of books or divided our shared room by stacking books as dividers. Early in elementary school, I began writing my own "books," even illustrating them in a rudimentary, almost hieroglyphic style. Yet nothing thrilled me more about this process than when I learned how to create my own makeshift binding; the contents of my imagined worlds spurred my creativity, but the physical shape of the final product satisfied me almost as much.

When I was a little bit older, I would head straight to the one tall bookcase at the Baldwin Hills Library dedicated to Young Adult novels and sat in the aisle with a freshly picked stack, staking my claim. I read about rebellious teenagers in parts of the country that I'd only heard mentioned on television, but related to them anyway as the heroes of these novels. Sometimes, I came across the stories of young people whose lives more closely approximated mine, and this element added another dimension to the experience. I learned about human development and sexuality thanks to this library; when I was ten or so, my mother took me on a special side trip to the health section to check out *What's Happening to My Body?* Not long after this, I exhausted the contents of the Young Adult selection, and then began to roam the general fiction section. I read thrillers alongside stories of Spanish *pícaros*, fainting English ladies, and, among my favorites, stories of the American West. These books didn't seem like "stuffy" classics to me. Nobody was forcing them on me. Instead, I was discovering all of these books on my own. They were all new and waiting to be transformed under my gaze.

As I started high school, the Baldwin Hills Library started to shift shape, becoming suddenly smaller; it was, after all, just one big room, nothing like the Central Library downtown, which I began to frequent in search of particular books. As I began to get more and more research projects or specialized assignments, my thumbing of the card catalog became more frustrating. I eventually stopped frequenting this library and have not returned since. There's something about this fact that I like. It is a space that is vulnerable to the shifting of my memory, but at the same time it is safe from too much judgment or too many comparisons that I might make after having access to some of the biggest libraries in the country. It remains a space that for me is totally separate from those other experiences in reading. It is more closely tied in my mind to the bookshelves in my home growing up than to the work I do now as a scholar.

I excelled in school in part because I made each of my subjects a running story, following the narrative mechanics of the books in which I immersed myself, in order to grasp the major concepts. Eventually, this became my ticket out of Los Angeles, something that my reading about distant places pushed me to desire. I received a scholarship to UC Berkeley. Far from the Baldwin Hills Library, I discovered the concept of *millions* of books all housed within a single campus. I spent a lot of time in the stacks that were so overflowing that the books were placed on moveable carrels to make room. At Cal, I began studying Italian and started spending time in a new area of the stacks with Italian literature. I also started getting into film, something that had only a negligible role in my cultural repertoire despite growing up so close to Hollywood. On days when I was supposed to be studying for finals, I'd take a break by heading to the basement of the Moffitt Library and, sitting at one of the private viewing areas of the windowless room, quickly going through the Italian neorealist archive. Surprisingly, my Italian study also gave me a better ability and confidence to start reading more books in my mother's tongue, another Romance language: Spanish. At Berkeley, I had the sense that anything I wanted to learn was accessible. Most things I could imagine were explored somewhere in those depths.

Though I toyed with the idea of other majors (history, mass communications, political science), my eventual major was perhaps predictable: English. In the end, my love of books shaped not only my imagination but eventually my career path. I am currently completing my doctorate in comparative literature, and I spend much of my days immersed in books of all stripes.

Lately, though, I notice that my relationship to libraries has changed. I enter big research libraries often, sometimes to browse but more often now as I finish up my dissertation with a "shopping list" derived from my searches of online library catalogs. I don't linger too long in the stacks, as my bearings in the library are more closely tied to the organization offered and detailed online. As so many sources go online, I wonder how our relationship to literature and libraries will change. In part, I am excited about these possibilities, but I also note a reactionary response in myself. In the future, when I direct my students to the web instead of the stacks for their research projects, I think I will mourn a bit. In the meantime, I think I'll stop by my local library to pick up a good noir on my way to the beach this summer.

Los libros de mi padre

Shanti A. Sánchez

M i curiosidad de saber mi idioma natal empezó con un libro de mi papá escrito por Gabriel García Márquez, *Cien años de soledad*. Mi mamá me prohibió desde chica hablar español o ver programas en español. Mi bisabuela hablaba conmigo en español y siempre estaba discutiendo con mi madre de que fue mi derecho saber de dónde vine y cuál es el idioma que debo hablar en vez del inglés. Los fines de semana, mientras mamá tomaba su siesta y mi papá trabajaba, tenía la libertad de hacer lo que yo quería. Frecuentemente iba a la cocina y en la mesa estaban los libros de mi padre. A los cinco años ya supe leer y escribir, pero en inglés, entonces cuando abría los libros, no entendía nada. No comprendía qué decían las palabras aunque lo intentaba pronunciar. Un día me ganó la curiosidad; fui al cuarto de mi mamá y la desperté. Le pregunté qué era el significado del libro y cómo se leía. Me dijo que era español, y no tenía permiso de andar cargando ese libro por dos razones: (1) era de mi papá, y (2) estaba en español. Diario me decía, "You are an American, and you will learn the language of an American, English!" y siempre pensaba porqué. En sí, dejé mi curiosidad por un tiempo. A los doce años volvió mi curiosidad de leer y escribir en español. Cuando llegaba de la escuela siempre iba al baño primero, y en los baños me encontraba the *Reader's Digest*, pero en español. Esta vez no me animaba a preguntarle a alguien que me lo lea, entonces decidí aprender yo sola. Supe que con el conocimiento del lenguaje en mi mente, no iba a ser difícil conocer el idioma que mi bisabuela dijo que era mío. Poco a poco pronunciaba las letras y palabras como yo pensaba que era. Y en las noches me pondría a ver Univisión y escuchar a la gente platicar. También memoricé cómo la gente charlaba en las novelas y veía mucho las noticias. Todo eso lo hice a escondidas, y a los catorce, casi para cumplir los quince, demostré a mis padres que yo había aprendido el idioma español; que lo supe leer y escribir. Mi mamá no estaba furiosa, me dijo que era inevitable y que tenía la sangre de una mexicana. Mi papá, por supuesto, estaba orgulloso y después de eso me compraba libros en español cada mes.

Hace tres años fui a Guadalajara, México y les presumí a mis primos que ya había aprendido y les agradecí por ayudarme en mi niñez. Ahora se me hace más fácil el español que el ingles, y prefiero ver la tele o leer en español. Mi sueño es regresar a México y hundirme en mi cultura mexicana. Soy chicana, entiendo, sé que me voy a llevar parte de los EE. UU. conmigo, pero me siento más conectada a México y los que ya están allí. Estoy aquí por la educación buena que ofrece EE. UU., pero algún día regresaría a la tierra de mis padres, a tomar cursos de psicología, tener una familia y disfrutar la vida.

My Father's Books

Shanti A. Sánchez

y curiosity to know my native language started with one of my
father's books written by Gabriel García Márquez, *One Hundred
Years of Solitude.* As a girl, my mom forbade me to speak or view
programs in Spanish. My great-grandmother spoke to me in Spanish and
was always arguing with my mother about how it was my right to know
where I came from, and what was the language I had to speak instead of
English. On the weekends, while mom took her nap and my father worked,
I had the freedom to do what I wanted. I would frequently go to the kitchen,
where my father's books were, on the table. At the age of five I already knew
how to read and write, but in English, so when I opened the books, I didn't
understand anything. Although I did not understand what they said, I tried
to pronounce the words. One day my curiosity won; I went to my mom's
room and I woke her up. I asked her what was the meaning of the book and
how to read it. She told me that it was Spanish, and I did not have permission to be carrying around that book for two reasons: (1) it was my father's,
and (2) it was written in Spanish. Daily, she would tell me, "You are an
American, and you will learn the language of an American, English!" and I
always wondered why. In fact, I left my curiosity for a while. At the age of
twelve, my curiosity to read and write in Spanish returned. When arriving
from school, I would always go to the bathroom first, and in the bathroom
I would find the *Reader's Digest,* but in Spanish. This time I was not willing
to ask someone to read it to me, so I decided to learn myself. I knew that

with the knowledge of the language in my mind, it would not be difficult to know the language that my great-grandmother said was mine. Little by little I would sound out the letters and words as I thought they should sound. And in the evenings I would watch Univisión and hear the people talk. I also memorized how people would talk in the novelas, and I watched the news a lot. All of that I did secretly, and when I was fourteen, almost fifteen, I demonstrated to my parents that I had learned the Spanish language, that I knew how to read and write it. My mom was not angry, she told me that it was inevitable, and that I had the blood of a Mexican. My dad, of course, was proud, and after that he would buy me books in Spanish each month.

Three years ago, I went to Guadalajara, Mexico, and I showed my cousins that I had learned, and I thanked them for helping me in my childhood. Now I find Spanish to be easier for me than English, and I prefer to watch TV or read in Spanish. My dream is to return to Mexico and immerse myself in my Mexican culture. I understand that I am Chicana and that I am going to take a part of the United States with me, but I feel more connected to Mexico and those who are already there. I'm here for the good education that the United States offers, but someday I will return to the land of my parents, take psychology courses, have a family, and enjoy life.

Note

Submitted in both English and Spanish by the author.

Reading Saved Me
from the Chaos

Shonnon Gutiérrez

R eading saved me from the chaos. I always remember my older sister
Terrie reading to me. Late at night, when we were supposed to be
asleep, she would pull out the flashlight and we would travel far
from all the problems at home. She'd read me *The Hobbit*, *The Chronicles of
Narnia*, and *The Illustrated Man*. I had trouble reading all through first and
second grades. It was painful when asked to read out loud in class. I had a
bit of a lisp and was sent to speech therapy. Things at home were always
hard; lots of abuse, Dad kicked the shit out of us at least once a day. I counted
on Terrie to take me away from home every night. Things changed when she
went to junior high; she no longer wanted to spend her nights reading to me;
she had friends and talked on the phone for hours. My speech got better and
I was determined to be a reader. I picked a book, *Little House on the Prairie*,
and a dictionary, and every night I read slowly but surely. I wrote down
every word I didn't know and the definition. I wanted to learn and be a good
reader. That summer of 1979 I read so much to escape the family life that was
so broken. I remember asking my brother Jaime, "What do you remember
about me when I was little?" Jaime said, "You were always reading, you
always had a book with you." I couldn't help but smile. I became passionate
about reading. I am an articulate and somewhat intelligent person. I have
no formal education; that is, I only went up to the eighth grade. Dad put me
to work to support him and there was no time for school, but I had books,

magazines, and newspapers, therefore I had knowledge. My writing grammar isn't great and I am a phonetic speller. I have worked all my life and am a single Chicana mother of three. My fifteen-year-old carries a book around with him everywhere he goes. My other two children love it when I read to them. I am a success thanks to reading. Whenever asked, "If you could be anywhere right now, where would you be and what would you be doing?" I always say, "In a comfortable chair with a good book." I will go back to school one day, but until then I will continue educating myself by reading.

—Chanata, from Aztlan

The Importance of Libraries and Chicano Literature

Veronica Ortega

Reading and books have always played an important role for me. As a child, my mother encouraged us to read. She read to us children's stories and would take my brother, sisters, and me to the local library, especially during summertime. We learned how to use a library card, check out books, and would sometimes even stay for story hour. Those trips really were a big event for us. We didn't have money and I was in awe as a child how the libraries could offer such a wonderful gift for free.

In junior high, I read the paperback *Viva Chicano*, and it excited me to find a story about a Chicano/Latino character. This went even further for me when, as if purposeful or by fate, I came across used textbooks on loan to my mother, by her sister, then a student at San Jose State, and the only one we had ever known to attend college. I read the pages of *Bless Me, Ultima* by Rudy Anaya and *Literatura Chicana*, where I discovered the epic poem "El Louie" by maestro and poet José Montoya.

I remember sitting on my bed surrounded by my sisters reading "El Louie" aloud, over and over because we loved the sound of the language, the images and the whole Chicano experience, which we couldn't really explain at the time, and how this poem told a story. Needless to say, I read the whole volume and was inspired to learn that Chicano writers were telling our stories. This was cultural affirmation for me, as a young Chicana, growing up in a society that pretended we didn't exist.

Nena

Vito de la Cruz

hroughout my life the only name I have ever used for her was "Nena." Everybody called her that—my grandmother, aunts and uncles, cousins, the neighbors who occasionally came by our house to have her translate documents from English into Spanish. She was my aunt, but, in ways that I cannot completely relate, she was so much more. She filled the spaces left vacant by my father, her brother, after he abandoned me when I was six months old, and by my mother, whom I never knew. Nena taught me to read before I formed memories of the accomplishment. When she first introduced me to the library, I also learned her real name and my place in her life. I remember that day because Nena stood by my side as we applied for my library card at the tiny library building in San Benito, Texas. More significantly, however, in the process she ingrained in me a love of learning that persists to this day as I slog through middle age.

Nena grew up, as did I, in San Benito in the lower Rio Grande valley of Texas—"El Valle," as most of the Latino residents called it. She was the first in our family to graduate from high school, attend college, and receive a bachelor's degree. She concentrated on elementary education and eventually earned a teaching credential. Her achievements came despite a multitude of obstacles that thwarted many of her classmates and, unfortunately, a majority of her siblings. Her father died when she was two years old, right around the year Nazi Germany plunged the world into catastrophic war. At the age of four, Nena saw my grandmother remarry a good man, but a coarse, uneducated, illiterate man who increasingly drank too much. By the time she entered the first grade, she was helping care for a string of half brothers and half sisters, seven in all, before and after school and on the weekends.

Nena witnessed times when Jim Crow laws affected Latinos as well as African Americans. Even though Latinos were a majority of the population in San Benito and south Texas, discriminatory laws and practices undermined the quality of the education and employment Latinos received and the housing they acquired. Most Latinos were systematically tracked into "basic" education classes and menial jobs despite the aptitude, talent, and desire for a college education. Barrios like El Jardín, where we lived, were our sanctuaries. Until the Supreme Court decided *Hernandez v. Texas* in 1954, declaring such practices unconstitutional, many Latinos, like Nena, were restricted from college preparatory courses in public schools. Hers was the first generation of Latino students that reaped the benefit of that court case and the opportunities that grudgingly became available.

Latinos in south Texas often remained mired in poverty. Our family was no exception. By the time my father deposited me into Nena's arms in the summer of 1959, our family had been migrating north following the harvests and earning subsistence wages every summer for a dozen years. Fortunately for me, Nena refused to migrate that summer in 1959. She stayed in San Benito to work part-time as a filing clerk and receptionist at the local water authority and complete some courses at the community college, twenty miles down U.S. Highway 77, in Brownsville. Her refusal to toil in the northern fields had been one of her first acts of defiance on the road to acquiring her college degree. She defied not only my grandmother but also her stepfather, who had little or no use for education. She also angered her younger half siblings, who interpreted her refusal to migrate negatively, as a manifestation that she believed perhaps that she was better than they. She did not, of course, but she did believe she was capable of more. That fall Nena migrated north from San Benito as she had the previous autumn, not to chase the harvests but to continue her studies at Texas Women's University in Denton, Texas, where she received her bachelor's degree. She never worked in the fields again.

When she was away, Nena wrote to me at least once a week. Two of my other aunts, who at the time were working their way through junior high and elementary school, read the letters to me until I was old enough and sufficiently literate to read them myself. I reviewed Nena's letters several years later when I was about to enroll in junior high school and realized that my aunt's correspondences were in fact reading and spelling lessons. She would pick a letter from the alphabet and ask me to send back to her words that began with those letters. It was utter genius. She was practicing with me what she would do later when she became a teacher in our barrio's elementary school.

When my aunt graduated from college and returned to El Jardín, I was almost four years old and still not venturing the three blocks to Frank Roberts Elementary. First grade for me was still two years away. We had no kindergarten in the barrio. Nena vowed that she would get me ready to succeed in school. Under her guidance I read everything that I could get my hands on, everything the San Benito Library could give me. Soon after Nena returned from TWU, she and I started walking to the library every Saturday morning.

The routine was quickly laid down from our initial trip to the library. Nena woke me at 7:00 a.m. to perform the chores she assigned to me—make my bed, arrange the two drawers in my dresser so that they didn't resemble a "writhing snakes den," as she would say. I took out the trash, swept the covered porch where I slept, helped collect the books she had checked out the previous week, and packed them in my morral and in her oversize canvas bag to return to the library. By late morning and once I had completed my chores, Nena and I ate a breakfast of *huevos con frijoles* and warm flour tortillas my grandmother had made earlier that day. I remember my grandmother spiked my glass of milk with a half cup of coffee, a practice she repeated occasionally, especially in winter. By breakfast's end, I could hardly wait for the walk out of the barrio, south across the resaca, past the small Latino-owned shops like Ornelas's *panadería* where on later trips we would often stop for pan dulce, then on to the library. The library opened at 10:00 a.m. on Saturdays, but we arrived around noon that day, a little earlier on subsequent visits especially during the hottest parts of the summer.

The library sat dead center on two square blocks of park-like grounds. It was one block south from the intersection of Sam Houston and Stenger, the two main streets that framed my small, rural farming town. Everything radiated out from the intersection—businesses, county and state buildings, a once-elegant hotel long past its prime where the valley's wealthy had lodged and dined and where the Veterans of Foreign Wars held their annual ball, the post office, the various neighborhoods that comprised the town. The library sat on the edge of one older neighborhood in particular where many of San Benito's Anglo citizens still lived in grand houses with wide porches and lush lawns and that in 1962 remained foreign territory to brown-skinned kids from the barrios north and west of town—kids that looked and spoke like me.

The manicured gardens surrounding the library were beautiful and full of adventure for anyone who liked to run, climb trees, and act out the scenes from the action stories that poured out of the books on the shelves inside. Thick, coarse Bermuda grass covered the open space between the rough-barked mesquites, smooth cottonwoods, and twisted, squat Texas ebonies that provided shade, shelter, and climbing opportunities. Red, yellow, white, and pink rosebushes occupied some of the raised, circular flower beds carved out of the ground and framed with flame-red brick retaining walls. Other flower beds sheltered colorful dahlias and sprawling, thick-stemmed geraniums. Some of the geraniums reached four and five feet in height and provided excellent cover from which to fire my imaginary arrows at shadowy, advancing enemies. Broad, curving walkways meandered throughout like rivers or moats leading invariably to the library entrance.

The building that housed the library was old and angular. It stood like a castle, a full two stories tall. Its burgundy-brown window and door frames contrasted starkly against the whitewashed, plaster exterior walls. A set of brick steps cemented into a wide, semicircular landing led up to the rounded arch and double doors of the main entrance. The steps were gently worn concave from years of boots and shoes coming and going. When it rained or when the grounds keepers set out and ran the sprinklers, small puddles collected on the steps that on hot summer days cooled my huarache-encased feet.

The library was cool, inviting, and mysterious all at once. Rose-colored tile fired in Mexican kilns covered the small foyer at the entrance, where the checkout desk alternately welcomed visitors and their returns or bid them goodbye while entrusting them with a good read or two. Scuffed, warped hardwood floors supported the ten-foot-high stacks of books that entertained me when I aged to preteen adolescence. The shelves in the children's section were no higher than eye level. This was fine with me when Nena first took me to the library, when she first showed me the worlds that came alive as soon as I cracked open the cover.

Our maiden visit to the San Benito Library was an adventure. The sweetness and significance of the memory has persisted for reasons too numerous to recount here. However, two things occurred that helped shape me and my lifelong relationship with my aunt—I learned Nena's real name, and she began bequeathing to me a passion for reading, discovery, and love of learning.

I spent that first journey reading through children's primers while Nena sat at a not-too-distant table. Toward late afternoon, when the heat of that south Texas June day had begun to dissipate, I collected the books I wanted to take home and tentatively approached the checkout desk. Nena lagged behind, almost by design I think now, as if to see how I would handle myself. When the librarian at the front desk asked me for my library card, I turned to face my aunt who was smiling broadly.

"Do I have a card, Nena?" I remember asking.

"Not yet," she replied, "but we're going to get you one."

Nena filled out the single-sheet application for a library card and asked me to sign it. Much to the surprise of the librarian, I wrote out my strange-sounding first name in awkward block letters. Right below my name I saw hers, and I read it aloud. "Iris de la Cruz," it said.

"What does Iris mean?" I asked.

"It's a flower but it's also my real name," she said. "But you don't have to stop calling me 'Nena.'"

She was about to hand in the application when I spoke up. "I have to finish my name." Nena looked over my shoulder as I wrote "de la Cruz" next to my given name. She smiled broader than I remember her ever smiling before that day when she saw that I wrote the word "son" in the blank space following my name.

Revisiting Nancy Drew

Beth Hernandez-Jason

I remember reading Nancy Drew books with a flashlight late at night under a blanket in bed. I was supposed to be sleeping, but how could I sleep when I knew that Nancy was close to solving a case? Besides, reading about her suspenseful discoveries at night made the experience much more exciting. I felt like I was Nancy—a petite strawberry blonde with a boyfriend named Ned, who was inquisitive, clever, likeable, and always safe from harm.

I would check out each Nancy Drew book at the Fresno County Library. My mom would drive me there, and while she was in her Agatha Christie section, I made a beeline to the Nancy Drew shelf. There I would sit, familiarly looking at my old friends, trying to find a book I had not already read. Did I read in numerical order? I can't really remember, but I think I tried to whenever I could. When did I first pick up a Nancy Drew book? Which one was it? I have no idea, but I think I read Nancy Drew while I was in first or second grade at Birney Elementary School, or perhaps in third grade at Bullard Talent, in Fresno, California. While I was in the first grade, I would visit my old kindergarten class to read to them, and I remember reading *Gus the Bus* and *The Little Engine That Could* to my younger sister. I only read the Nancy Drew Mystery Stories series, not the Nancy Drew Files or any other versions. Instead, as I got older, I began reading the Sweet Valley High series (I felt a strong connection to Elizabeth Wakefield, the older, more responsible twin who reads and writes).

Today, as a graduate student studying Chicano literature, I pick up Carolyn Keene's *The Clue in the Diary*, number 7. I have probably not read (or reread) a Nancy Drew book since I was ten years old, and I am now twenty-six years old.

I read the short blurb that acts as an introduction to the latest mystery and don't remember this synopsis. It even explains Nancy's motivation for wanting to discover the truth behind "the explosion and burning of a beautiful country mansion"; Nancy cares for the daughter of an inventor who might be framed. We then are told that it will end well: "How she accomplishes this makes another exciting Nancy Drew mystery." I wonder if this is why I was able to read these suspenseful stories as a young girl. I hate scary and suspenseful movies, but I loved these books. Was it the guarantee from the very beginning of a happy ending?

As I continue to read, I am surprised by the vocabulary words—"unscrupulous," "exonerate," "insoluble," "titian." I do not even know what "titian blond" means, and I surely did not know then. However, if in other books her hair was described as strawberry blonde, I must have simply guessed what "titian" meant at the time.

In doing some research online, I have found out that the Nancy Drew Mystery Stories numbers 1–34 were revised starting in 1959. Looking at the different covers from different years, I know I read the revised editions, but at the time, I didn't even realize that there were different versions.

2

ORAL INTERVIEWS
from the
CHICANO/A READERS
ORAL PROJECT

Introduction

art 2 consists of four oral interviews from the Chicano/a Readers Oral Project (CROP), discussed in this book's introduction. These sample interviews are intended to complement the written submissions in part 1, and they represent Chicano/a readers of diverse educational backgrounds. Their inclusion in this volume contributes to the diversity of the contributors' overall background, which in part 1 tends to lean toward the academic.

In addition to their publication in this volume, these and other interviews will be available in a database and website currently under construction for the CROP, both as audio files and in transcript form. Anyone interested in being interviewed (or in submitting a written statement on the topic for inclusion in the database) is invited to email his or her materials to me at mmartin-rodriguez@ucmerced.edu.

In the field of Chicano/a studies, oral histories have long been used for different purposes and toward different goals. My purpose here is to give voice to Chicano/a readers and to further contribute to documenting the history of how and what Chicanos/as have read over the years.

The first three interviews in this section were conducted by Carolina Valero, then a student at the University of California, Merced, and now a graduate of that institution. The fourth interview, with Helen Fabela Chávez (César E. Chávez's widow), was submitted by Lucía D. Vázquez, a former graduate student of mine. In transcribing these interviews and in publishing them here, we have maintained the rhythm of the different conversations. As is to be expected from oral interaction, the kind of information that these interviews provide, and the manner in which they provide that information, tend to differ from the essays submitted by other readers. In any case, they remain an extremely valuable indicator of reading patterns, experiences, and histories that make this volume richer.

Fernando Vázquez

FERNANDO VÁZQUEZ: My name is Fernando Vázquez, and we are in
Tehachapi, California; I've just met Carolina and have agreed to respond to
some questions regarding a study. You want to know about what I read as a
child and how that led to what I read later on in life.

When I was growing up, prekindergarten age, we were working in the
fields, and initially there wasn't a lot of reading going on. I remember my
father reading the newspaper, *La Opinión*, and I started to learn to read
in Spanish first, with my mom and grandparents. By the time I started
first grade at Holy Family School in Visalia, I was reading at about a fifth-
grade level in Spanish, before I ever started to read in English. The transition was not difficult because I already knew the very basics of what a lot
of the other kids were learning for the first time: the alphabet, the sounds
of the letters, that you go from the left to the right . . . you know, the basic
concepts. Though I had been reading phonetically in Spanish, the transition was easy. What I believe really helped was that most of the nuns were
Hispanic, and there wasn't anybody correcting me in a harsh manner, it
was a loving transition and I learned from their correction. Well, even an
automatic response, like reacting to being pinched by a desktop: "Ay!"
and the teacher correcting me by saying: "No, en inglés decimos 'auch'";
so the recognition that even a spontaneous response had to be couched in
the language we were speaking was enlightening. Well, that was part of
the less painful transition from Spanish to English. That is when I started
learning more English and really getting into reading. It became obvious
that I and a couple of other Chicanos that had learned to read in Spanish
first were well ahead of the class. Of course, the reason became evident

only in retrospect. When we were little kids, and working in the fields with our parents, we became exposed to comic books in Spanish, usually brought by some of the migrant teenagers picking fruit and cotton alongside us. That is when I also became acquainted with comic books in English and started making the storyline transitions. I became even more interested in following storylines after talking to my tío Johnny. My father's youngest brother criticized my accidental choice of reading material and introduced me to beginning literature. Though it was more advanced than my grade level at the time, I was drawn to horse books by Walter Farley and later cowboy stories by Zane Grey. It was difficult because they were talking about the color of sunsets, and these gullies and the smells of sage, and I was fascinated by my initial lack of understanding and frame of reference. It was not until later that I realized that the "greasers" they were talking about were mexicanos, and all of the other derogatory terms and attitudes that were prevalent that had escaped me. I didn't understand that they were looking down on us and how negative those misconceptions were.

Besides those books, I was introduced to the Bobbsey Twins, and a character I only remember as a kid detective that used to make me want to be a cop when I grew up. Later on there was a TV series about Spin and Marty that would remind me of the books. I used to read much of this while staying in Los Angeles at the home of my grandparents. My uncle John, who was in high school at the time, would come and quiz me about the books I was reading and pretty much supervised new selections. If he was not satisfied with my responses, I would receive an assignment for the next day. I was to go back and find those paragraphs where he thought I had made a mistake and to read it over and come back to explain to him how I could have been mistaken or why I had that perception. So, I'm six, and seven, and eight years old during these times and had no idea of the value of what was being imparted. I also doubt my tío Johnny realized the magnitude of his gifts. Who consciously teaches kids this age about concepts? I credit my tío Johnny for much of my early childhood education. He was a real taskmaster and many times not appreciated. He led me through the entire Black Stallion series by Walter Farley. Our family economic situation had improved, as we had left the fields as a primary source of income and my father was working on a cattle ranch. That just confirmed my desire to be a cowboy like my father, and I kept reading cowboy books. As I learned to rope and ride, I continued to read books that related to ranches and horses and cowboys. So, you see, the negative stereotypes that were popular, that mexicanos were always bandidos, were troublesome because I knew my dad wasn't a bandido, and he rode horses. It wasn't until later that there were more positive images like the Cisco Kid and Pancho; still stereotyping, but superficially much more positive. There were also the good guys like Roy Rogers and Gene Autry. I enjoyed reading about them and the "cowboy ethic" and the "cowboy code" that they publicly espoused. It was amazing that they actually encouraged kids to be kind to everyone and not take advantage of a smaller person and accept people of all races. I never dreamed that I would ever get to meet them as an adult and actually ride for Roy Rogers before his death. This stuff became more important to me than the Boy Scout Oath because I could personally relate; it was simple, direct, and grounded in my own reality. I continued to read about Western lifestyles, but as I went on to high school, also broadened to include knights, chivalry, and honor. This also brought back ideas that my uncle John (Tío Johnny) had drilled into me as a child about honor and the value of your word. Why did they call this knight "el desdi-chado"? The whole concept of the Knights of the Round Table took on major proportions. I began to realize then that these guys weren't just English speakers. That the Spanish knights were fighting the Moros and that "el desdichado" wasn't just a disinherited knight that had gone on the road as a warrior having lost his ancestral lands. It gave a whole different perspective to Richard the Lion-Hearted and El Cid, and just swelled me with pride.

CAROLINA VALERO: All of these books, where did you have access to them? Was there a library nearby? Or, did your parents have their own? Where did you find all of these books?

FV: My uncle John had a collection of books in the basement of my grand-parents' house in L.A. and my tíos and tías had read a lot of them and that was where the family kept them. From here they would recycle them for the rest of the family, like a library. This is where my uncle John had his room, in the basement, and some of my other tíos and tías lived upstairs. I guess you could consider it a library, but he had such a love for the books that I came to recognize them as really important.

CV: Do you want to share any stories that you've had with finding a certain book or . . . I know you had connections with different books and it was fun for you and you identified with. It kind of related to your family, how

your parents . . . how your dad taught you. Did you have any . . . trying to
find a book? Or any story that you want to share?

FV: Well, once we left the fields and my father started working on the cattle
ranch, we finally had a house on the ranch and gained some stability. We
also gained a garage where many books were kept. Besides what my parents
were reading, and magazines, my mom would read these novelas. She also
read (prayed) from novenas at church. I never got into those much, but
there were also many books that were given to us by family and friends,
including many from Tío Johnny. I would be out there in the garage many
times until dark after my evening chores were done and it was time to
come in the house. I spent a lot of time out there because I was the oldest of
nine and my younger siblings could be quite noisy and distracting, so it
was less of a hassle to just hide out in the garage and read. We were living
in the country, about twelve miles from town, and didn't have a nearby
library. In the summer, when school was not in session, the only way to get
books was to meet the bookmobile on the elementary school grounds.
Never heard of a bookmobile? It was like a mobile library . . . a big van or a
converted RV (before there were RVs) packed with books and scheduled to
make weekly rounds of all the country schools during the summer. Well, I
and the other kids, the patron of the ranch that dad worked for had three
girls, and two of my brothers would saddle the ranch horses and ride the
six miles or so to the school to meet the bookmobile. The Tulare County
librarian driving this rig would be there before it got too hot in the day. We
would saddle up and ride out there with a gunnysack tied to the saddle
horn in which to carry our returning books and to pick up our new ones.
After selecting our new treasures to put into the gunnysacks, we would ride
home. The rule was, you had to do a certain amount of work in order to use
the ranch horses. It amounted to feeding cattle, cleaning poop, weeding,
and whatever else was needed. These were the same horses we used working cattle on the ranch, but we had to earn their use for a pleasure ride such
as going to meet the bookmobile. It was great fun for us as we were excused
from our regular chores, got to pleasure ride with the girls, and were able
to replace the books we had read the previous week with new ones. We
must have been ten, eleven, and twelve years of age during this time. I was
still reading lots of horse-related material and had developed an interest in
becoming a veterinarian. I would talk to some of the ranch hands and
some of the viejitos about animal medicine. They were probably not really
viejitos, but seemed so to me at the time. The old horsemen did share with

me some of the herbs and what properties they contained that were necessary for medicating animals. They were interested in my finding out and
reading to them about current medicines that might improve on their
remedios. This was not usually the case. One time there was a horse that
had incurred a pretty serious wire cut on a shoulder and it was going to be
a week before the regular vet visit to the ranch. One practitioner came by
and said, "You know, it looks pretty bad, we might need to stitch him up,
blah, blah, blah. If we stitch him up the wound is going to infect and, well,
none of the medications we have are going to help." Dad said thank you,
and as soon as the veterinarian left, he described a plant that looked like
sour dock and told me where I could find it growing in a grove of *álamos* a
few miles from the ranch. When I got back, he mixed this plant with some
others he had, added some grass, and then mashed them all together. He
asked me to dig a small hole in the ground and then to urinate in it. He put
the prepared plants in the hole, mixed all the elements together, made a
muddy poultice, and placed it in a bandage, which he applied to the horse.
When the veterinarian returned the next day, he said, "This is amazing,
what did you use, I know it wasn't the ointment I gave you?" So my dad
said, "No, it didn't work, so I used my own," but he didn't tell him what it
was. So, for a long time after, I knew I wanted to be a veterinarian, but
using *all* medicines available. I would read all this stuff and when I'd come
home, Dad would ask me, "What did you learn today?" "How can we do
this?" Well, I was in high school for Christ's sake. What did I know? Yet,
after all he knew from a lifetime of hands-on experience, he still had
respect for formal education and the written word. He thought I could
learn this stuff one day and be ready to apply it the next on horses and cattle. Actually, the exposure he gave me to ranch animals made me more
curious, more eager to read and learn, and led me to go to work for a veterinarian when I graduated from high school and started college. I was
enrolled at the College of the Sequoias, lived at the veterinary hospital, and
got to sterilize equipment, do general cleanup, and even assisted in emer-
gency surgery. I eventually ended my pursuit of a veterinarian credential.
UC Davis only accepted the equivalent of one student per county for the
state of California. These fifty-two new vet med students had to have the
sponsorship of a practicing veterinarian, top grades, and field experience. I
was close with the grades, but there were others that were better. I had
more experience than anyone else, and my employer seemed very supportive and praised me publicly for my performance. Privately, I overheard him

tell a wealthy client that I would never finish college despite my ability because my father had only completed the third grade and that we couldn't possibly have the respect for formal education that professional people required. This was the person upon whose sponsorship I had depended and whom my father had personally mentored and taught to rope. The final kicker was that this occurred before the creation of the plethora of education grants that came later, and there was no money to pursue such a course of study. You had to have an "in." It was all part of the *política*. If you weren't considered part of the dominant community culture and accepted at that level, you were out. Regardless of how much your father may have been lauded as a champion cowboy, a man that created an exemplary breeding program as the foreman of a cattle ranch, and an admired family man, he was still an uneducated laborer whose progeny was doomed to follow his steps. My father, while raising my eight younger siblings, did not require me to stay and help him provide for the family as was the custom. He pulled me aside when I graduated from high school and said, "All I can give you is the freedom to go and do it, but you have to put yourself through, you have to earn it." So that was his big gift, and a major relief for me, taking away the guilt from pursuing a college education. I ended up not going to Davis.

You asked about what other things I was reading that gave me pride in my family and my culture. That had to be the combination of theory and practice of the cowboy and vaquero lifestyle, both historical and contemporary. The vast majority of the cowboy stuff I'd been reading had roots in the Mexican vaquero and charro culture. All of this terminology in popular use that was being mispronounced had genesis in our culture. This just encouraged me to excel in this area. Not just as an intellectual practice, but in actual competition. I had been riding calves as a kid and doing the regular ranch work, but that is when I started competing by riding broncs and bulls. There wasn't anything more fun than beating the *gabachitos*. Some of the kids that beat me on a regular basis were the *inditos* from the reservation. They were the best! I continued to read everything I could get my hands on.

cv: Any book in particular that you remember, and that you liked and stands out?

fv: Well, most of the readings were in English. As a kid, my favorites were the Walter Farley series on the Black Stallion. Later, Zane Grey and Louis L'Amour before I started college. Out of necessity, that changed after a short military break, when I began focusing on social psychology, graduated from Fresno State in sociology, and was awarded a National Institute of Mental Health Fellowship to Cal Berkeley. That fellowship was the result of some writing I had done while an undergraduate. I began reading what was popular and/or controversial with the Department of Sociology at Cal at the time, not only in sociology but also social anthropology. Albert Memmi, *The Colonizer and the Colonized*, was one of those points of contention. I was interested in methodology, therefore I became a big fan of Erving Goffman. It was during this time that I developed a hatred for Oscar Lewis and all his bullshit about the Sánchez family. In writing *The Children of Sánchez* and related socioanthropological pieces, he applied George Foster's theory of limited good, not considering that it was developed from preconceived premises of a culture, a skewed sampling of subjects from a very narrow geographic area, subjective notes that were culturally laden, and then he attempted to extrapolate an inherently faulty theory from a minuscule sampling to a national culture. It was an uphill battle for a new graduate student to challenge a tenured professor, even using accepted methodological tools. Then too, Oscar Lewis had just recently died (1970), and George Foster was a former chair of Cal's Department of Anthropology.

One of the highlights of my time in Berkeley was a meeting with Paulo Freire after I had read his *Pedagogy of the Oppressed*. I found out he was going to be in Berkeley in a roundabout way. He had visited a *cooperativa* in New Mexico, with some guys I knew that were hiding out in the hills. Not a lot of people knew he was going to be in the country "because his life was in danger." He spoke at the home of Jack London. No, not the original Jack London, I'm not that old. This Dr. London was the chairman of the English Department at Cal. I got to meet Dr. Freire and talk to him after reading his book, and we discussed some of his other books and articles. He said he wanted to apologize. I was blown away and asked for what reason? He said, "At the time, I was writing for colleagues, I was writing for other college professors and it was after that, that my life changed." It was at this time, I realized, that he actually began to live his theory of "praxis." It was his work with adult education that caused a melding of theory and practice. The process of educational theory was not complete until it was consummated in practice. In this case, the streets of Brazil and the communities of Colombia. He responded to a request from Chile to set up the same model of educational systems he had established in the other countries. This had to do with a necessary government intervention at every level. If education was being made available to illiterate adults, it had a great impact on the attitudes and education of the nation's children. What happened was that there was a documented improvement not only in academic achievement, but the retention rates improved. The result of educating the masses was that there was greater interest in informed governing, a greater participation in government, and the economy prospered. So when he arrived in Chile attempting to replicate his education model at the invitation of Allende, he faced opposition as a goddammed communist. It was shortly after this that Allende was assassinated and Paulo Freire was forced to go into hiding with a price on his head. Dr. Freire went to work for the World Council of Churches based in Switzerland and from there came to New York, then Nuevo México, stopping to visit with César Chávez in La Paz before arriving in Berkeley. Before he left California, he was scheduled to speak at a community meeting in San Jose, and I was invited to attend. The manner in which he spoke was impressive. It was quietly passionate, deliberate, and penetratingly multilingual. The delivery was a mixture of predominantly English, Spanish, and Portuguese, with a little punctuation of French and Italian where appropriate. Amazingly enough, though I don't speak all of these languages fluently and only understand a few phrases, I could understand his every point and was blown away by it. It was an incredible experience that only got more intense. There were two or three young guys there whose primary language was Portuguese, and they seemed to be looking after Dr. Freire. I did not really know them but had seen them around campus before. One of these young men approached me and asked: "Could you do us a favor? Can you take the maestro?" Of course! They had asked me to give this man a ride, great! So he says, "When the program is over, *mira*, bring your car over here, everyone will be getting ready to share a meal at the hall, but take that time to bring your car in facing in this direction and we'll tell you where we're going then." I thought nothing of it and pulled into the Guadalupe Church parking lot as the reception was ending. Paulo Freire got into the back seat of my car and one of the other young men sat in front and said, "Quickly, let's go," pointing between buildings. A quick right turn out of sight and he said, "Stop right here." Dr. Freire quickly got out, and the third young man, José Luis, got in the car wearing the same style and color of hat and overcoat that the maestro had been wearing. Dr. Freire, keeping his head down, quickly got in a dark van and was driven away. I immediately drove around the building, slowly drove past the people from the reception and out of the parking lot, heading toward Oakland, opposite the direction the van had taken. "What is going on?" I had asked. Once we were away from the neighborhood and they didn't believe we were being followed, they said, "OK, look. The maestro's life is in danger; I'm sorry we didn't tell you but you couldn't know then." We drove to Oakland with them directing me to a downtown neighborhood, and into an alley where they said, "Just take off, go back." That was the last time I ever saw José Luis. He came up missing, wearing Paulo Freire's hat and coat in that alley in Oakland. What I remembered about Paulo Freire was his apology about what he had written, because it was not in keeping with his later philosophies, that written material had value only if it could convey a message, an understanding, and cause a positive action, not to confound or impress because it was flowery or erudite. Rhetoric does not get to the crux of things; you want people to understand, you write plainly, you speak plainly and get your point across.

cv: Well, I'll just leave it up to you, if you want to add anything about whatever you want.

fv: The love of books has been a lifelong affair for me. Some of the interests that I had as a kid I still have now. It just seems that some of these perspectives have a more universal appeal. People in general, I believe, have a greater understanding of the value of cross-cultural learning. For example, have you read *All the Pretty Horses*? That trilogy includes *The Crossing* and *Cities of the Plain*. Cormac McCarthy is amazing. So, here you have a guy from the South or somewhere. What does he know about our culture? Then, I started reading *All the Pretty Horses*. He would switch from English to Spanish, and speak about the lobo and the horses . . . about getting up early in the morning; describing the smells of the sage . . . it would remind me of being a kid and smelling the sage at dawn. Or when we would load up the horses and ride up into the mountains with Dad to gather cattle. . . . Then he starts describing the smell of leather, the creaking of saddle leather or what a hoof sounds like when it hits the ground when it still has dew on it . . . and how it's going to be different in the heat of the afternoon, when the acrid, you know, acidic properties of the sage are prevalent over the sweeter morning smell. Once the sun has dried this out in the afternoon, you feel the heat on your neck under your hat. When you read this, you know the guy has been there, he knows it, and he understands it and has the ability to communicate the full essence. That is the beauty of the written word, and I hope to be able to convey some of my own thoughts in writing at some point. I hope I was able to pass on some of this love to my children. All four of my kids write very well and I think all have published poetry, or short stories. My oldest, Anna, has published poetry and is currently reading children's books for publication in DVDs as well as some Shakespeare. My son Mateo has been published since he was in grade school. My second son, third child, Fernando, is stationed in Riyadh with the State Department and has also written all his life. I am amazed by his e-mail descriptions of everyday existence in the Middle East. My youngest, Andrea, is also a gifted storyteller. She wrote and then performed short plays in high school, some that were recorded on film. She has written and edited while interning for extreme sports magazines as part of her journalism minor. I believe that with Pat, her starting out as an elementary school teacher and all, and both of us working with our two youngest in particular, they've all developed an appreciation and an affinity for the written word. We may have placed them on that path, but they've done very well on their own.

Cuauhtémoc B. Díaz

CAROLINA VALERO: Quisiera saber lo que . . . cuándo aprendió a leer y qué tipo de libros [eran] los que usted utilizaba, o cómo fue cuando aprendió el español, el inglés.

CUAUHTÉMOC B. DÍAZ: Cuando yo aprendí a leer, aprendí en base precisamente a los libros que estaban; eran los libros de texto autorizados en el sistema educativo allá en México. La mayoría de mi educación ha sido en México y había anteriormente un sistema de libros . . . , estuve, por ejemplo, en el kinder. En el kinder había algo así que era como un . . . le llamaban un silabario; silabario porque permitía que juntáramos letras y poco a poco la *M* con la *A*, *MA*, la *P* con la *A*, *PA*, y eso era el silabario. Un libro pos muy chiquito, lógico; la edad, cinco años, seis años, también era correspondiente. De ahí, pues el primero, segundo y tercero grado de primaria había libros que, como dije, de texto, muy sencillos, de muy fácil asimilación, y uno de los profesores . . . uno iba por ahí; primeramente, leyendo meramente los subtítulos que había en los cromos o fotografías de los libros, pero posteriormente había varias técnicas para la lectura. Una era la lectura de rapidez y otra era la lectura de comprensión. La lectura de rapidez, pues había que leer la mayor cantidad de palabras posible en un tiempo determinado, y la lectura de comprensión había que leer un párrafo y explicar aquello que habías entendido de él, o la idea principal del autor. Pasó así la primaria y poco a poco pues, en lo personal, me fui adentrando al partir del quinto grado, especialmente, en leer libros en inglés. Porque, aunque estuve por allá en Tangamandapio, Michoacán, tuve la oportunidad que la maestra de quinto grado nos indujo poco a poco a aprender inglés. Pienso yo que ella había vivido en los Estados Unidos. Entonces decidió que nos

iba a enseñar un poco de inglés y pues yo pienso que, de los treinta y seis
compañeros que tenía, nadie vio en el futuro que podía haber hecho con
ese inglés. Yo, en lo personal, a mí me gustó porque, aparte de que tengo
una familia acá en los Estados Unidos, pues tenía una creencia de que
podía aprender inglés, que ya era para mi un segundo idioma, y que actual-
mente me iba a servir de algo. Y así terminé mis quinto y sexto grados de
primaria, pero cada pieza de literatura que caía en mis manos en inglés,
pues la devoraba, aunque lo que hacía era leer palabras, consultarlas en el
diccionario y, aunque no sabía cómo se pronunciaban, simplemente sabía
lo que significaban. Este . . . eso me valió bastante a mí en lo personal,
porque desde entonces en la secundaria, que viene siendo *junior high*, y
luego la preparatoria, y realmente nunca tuve la necesidad de hacer
exámenes de inglés, por que yo era el único que más sabía y sabía porque
solamente había aprendido palabras sueltas, no tenía acceso a conversa-
ciones. Escuchaba canciones. He tenido dificultad con el oído desde
pequeño, entonces escuchaba canciones; me gustaba una que otra letra o
palabra, la identificaba, pero más bien buscaba la letra para saber de qué se
trataba la canción. Este . . . de ahí, como dije, la mayoría de los muchachitos
que empezaron conmigo, no se dieron cuenta qué tanto podían haber
hecho con el inglés. Pero a mí se me fue quedando, ahí me fue gustando,
empecé a venir a los Estados Unidos desde la edad de once años; entonces
venía y para mí era un contento el leer todos los letreros. Venía por el *freeway*, mi hermano manejando y yo venia viendo ahí que decía *Coke*,
Hamburger, más para delante que decía *Exit Only* y todo eso me lo iba registrando, registrando, registrando a tal grado que aprendí principalmente
una gran cantidad de palabras en inglés. Tengo, podemos decir, que un lé-
xico muy amplio de palabras en inglés, que la mayoría o el estándar de
estudiantes no lo tienen, y las utilizo ocasionalmente porque hay necesidad,
pero siempre que alguien me pregunta: "¿Oye, papá, eso que se significa en
inglés?" O alguna persona: "Oye, y ¿esto que quiere decir?" Ya conozco y
tengo el concepto de lo que es la palabra, porque aunque no la sé ni pronunciar, pero sé lo que quiere decir. ¿Verdad? Entonces eso fue la primaria.
También quería decir que en la primaria, desde que estaba en el sexto
grado, como le dicen, no sé, pero siempre he sido muy *resourceful*, y por ahí
me encontré una tarjetita para subscribirme a la revista *Time*, y desde sexto
año empecé a recibir la revista *Time* y me encantaba leer pedacitos, porque
era todo lo que entendía, pero siempre fue bastante motivacional para mí el

poder tener acceso a la revista en inglés, porque me daban a mí la oportunidad de sentirme que pertenecía a dos culturas diferentes.

CV: ¿Algo que quiera agregar?

CD: Bueno, posteriormente . . . antes, más bien dicho, durante mi época de la escuela primaria, del primer grado al sexto grado, leía mucho revistas cómicas que tenían que ver especialmente con personajes de Walt Disney como el Pato Donald, los Chicos Malos . . . era algo que era yo muy hábil lector. Iba ahí a un puesto de revistas y ya me apartaban los más nuevos. Todos los leía, me encantaba este . . . , ver ese tipo de revistas porque siento yo que (estoy hablando de 1965 al 75 más o menos, diez años), este . . . todavía estaban muy sanos. Influían en mí, por ejemplo, que vivía en México, porque el tipo de vida que desarrollaban los personajes de la historieta era la vida de los Estados Unidos. Por ejemplo, salía, no sé, el Pato Donald y era cartero, era *mailman*, o salía y era policía, o salía y era militar. Y de ahí empecé yo a tener, ahora sí, que mi propio héroe o mis propias metas, qué era lo que yo quería ser cuando fuera grande. De hecho, yo sentía que el ser cartero en los Estados Unidos era algo muy loable. La revistita ésa me tenía a mí encantado con el ser cartero.

Cuauhtémoc B. Díaz

CAROLINA VALERO: I would like to know . . . when did you learn how to read, and what type of books did you use? Or, when did you learn Spanish, English?

CUAUHTÉMOC B. DÍAZ: When I learned how to read, I learned precisely with the books that were available. These were the textbooks authorized by the educational system back in Mexico. Most of my education was in Mexico, and there used to be a textbook system. . . . I was . . . for instance, in kindergarten. In kindergarten there was something like . . . they called it *silabario* [primer], silabario because it allowed us to put letters together and, little by little, *M* and *A* made *MA*, *P* and *A* was *PA*, and that was the gist of the silabario. A rather small book, logically. Our age, five or six years, was in accordance. After that, in first, second, and third grade, there were textbooks, like I said, very simple, easy to understand, and one of the teachers . . . that's how we did it; at first, just reading the subtitles to the illustrations or pictures in the books, but then there were several reading techniques. One was for fast reading, and the other for comprehension. As for the fast reading, well, you had to read the maximum number of words in a limited time; for comprehension, you had to read a paragraph and explain what you had understood, or the main idea of the author. That's how elementary school went. Little by little, starting in fifth grade, I personally started reading books in English. Even if I was in Tangamandapio, Michoacán, I had the good fortune that my teacher made it possible for us to learn English little by little. I think she had lived in the United States. So, she decided she was going to teach us some English, but none of my thirty-six classmates, not one of them, thought of the future that English could have meant for them. Personally, I liked it because, aside from the fact that I have family here in the United States, I thought I could learn English, a second language for me, that was actually going to be useful. And so I finished the fifth and six grades, but if I stumbled upon any literary works in English, I devoured them, even if all I did was read the words, look them up in a dictionary, and, though I did not how to pronounce them, I just knew what they meant. So . . . that was very valuable to me personally because, after that, in secondary education (the equivalent of *junior high*), and then in high school, I never had to take any English exams because I was the most knowledgeable student; and I knew because I had learned isolated words, I never had access to conversations. I listened to songs. Hearing was difficult for me since I was little, so I used to listen to songs. I liked this or that lyric or word, I identified it, but, mostly, I would look up the lyrics to know what the song was about. So . . . as I said, most of the youngsters that started when I did never realized what they could have done with English. But in my case, I would memorize it, I started to like it, and I started coming to the United States when I was eleven; so, I would come here and it was a pleasure to be able to read all the signs. On the *freeway*, my brother would drive and I would notice that [a sign] would say *Coke, Hamburger*; another one, later on, would read *Exit Only*, and I would take notice of all that, it would sink in, sink in, sink in to the point that I learned a great number of words in English. One could say that I have a vast vocabulary of words in English, better than most students or the average, and I use those words occasionally when I need them; but anytime someone asks me, "Listen Dad, what does that mean in English?," or someone asks, "Say, what does that mean?" I know the meaning of the word because, even if I don't know how to pronounce it, I know what it means, right? So, that was elementary school. I also wanted to say that when I was in sixth grade, as they call it . . . I don't know, but I have always been very *resourceful*, and I found a subscription card for *Time* magazine, and since the sixth grade I began receiving *Time* magazine, and I loved to read little bits, because that was all I understood, but it was always very inspiring to have access to that magazine in English, because it allowed me to feel I belonged to two different cultures.

cv: Anything else you would like to add?

cd: Well, later on . . . actually it was before that time, during my elementary school years, from first grade to sixth grade . . . I used to read many comic books, especially those with Walt Disney characters like Donald

Duck, the Beagle Boys . . . that was something I was good at as a reader. I would go to a newsstand, and they would save the new ones for me. I read them all, I liked . . . to see that type of magazine because I think (I am talking about the period from 1965 to 1975, more or less, those ten years) that . . . that they were very wholesome. They had an influence on me, for instance, as someone who lived in Mexico, because the lifestyle of the characters in the comic strip was the life of the United States. For example, there was, say, Donald Duck, and he was a *mailman*, or he was a police officer, or a soldier. And from then on, I started to have my own heroes and my own goals, what I wanted to be when I grew up. In fact, I felt that to be a mailman in the United States was something praiseworthy. That little magazine sold me on the idea of becoming a mailman.

Note

Translated by the editor. I have tried to capture the spirit and the flow of the conversation, but the translation is not intended as an artistic or exact rendition of the original; rather, my goal has been to convey the original information as exactly as possible. I have used italics for words that Mr. Díaz used in English in the original interview.

Lupe Rodríguez

LUPE RODRÍGUEZ: I'm a Latina girl, and I don't remember exactly when I learned how to read in Spanish, but I think I knew how to learn . . . how to read in English before I learned Spanish. I wanted to learn the Spanish so much because my mom used to read these Spanish novels and I wanted, I really wanted to learn . . . know what was in those Spanish novels. So, my mom would tell me: "Well, if you want to learn what's in those novels you are going to have to try to learn how to read"; but I don't remember exactly if she taught me how to read, but I just kind of like tried to phonetically . . . tried to do it myself. But I was really interested in those stories in those magazines. So, I really don't know exactly how I did learn how to read, but I know that I already had some English part, because I know I learned how to read when I was in probably in first grade, because I learned how to read the English language in first grade, when I was in school. I started school kind of late, because of my sickness. I remember . . . as far as I remember, reading in the English language. I remember the teacher: she didn't have like small . . . I mean, like one-to-one groups, you know. Sometimes one of the groups would read with her and the other groups were in different other groups doing like more oral language type of things in English, in stories, retelling stories and doing like plays. That's as far as I can remember in learning the English language. It's been such a long time that I really don't remember exactly how I learned, but I know that I did learn how to read. And then I continued with my Spanish, because I wanted to know what those magazines said. So, I guess my mom would probably read to me. She probably taught me a few of the Spanish phonetic sounds and then that's when . . . then I got my start there, and I was so happy that I learned how to read because I was able to read all of those magazines, and I was looking forward every week to reading those magazines.

CAROLINA VALERO: What kind of magazines? What were the titles of the novelas?

LR: There were Spanish novelas like *Lágrimas y risas, Memín Pinguín,* and there were Spanish novels, telenovelas, but there were articles and magazines, not in the television.

CV: Is it the only kind of books or magazines that you read, that you remember?

LR: In that age time yes, that's the only thing I can remember. But later on I read like those . . . when I was older, like in high school, I remember reading like those romantic novels, what were they called? Anyways, those romantic novels. I was there like two or three chapters. Well, there was a big book. I remember reading a lot back then, but as far as now, no. I just read a few articles sometimes when I'm in the . . . when I go to the doctor's office, or the dentist's office, you know, I do read the articles there. But even though I know the language, you know, the Spanish language, I still feel that I do more in the English language, I don't know why but, you know, because I understand it more and though I am able to speak Spanish very well, phonetically I understand more the English language. I kept more the English than the Spanish, but I do get around.

CV: And those novelas were in Spanish?

LR: Yes the novelas were in Spanish. Yes, but it's different from a novela than to . . . like when you go to a doctor's office and read an application, signing an application, you know, that's just more . . . the language there is just harder, you know. So, I didn't have the full understanding. Even in the Bible sometimes, when my mom would read the Bible (she read the Bible a lot), sometimes she would want me to kind of like assist her in reading the Bible, which was in Spanish and, you know, ask her questions and stuff like that, because where she was attending (in our church group), she had to do like what we call . . . they had to do like an act, you know, trying to give like a sermon to the other people so they can know what the benefits are. So, a lot of those Spanish words that were used in biblical times, you know, I had a hard time understanding.

CV: Anything you want to add, when you were learning? Like any kind of library that your family had? Like books that you remember? Or your brothers and sisters?

LR: No, I don't remember too much. I do remember my brother, he enjoyed reading; every time he was reading books; could be in the bathroom—and that was his main area to read—and I said, "What the . . ." But you know, that was one thing for him, he was . . . he just loved reading. And on the other hand, I learned how to read . . . well, just for the benefit, that I had to learn how to read for certain things, but not that I loved it.

CV: Were your brother's books mostly in English or Spanish?

LR: My brother's were mostly in English.

CV: And yours were both?

LR: Yeah. Well, kind of both, because right now I'm still speaking both languages. I work for a school and I have to speak basically more Spanish, because I work with a lot of ELD students. So that's my background there.

Helen Fabela Chávez

LUCÍA D. VÁZQUEZ: I'm sitting here with Helen Fabela Chávez, who is recuperating from her surgery, so we don't know how her energy is going to be, and I know I'm louder than her so I'm going to put [the tape recorder] closer to where she is; but I asked Helen . . . I told her how important reading is, and that some publishers don't think that Latinos read. And that's our question for today, if she's a reader. So, I'm going around the country-side (OK, I'm not going that far, but I'm going around) asking people about their reading history, if they like to read, if they used to read, if they read, what they read when they were kids, that kind of stuff. So, Helen, you said you don't read as much anymore, or you used to read?

HELEN FABELA CHÁVEZ: No, I don't read anymore; my eyes are bad. But I used to read whatever I could get my hands on. A lot of union books, a lot of history stuff. But César [E. Chávez] was a reader; he loved to read. He would read day and night if he could.

LV: Do you do any of the big book readers? Does that help at all, any of the large print [books]? Have you tried that?

HC: No, I haven't. Because I've been sick, and I have no energy at all for anything.

LV: But maybe after you start walking and get your diabetes under control that will be better.

HC: Yes, maybe I can start doing that again.

LV: Maybe we can get you some books on tape too. That's what I do when I travel: I put books on tape, because it's kind of . . . like reading, but not quite.

LV: So, when you said you could read everything you could get your hands on, when you were a kid, were you a big reader?

HC: When I was little? Yes, but not very much; just what they gave us in school.

LV: Because you didn't have a lot of access then.

HC: Right.

LV: What was your favorite book in school that you can remember starting?

HC: God, I don't remember! It's been so long ago, Lucía, I don't remember.

LV: How about when you say the union stuff; what do you mean by the union books?

HC: Some of the books that had been written about the union; the biography of César, and different books that have been written.

LV: And when you read them, do you say, "That's not true!"

HC: Some I do.

LV: Was there anything you thought, "No way! that's not the way it happened!"

HC: Yes.

LV: "I was there!"

HC: Yes, that happens a lot of times in some of the books.

LV: Can you give me an example?

HC: Well, like they'll say things that are not true, you know? Things that I know were not really true, and it upsets me, so I stop reading.

LV: Ah, that's not good. Have you thought about correcting it, maybe have somebody write down the things that were true and . . . "Oh, excuse me but that's not the way it happened: I was there."

HC: Yes, Marc Grossman does that.

LV: Oh, he does?

HC: Yes. When we see something that's not right, we call him, and he'll make a correction and send it in.

LV: Oh good, very cool. I haven't seen him in a while.

HC: He was here Saturday, came back to visit me.

LV: And will all the kids be here this weekend?

HC: Not all of them, some of them are staying home.

LV: Anyway, it's getting close to Thanksgiving. Were any of your kids real big readers?

HC: Paul is, he is a big reader. I don't know about the others but Paul, I know, loves to read.

LV: Anything in particular?

HC: He reads anything he can get a hold of, biographies . . . I like biographies.

LV: Oh, you like biographies too, because it's a part of your history? What biographies have you read?

HC: I read the Kennedy, some of Sister Teresa, some of . . . I don't know, some that I have at home that were given to me.

LV: Would you get stuff from César when he would read? Would he come to you and say, "Oh, try this one, read [this] one." Because I know his library; I would always go and wanted to get stuff from him; he would . . .

HC: Well, yes; he would get mad because we wouldn't read. He would scold the kids and me, because he said, "You've got to read so you can learn," and said we could learn anything by reading, which is true.

LV: Lots of good stuff out there. Do you do any of the Internet stuff?

HC: No.

LV: Haven't had a chance to get on there? How about your grandkids, do your grandkids read?

HC: I think they do.

LV: Do you ever get them to come read to you?

HC: No.

LV: Well, there you go; since you can't read, you've got to get them to start reading to you.

HC: Yes.

LV: That'll work. Oh, they'd love to come read to Nana.

HC: Yes.

LV: Was there anything in particular that César would bring to you and say, "Oh, you've got to read this, I love this," or make suggestions for you?

HC: Everything, everything.

LV: He would come and talk to you about everything he read?

HC: All the books in his library that he would read, he would tell me, "You should read them, you can learn something."

LV: Like his dog books. I have a German shepherd now you know.

HC: Oh, do you?

[. . .]

HC: Oh, you're not working?

LV: No, I'm between jobs, because I graduated and I haven't really found anything yet. I'm doing a little consultant work here, and I'm waiting for another project to come through, but I'm not working right now, so that gives me time but . . . I love reading.

HC: That's good.

LV: I love reading, and I finally got my daughter to read more, but we had to get rid of the TV. Because with the TV, forget it.

HC: I know.

LV: I'm addicted to it; it's like, "Oh, look!," I get all excited.

HC: You're like me; I'm addicted to novelas.

LV: Oh yes?

HC: Five and six, I watch them faithfully.

LV: Even at 5 p.m. . . . ? You didn't have any books that were like that, that you would want to read one after the other? Any kind of series, or detectives, or any of that stuff?

HC: Yes, I used to like to read detective books.

LV: Yes? Like what? Like who?

HC: You know, about different murders and stuff like that that would happen. I wanted to find out why they did what they did, who, what.

LV: There's a Chicana detective, you know, that . . . She writes Chicana detective novels. I'll have to see if she has it in big print. Her name is Lucha Corpi and her first book starts at the Chicano Moratorium, but there's a death there. It talks about all the stuff that happened there. It'll be kind of cool, you like detective novels. I'll have to see what's available in big print for you, maybe you can try that, maybe get the kids to read to you. It'll be fun.[1]

Notes

For this publication, we have edited out a few personal comments that were not related to the topic of reading.

1. The interview ended here, when Helen F. Chávez expressed her need to rest.

3

READING
IN THE PAST
Personal Libraries and Reading Histories

Introduction

The five pieces selected for part 3 address issues of book ownership and cultural/literary recovery. The first two do so as exploratory essays on the meaning and value of books and newspapers as cultural capital; the last three are examples of the analytical cataloguing of private and institutional libraries.

Carlos Morton, in "El don de Olegario (Olegario's Gift)," wonders about the possibility that his own literary career may have been influenced by his maternal grandfather's interest in journalism and letters in general. A mystery to him at first, grandfather Olegario's activities become better known as Morton guides us through archival and family research that allows him to reconstruct Olegario's activities as a printer and journalist. Morton embarks on a journey in which reading the past becomes the pathway to illuminate the present.

A. Gabriel Meléndez's contribution, in turn, is a reflection on the power of books and book ownership. Meléndez first considers the general scarcity of books in his native (northern) New Mexico in order to then reminisce about his family's private library. The (trans)formative effect of those books on Meléndez is the subject of much of his essay, which also pays attention to literary developments in the state, with an emphasis on the career (and the significance) of Felipe Maximiliano Chacón and other writers. The epiphanic connection that the adult Meléndez is able to trace between his small family library and the public careers of local writers and scholars (himself included) is a powerful reminder that the private and the public are not separate but are complementary spheres when it comes to the preservation and the transmission of knowledge.

As the essays by Morton and Meléndez make clear, much of the Chicano/a cultural past remains elusive because of the difficulties involved in locating historical records. Like these two authors, a large cadre of scholars has worked diligently during the past few decades to better document the Hispanic heritage in the United States. As a result, we have seen great advances in the reconstruction of the history of writing (and publishing) by Mexican Americans and Chicanos/as. But the same cannot be said about those other areas of the cultural sphere (such as reading, book ownership, family libraries, and others) that illuminate reception rather than production. The last three chapters in this section (written over a span of seventy years!) take up that challenge and, together, offer us a panoramic exploration of libraries in New Mexico, from 1598 to the mid-twentieth century.

As I suggest in my essay on the family library of Miguel A. Otero, the study of private libraries (and libraries in general, I would add here) is one of the most effective tools we have to document what individuals or groups have valued and treasured for their own use and for the purpose of future preservation. Through the analysis of these collections, we can study literary taste and preferences, the access that their owners had to certain print materials (or lack thereof), and many other related aspects such as the type of education that parents wanted for their children. Meléndez's recollection of the Compton's Encyclopedia at his home offers a glimpse in that latter regard, and my own study of the children's books in the Otero library will give further details.

Because the section opens with two testimonials from the twenty-first century (those by Morton and Meléndez), I have decided to arrange the three library studies in reverse-chronological order, starting in the nineteenth- and twentieth-century period with the Otero library, then moving back to the eighteenth century ("Two Colonial New Mexico Libraries"), and ending with "Books in New Mexico, 1598–1680," which brings us back to the period in which books were first introduced in the area. These last two chapters were originally published in the *New Mexico Historical Review* and are reproduced here by permission. Upon the recommendation of early readers of this book (when it was in manuscript form), I am reprinting them here without the extensive book catalogs in their respective appendixes. For readers interested in those catalogs, I would recommend consulting the original *New Mexico Historical Review* essays.

El don de Olegario
(Olegario's Gift)

Carlos Morton

GROWING UP

When we were growing up, my mother and tías always told us *primos* that our maternal grandfather, Olegario López Luján, was "un escritor y espiritista." This never meant much to the half dozen or so primos because there was no visible proof that he was "a writer and spiritualist." What kind of writer was he and where was he published? What was a spiritualist and how could they "see into the future" and predict things? For years, the three sisters repeated the mantra that our grandfather "hypnotized people and dabbled in the occult."

Olegario López Luján was born in La Habana, Cuba, in 1891. As a youth he studied medicine, although he didn't finish his studies. He later worked as an apothecary in Mexico, so he knew something about medicine. He grew up in a well-to-do family whose fortune was in export/import. Legend has it that the family wanted him to marry an attractive but older woman with a title, but, rather than be forced into this marriage, he left for the United States.

After leaving Cuba he traveled to Mexico and the United States, where he met and married our Mexican grandmother, Emilia Tejada Cuéllar, in 1920 in Detroit. They met outside a movie theater where he "followed her home" and, months later, asked her father for her hand in marriage. They were married in a civil court in Detroit and then went to La Habana for the Catholic marriage.

We can track their wanderings by the births of their children: the twins (Héctor and Hilda) were born in Cuba in 1921 (Héctor died several years later), Hortencia in 1924 (San Luis Potosí, Mexico), and my mother Helen in 1927 (San Antonio, Texas). López Luján was an eccentric man, insisting that his children be given names that began with the letter *H*. Hilda, the oldest, described him as being very loving and affectionate, but with certain strict rules. For instance, once when he caught Hilda whistling, he admonished her by saying, "No young lady or civilized educated person should ever be caught whistling."

THE TEXAS YEARS

The years 1927–1929 must have been an exciting time for the Hispanic community in Texas, a time of political activism mixed with literary flowering. The League of United Latin American Citizens (LULAC) was founded in Corpus Christi in 1929, and there was a flourishing amalgam of Spanish-language newspapers that extended from McAllen (*Diógenes*) and Laredo (*Revista Semanal*) along the border to little towns like San Diego (*La Libertad*), Kingsville (*Milicia*), and Falfurrias (*La Verdad*) in the valley. The largest and most influential newspaper was *La Prensa* of San Antonio, but Corpus Christi's prominence was marked by the fact that it had two Spanish-language newspapers, *El Paladín* and *El Puerto*.

After Helen was born, the family moved to the bustling port city of Corpus Christi, which was then undergoing a boom with much construction and business activity. According to my Aunt Hilda, her father "had some capital and decided to invest in a newspaper, which he started with a partner." It seemed like a good place and time.

Little did they know that in 1929 the stock market crash would precipitate the Great Depression. This must have taken a terrible toll on *El Puerto* and other small businesses. After the paper folded, my grandfather and his family packed up and moved to Villa de Arriaga in San Luis Potosí, Mexico, the ancestral home of Emilia. Aunt Hilda told me that her father "sold his interest in the newspaper to a partner (unnamed) who cheated him out of his money." Olegario López Luján died at the age of forty-two and was buried in the Masonic crypt in San Luis Potosí, Mexico. The family went from a comfortable middle-class life to one of destitution.

A LITERARY DISCOVERY

Emilia had to struggle to raise her three daughters, but she instilled in them a love of learning. The sisters were prolific readers (*en español*) and listened to different kinds of music, danced up a storm, and loved attending the theater and movies (especially from the "Golden Age" of Mexican cinema).

Reading rubbed off on us; my cousin Shylda Álvarez graduated with an MFA degree in creative writing from UC Irvine, and I wrote poetry and short stories and settled into a career as a playwright and professor. I remember vividly the first book my father bought me, a hardbound copy of *Tarzan of the Apes*. After that, I went on to read every book Edgar Rice Burroughs ever wrote.

In 1980 I was visiting my Aunt Hilda in Los Angeles when she mysteriously produced copies of several dozen newspaper articles written by my grandfather and posted in a makeshift album. She never showed the album to any of the primos, not even her own daughters. Along with the articles glued in a catalog was a copy of a business card.

717 Waco St.   Phone 33

EL PUERTO
A Spanish Weekly Newspaper
Olegario Lopez   Corpus Christi, Texas
Director

The writing was a mixture of articles dealing with Corpus Christi and its growth as a city, as well as a series of columns ("Tópicos Semanarios") discussing the times in which they lived, including Prohibition, lynching of blacks, Mother Jones, the Texas Rangers and their mistreatment of Mexicans. Some of the columns were written with a dry humor reminiscent of Mark Twain.

Regarding his alleged "spiritualism," a separate newspaper article (undated, with no byline) featured a headline that reads "Como fue el Vaticino de la Muerte de Sr. Rangel" (How the prophesy of the death of Mr. Rangel came to be). My aunt Hilda remembers this being from a newspaper in San Luis Potosí, Mexico, that reported the "sudden death of Don José Rangel foretold by the Cuban spiritualist Olegario López Luján." The article goes on to state that six or seven men were present when López Luján wrote on the wall "not only the date in which the prediction was made" but the date in which Mr. Rangel would die.

One of the informants, Juan Lastras, told the writer "with frequency he would see Mr. Rangel who would laugh with good humor and say, 'do you see how Olegario lies, instead of dying each day I am getting fatter.'" When the reporter sought him out at his home, López Luján replied that he wrote the date on the wall "because Rangel kept insisting."

According to my cousin Shylda, her mother, Hilda, recalls that Olegario tried for years to get Emilia to quit smoking, but to no avail. His extrasensory perception (ESP) was evident in small ways. Emilia would hide her cigarettes in unusual places, but he would always find them. Once she hid some cigarettes in one of the small terra-cotta jugs hanging on the wall, and he walked into the room and immediately went to the jug that contained the hidden stash.

RECOVERING THE HISPANIC HERITAGE

In 2001 I received a grant from Arte Público Press and went to Texas hoping to find more information about the literary career of my grandfather. I contacted Dr. Thomas H. Kreneck, associate director for special collections and archives at Texas A&M University–Corpus Christi, for help in locating copies of *El Puerto*. The 1930 Corpus Christi telephone directory listed *El Puerto* as a "Newspaper Business" on 717 Waco Street with the telephone number 33. The Corpus Christi city directory of 1929 also had the following listing:

López Olegario (Emilia, home, 420 Staples)

I felt a deep sense of emotion seeing my grandparents' names and discovered much more about their stay in Corpus Christi. According to Kreneck, the area where they lived and worked was considered the "Mexican part of town on a bluff overlooking the port." Texas had been a part of the Confederate States of America, and separate parts of the city were designated as Mexican, Negro, or White. Even the cemeteries were segregated.

I brought a photo with me which was stamped "Swafford Company Photo," which appeared to be taken in front of "Garza's Grocery Store." Pictured were Olegario, Emilia, and their three daughters; he was wearing a white suit with white hat, and she was dressed in a fashionable "flapper" outfit with high heels. Also pictured was an unknown man in a suit, with three children beside him. We can only infer it was the shop owner, Mr. Garza. From the numerical listing telephone directory it was "Garza's Grocery no. 11" at 419

Staples Street. Mr. Garza owned at least twelve grocery stores in town and was a prominent member of the Mexican community. As a newspaper editor who solicited businessmen to advertise in the newspaper, my grandfather must have dealt with people like him on a daily basis.

During my stay in Corpus Christi, Tom Kreneck introduced me to Rosie Garza (no relation to the grocery store owner), whose family owned an existing newspaper, *El Progreso*, in Corpus Christi. Mrs. Garza gave us further evidence of the existence of *El Puerto* by showing us a copy of the November 2, 1930, edition of a magazine titled *La Calavera: Revista epitafial de las Necrópolis de La Raza* (loosely translated as The skeleton: Magazine of the epitaphs in the Necropolis of the Mexican race).

On one of the pages was a series of *calaveras* under the subheading "Panteón de los Pasquines" where they lampooned all the newspapers in south Texas, including one dedicated to *El Puerto* that read:

No hechaba muchas mentiras,
Tan solo las que podia:
Como que sabían sus TATAS
Que sólo así se vendía.

Translation (mine):

It did not print many lies,
Only those it could
Because their grandfathers knew
That's the only way they could sell it.

During the Day of the Dead festivities, the Mexican community has a tradition in which they lampoon friends and associates by publishing calaveras, or rhymed couplets, poking fun at death and immortality.

El Puerto took out an entire page in the *Revista* advertising its printing press with the following information: "Specializing in all kinds of printing, envelopes, stationery, notices (mortuary), weddings, business cards, fliers, and bylaws." This was significant proof that it was more than a newspaper—it was an actual printing press.

Our enthusiasm was further inflamed when Kreneck remembered that he had discovered an interesting book years ago published by Casa Editorial El Puerto dated 1930, Corpus Christi, Texas, which he produced from the special collections. I was told to "handle the book with care" as it was "an extremely fine and rare volume," perhaps the only copy left.

The title, *Andrew Almazán: La Reconstrucción de México y el Crimen del Vasconcelismo*, was written by J. Manuel Corro Viña and dedicated to "Manuel Ortiz Guerrero, the inspiring intellectual from Guanajuato; José Rocha, the untiring worker and businessman from Monterrey; and General Lázaro Cárdenas, the loyal revolutionary, true to his principles, and to his friends and country."

The special collections had a microfilm copy of *El Paladín*, "the official organ of the League of United Latin American Citizens." I did a search, hoping to discover more about *El Puerto*, but to no avail. There was, however, mention of "the eminent Mexican writer Manuel Corro Viña," who is described as a "youthful orator . . . a real and prestigious intellectual . . . humble, modest, and simple, unpretentious nor vain." The anonymous writer goes on to say that Corro Viña has "published many meritorious books" of philosophy and is "currently writing one of his most tragic modern novels, 'Lover and Sister.'"

That was about as far as I got, spinning through the microfilm that contains copies of *El Paladín* from 1929 to 1930. The Hispanic intellectual community of Corpus Christi and south Texas was obviously aware of events that affected the community. The fact that *El Puerto* printed Manuel Corro Viña's novel and *El Paladín* wrote several glowing stories about this Mexican writer is proof their paths converged.

CONCLUSION

I wonder if literary aspirations run in a family. My first career choice as a teenager was journalism, a kind of Mexican American Clark Kent who would save the world. I recall the first time I ever wrote something for the high school paper in Battle Creek, Michigan; the words seemed to glow out from the page, emanating a sense of power. While still in high school I wrote articles for the *Battle Creek Enquirer and News* and later worked as copyboy, editorial assistant, and teletypist for several Chicago-area newspapers. Was this a gift my grandfather sent me from beyond the grave?

Growing Up

Book Culture in the Land of Scarcity and Want

A. Gabriel Meléndez

W ell into the 1970s, even some years after Woodstock, northern New Mexico had the feel of want and scarcity in terms of most material things. Of course this was decades before the massive restocking of inventories that happens routinely in the present age of Walmart and other big-box stores. When I was growing up there was more to this want than the absence of dry goods in intermittently stocked mercantile stores, their shelves gaping wide-mouthed awaiting shipments of household goods and hardware that arrived only sporadically. Scarcity was neither absolute nor complete. Modern things like chainsaws, hay bailers, sewing machines, and other manufactured goods had been leaking into the region since at least the railroad penetrated New Mexico in 1880, but the scarcity of material goods did affect many aspects of living in the rural towns and villages I grew up in. Classroom and library shelves could be as bare as winter kitchens or their adjoining *dispensas*. And to this extent the *gente, los manitos de Nuevo México* simply went on making do with what they had at hand. Planned obsolescence was unimaginable; hoes, shovels, axes, hay bailers, doors, *compuertas, guarniciones de caballos* were used and reused until they were wore thin, and if they hadn't broken down altogether, they were mended, wired together, and brought out to do some other work. Things were changing of course as money from salaried workers trickled into the villages and some people were enticed to buy on the credit plan, and so the occasional new truck, car, wringer-type washer, or TV started show-ing up in towns and villages.

Like other things, books and other printed matter lived on well beyond the time in which they were fashionable—missals, breviaries, calendars, newspapers, handwritten *cuadernos* made up the whole of the texts that peo-ple kept in their homes. If someone had the good fortune of owning a few books of local color, things like *Vicente Silva y sus cuarenta bandidos*, Manuel Cabeza de Baca's tale of the gruesome misdeeds of Silva and his gang of out-laws, or his *Noches tenebrosas*, an 1890 treatise on the Gorras Blancas, people were expected to pass the books back and forth among friends and neigh-bors, who first wanted to see if C. de Baca knew his stuff, and so they com-pared what he had written to the tales people told in *pláticas* about those days of violence and trouble that had visited so near to their pueblos. In matters connected to learning, things went beyond the problems of uneven distribu-tion and material poverty; scarcity was in some crazy way a cultural feature of growing up Chicano in northern New Mexico. On this front, things started to change a bit after World War II, when a few families began to sub-scribe to *Life* and *Time* magazines, *True Detective*, *Reader's Digest*, the *Catholic Register*, the *Santa Fe New Mexican*, and few other state and national publications.

In my town, Mora, a village ninety miles north of Santa Fe, there was no public library; textbooks carried the stamp of the Mora Public Schools or Saint Gertrudis High School, and they were returned year after year to school storerooms only to be issued the following year, a bit more tattered and a bit more frayed, to a new group of students. My older brother, the one who went to public and not Catholic school, had a couple of these books around which he never returned.

Right about the time I was seven and reached the age of conscience by Church edict, I began to be aware, at least in a most basic and elemental way, of the power of books and of stories. In the spring I got my First Communion prayer book, but I also began to understand in some sense that the village that was raising me loved to tell stories. It didn't matter if the stories were new or old, and sometimes this was confusing to me because I often couldn't always tell the difference between the old stuff, cuentos, and the new stuff, *chismes*. There were so many cuentos and chismes going around that written texts were seldom ever referenced. Things were changing, of course; televi-sion entered most homes by the mid-sixties and this brought about the shift from oral to media culture. Television certainly killed off the cuento, as the *ancianos* of the pretelevision, preradio, pre–everything modern vintage began to die off. Still, TV was no match for the chisme, mitote, and *mentira* telling that just kept on going like excrement through a *ganso*. The small screen did make clear to me that chisme and mitote were mostly about the contingent now when your neighbors' past or current habits could always be invoked and indicted if the circumstances warranted it, but the business of ogres, monarchs, princesses, *duendes, espantos, encantos, lloronas,* and legendary pícaros were shelved for the most part. I now realize that despite the heavy emphasis on story narrative in my *placita*, that whole of my rural upbringing had long ago been staked out by the written word and more specifically by the printed word. Now, I see that the scarcity of books and printed texts was only the stump of the tree of book knowledge, a tree that had been planted in my part of the world centuries before as the result of the large-scale global change that Western contact with the Americas represents. True, the tree of knowledge was withered, tattered, and unpruned, just like the *manzanos* in many of our neighbors' *arboledas*, abandoned when families moved away to become a part of the wage labor sector that cities offered.

For some reasons peculiar to my family, we seem to have gathered a bit more of the fruit in the way of the odd assortment of books and reading matter that were in our home. My father, Manuel Santos, and mother, Adela, moved the family to San Pedro, California, during World War II. There, my father took a job as a foreman in the civil defense shipyards that were cranking out a new fleet of ships for the Pacific theater. My mother was at home raising a newborn and four other school-age children. Just as the war ended in 1945, my family moved back to New Mexico. This was a good thing for me since it led to my being born a few years later. I still wonder why my parents willingly chose to leave California, a coastal paradise that was experiencing an unprecedented post-war boom in jobs, housing, and education. Why, I ask, did they walk away from this bounty to go back to the scarcity I have already talked about? Now I realize it had something to do with querencia, that sense of love and reverence that New Mexicans have for their *país*, their homeland, and for the people they grew up with. Well, at least they went back prepared, stocking up and taking things with them to use on their return to rural life. The cuento is that my father bought two GI-surplus trucks and drove them back across the desert to New Mexico. His plan was to convert them to logging trucks to haul timber down to the sawmill he was intent on starting. Then, too, there was no need for a mover; the family simply loaded up all their possessions on the beds of these green behemoths and got back on Route 66 heading east. He also bought a large Case gas engine that he would use to run the saws, sidecar, and edger of the sawmill he would build. My mother bought a pedal-type sewing machine and a few other labor-saving devices. Importantly, she also returned to the land of scarcity with the latest edition of Compton's Encyclopedia.

Now, when I think about our home library, I am also reminded of the Compton's encyclopedia set, since I recall there were rainy days somewhere in my childhood when I began to flutter through their pages, fascinated it seems by the pictures and illustrations of two-hump camels, snowy peaks, and ancient and modern ships—encyclopedias having a kind of "believe it or not" quality that they brought to the study of world cultures. I continued to use them even after we moved to Albuquerque and I was in high school. By then they were sorely outdated: their maps still carved up Europe between the Allies and the Axis powers, bold arrows marked Rommel's invasion of North Africa. They had illustrations of propeller-driven airliners, jet propulsion still only considered a theoretical possibility. The last time I made use of them, I was living in the time of JFK's New Frontier, Sputnik, the Space Age, a time when modern weaponry had gone from the atomic bomb to the nuclear arms race; none of these items were indexed in our home encyclopedia, but I was being bombarded with so many current events—civil rights, Vietnam, the Tijerina rebellion in New Mexico—that I was inoculated from ever thinking the Compton's were up to date except in the most general way.

In my mind, the encyclopedia, like our television set, was a harbinger of change and modern American life, but it was those few other books we kept at home back in Mora that eventually confirmed for me that Nuevomexicano culture was bounded by books and by book learning no matter how far our villages had fallen away from the tree of learning. At home we had two copies of the New Testament, one in English and one in Spanish, and a copy in Spanish of the Bible that included a family tree one could fill in with the names of forebears. My mother faithfully updated it, listing the names of the dead and the newborn members of the family. Most families in Mora did not have books, beyond the commonplace Bible and prayer books. We had a few more secular items, one was a book called *Modelo para cartas, en español y en inglés*, published by the R. D. Cortina Company in New York in 1920, a book I know my father made use of to double-check the etiquette of good letter writing. The other was a hardbound copy of *Cuarenta años de legislador*, a book that included a generous assortment of photos of people who looked like my neighbors and relatives. I later came to know that *Cuarenta años* was subtitled *La vida de don Casimiro Barela* and that José Emilio Fernández of Trinidad, Colorado, had authored the biography.

As a very young child, I must have leafed through *Cuarenta años* not able to read it and not having any idea of what it was about. I know I laid my hands on it, since I later came to see where I had taken pencils and pens and scribbled away in the margins and across some of the photos. For a time, our home library also included Charles S. Peterson's *Representative New Mexicans*, a book containing some four hundred photographs and biographies of men resident in New Mexico. This was a book published to commemorate New Mexico statehood in 1912, which my father borrowed from his first cousin, prima Lucía, to see the biography of his uncle, Tito Meléndez, a prominent businessman, the owner of a steam-powered sawmill, and a savvy local politician. The book stayed in our house for years, taking up permanent residence there despite the constant requests from prima Lucía to return the book promptly. It wasn't until we got ready to move to Albuquerque that my father, at the insistence of my mother, finally deigned to return the book to his cousin before departing the Mora Valley for life in a bigger town.

In conversations with other village men, Santos would often note that men of his uncle's generation, those Nuevomexicanos like his uncle Tito in Peterson's book, had what he called "el don de la palabra." By this, he meant that they were outstanding orators who lived in an age when public speeches moved the hearts and minds of communities. Santos always made sure to mention Tito to his neighbors, no doubt because he found in him a model for his own dream to run and operate a lumber and sawmill business. But there had been others he could have mentioned had he not been so expressly concerned about saying good things about a close *pariente*. Sometime in the late 1990s, a good friend and a very capable grassroots researcher, Anselmo Arellano, clipped an item from the *Santa Fe New Mexican* that he thought would be of special interest to me. It was a short article published in May 1919 that reported on the closing exercises for the eighth-grade graduation at the public school in Mora, a school then run by the Sisters of Loreto. The report gave an account of how Felipe Maximiliano Chacón, the editor of the Spanish weekly *El Eco del Norte*, had given a rousing talk exhorting the young graduates to continue their education. There, among the twelve graduating eighth graders, sat my father, Manuel Santos Meléndez. The children listened to Mr. Chacón deliver a talk in eloquent and formal English. Chacón exhorted, "Don't be contented and satisfied with the degree of education you have thus far attained. It is but one of the first footsteps in the stairway of life," and then went on at length: "One of the curses of the human race seems to be moral and social relaxation. To counteract and crush both, we must be superior to them, and this cannot be done without effort. Idleness is the road that leads to every vice and sin known to mankind. Shun it, then, and avoid it, or rise and crush it. If you would be good, great and successful, you must conquer the hydra-headed monster, and this you can only do through effort." Now we see that Chacón's speech was loaded with moralizing zest, surging in its zealous condemnation of slough, making it a typical of turn-of-the-century boosterism of the kind one would expect to hear at just such ceremonies across the United States in 1919, but it is important to note how this was coming from a solid member of the Nuevomexicano community who had a good number of accomplishments aided by education and that his audience of students, parents, and teachers were residents of one of the poorest Hispano rural communities in the nation. Manuel Santos would indeed complete his high school education and keep turning to books for the rest of his adult life, even while their scarcity could only give him access to *Modelo para cartas* or gave way to private harangues over who was best disposed to hold on to *Representative New Mexicans*, Santos or prima Lucía. Three years after his talk at Mora, Felipe Maximiliano Chacón would become the editor and general manager of *La Bandera Americana*, a newspaper in the Barelas neighborhood in Albuquerque. A year later, in 1924, Chacón would publish *Poesía y prosa: Obras de Felipe Maximiliano Chacón, el cantor nuevomexicano*. *Poesía y prosa*, as far as has been verified, is the first collection of poetry published by a Mexican American author. Quite expectedly, the book had a very small run of copies. Readers of *La Bandera Americana* were asked to remit an order form along with $3.50 in cash. The case points to the fact that a system of self-publishing and self-distribution of books was unfortunately still at work in Chicano communities nearly eighty years after New Mexico became a U.S. possession. Here, too, scarcity ensured that the only way a copy of this book would make its way up to, say, Mora, would have been through a sheer act of spectacular luck. Perhaps this is why I so value the three or four books I have talked about here, because they, against so many vicissitudes, got to my hands *de pura chiripada*, or serendipity in a Chicano way of saying.

And it is only now that I have thought to admit just how much my own career as an educator and cultural critic is built on serendipity and how so much of my claim that Nuevomexicano culture and Chicano culture more generally has always been precariously bound to books also results from a series of unpredictable coincidences. With the exception of the Compton's Encyclopedia, which got sold long ago in a yard sale, and *Representative New Mexicans*, which went back to prima Lucía's side of the family, the remaining books that formed our family library are distributed among my siblings. I managed to get hold of the more secular grouping of tomes, and as things have turned out, I have done a whole lot of research and writing on them.

When I was researching my book *So All Is Not Lost*, a history of Spanish-language journalism in the Southwest, I ran right into Felipe Maximiliano Chacón as his name surfaced at every turn of the research. His story could not be ignored. I came to find out he had been born in Santa Fe in 1873, that his first cousin, Eusebio Chacón, was a gifted novelist, a poet, and a Notre Dame law school graduate. Felipe began hanging around *La Aurora*, the newspaper his father worked for in Santa Fe, when he was ten or eleven, and he managed to contribute some early verses of his own making to the paper when he was fourteen. Felipe graduated from Saint Michael's College, a kind of parochial prep school in Santa Fe, and went on to work in mercantile stores while pursuing a part-time career in journalism. It didn't take long for him to come to the attention of other Nuevomexicanos, who dubbed him an able editor, orator, and writer. He spent most of his adult life in journalism, as editor and sometimes owner of newspapers across north-central New Mexico. He was at *La Voz del Pueblo* (Las Vegas, New Mexico), *El Faro del Río Grande* (Bernalillo), *El Independiente* (Las Vegas), *El Eco del Norte* (Mora), and *La Bandera Americana* (Albuquerque). His culminating effort being *Poesía y prosa*, a work that still needs to be studied, translated, and recovered for future readers.

When I was a graduate student at the University of New Mexico in the late seventies, it was then possible to visit the Coronado Room, Zimmerman Library's rare book section, and browse through its open stacks. One signed in, left one's belongings at the door, walked in, and leisurely perused the greater part of the university's collection of rare books. On one visit, I came upon an original copy of the slim tome holding Eusebio Chacón's two novellas, *El hijo de la tempestad* and *Tras la tormenta, la calma*, published in Santa Fe in 1892. Here was an important installment of work from a generation of Nuevomexicano orators that I had not known about. I was staring at the backside of the serendipity and scarcity coin, the side that had kept me unaware of such material until the late stages of my doctoral studies. On another visit, I ran into an old friend in the form of a copy of *Cuarenta años de legislador*. I was astounded to learn for the first time that others knew as much or perhaps more about what I assumed to be a family heirloom. When I dug deeper, I learned that the book was in the stacks, because Arno Press, a small, independent outfit, had begun to reissue titles on Chicano subjects to meet a renewed interest in Mexican American Studies. Arno didn't bother to do much with the titles it was lifting out of obscurity. Arno's edition of *Cuarenta años* was simply a photocopy of José Fernández's 1911 book, sandwiched between a new hardcover and cataloged in the library holdings as a work relevant to the Chicano and Mexican American experiences. For me, the find told me that there might be interest in this book beyond my own family and community. Still, the question persisted in me about what its content and story could mean in a larger context.

Once again, it was during the time I was researching my book that I finally was able to make the connections between the meager list of books in our family library and larger social concerns about learning, education, and identity for ethnic minorities in the United States. The research produced countless epiphanies. Finally it dawned on me that Casimiro Barela, the subject of *Cuarenta años*, had been born in my hometown. "Oh," I thought, "the book was around because he was a native son." Soon after, I began to associate the book with the story of Spanish-language publication. In addition to having served in the Colorado legislature for forty years, Barela had amassed wealth and had come to own two newspapers, *El Progreso* in Trinidad and *Las Dos Repúblicas* in Denver. His biographer, José Emilio Fernández, had been a teacher in southern Colorado and an editor of *El Progreso*. "Oh," I slapped my knee, "he was a ghost writer for Barela, paid to write up his life story!" There were more connections; Eusebio Chacón, the first Mexican American novelist, had married Sofia Barela, don Casimiro's daughter. Felipe Maximiliano Chacón had also worked as the editor of one of Casimiro Barela's papers. After this, I concluded that *Cuarenta años* ended up in a few New Mexican households because it told the story of another Nuevomexicano, born into poverty, scarcity, and want, who had led a life worthy of emulation. The purpose couldn't have been any clearer; José Emilio Fernández did not equivocate on this point when he wrote: "Here (readers) will find how a young man of humble birth, with limited education, and of a financially impoverished background, has come to distinguish himself not only among his countrymen, but before all the world . . ." [1] High praise indeed! Even before I had finished writing *So All Is Not Lost*, I made the commitment to recover the Barela biography for contemporary readers. In 2003, the

University of New Mexico Press published my annotated translation and critical introduction of the Barela biography. Now, it's not that I meant to ignore Fernández's status as Barela's salaried employee, nor his tendency to cover his subject with high praise. I knew that what had long ago been shelved away in our home was a very subjective, very partial, very unblemished account of Casimiro Barela. I was in fact looking for the ultimate meaning of the book in its very subjective nature and in its very form as unabashed self-representation. In reintroducing the Barela story, I situated it among the work of a generation of Mexican American authors in New Mexico who came to understand quite clearly that the social, political, and economic rules had changed for their community after the arrival of American power and rule. Everything they said, did, and wrote about, along with every aspiration they held for themselves and future generations, became pregnant with meaning. This is how I saw it as I wrote a new introduction for the Barela biography: "For Hispanos in New Mexico and Colorado during this period, every social act and every inscription of action in print is complicated by a politics of conquest and by the subaltern status they occupy after 1848".[2]

If the whole of Spanish-language publication in the Southwest could be reduced to two or three straightforward aims, the top three would be, first, to use the press to express the accumulated frustration and grievance Chicanos felt as a result of their social and economic decline after 1848; second, to showcase the power of literacy and education in the very pages of the newspapers Chicanos were founding from Texas to California; and third, to showcase the potential of a people by publishing symbolic biographies that recorded the hopes, aspirations, and accomplishments of Chicano elected officials and public persons.

It is only now clear to me how important are those few books that ended up on our bookshelf in the land of scarcity and want. What was passed on to me is more than the content of these four or five tattered texts; rather, by them I had laid hands on the last examples of a literary movement, a wellspring of thought, that had operated in the Mexican American community forty, sixty, eighty, sometimes a hundred years before the Chicano renaissance of the 1960s. Through these surviving texts, *el don de la palabra* of a generation was passed forward, even to those of us who would never hear the power of the silver-tongued oratory of a Eusebio Chacón, an Aurora Lucero, a Casimiro Barela, or an Octaviano Larrazolo, and yet some portion of that energy resides in the texts they bequeathed to posterity.

In 1995, I had the good fortune of interviewing Herminia Chacón González at her tidy Jewish Housing Federation apartment in El Paso. The daughter of Felipe Maximiliano Chacón, doña Herminia was ninety-two years old when I met her and represented one of the last vital links to a world of editors and writers that had been the active agents of Nuevomexicano publishing in the Southwest. My hope was that she would provide information on the years that her father had been active in the Spanish newspapers in New Mexico. But I had my doubts. As I drove to El Paso to meet her for the first time, I wondered if anything might come from the interview: would she in fact be able to remember events that had transpired nearly three decades before her father's death in 1949?

As he had for each of his children, Felipe Maximiliano wrote a poem for Herminia on her third birthday. The poem as it appears in *Poesía y prosa* reads in part:

El cielo nos la preste	May heaven entrust her to us
Con alma pura y bella,	with a pure heart and radiant soul
Estímulo de dicha	the cause of our ideal,
Sin límite, ideal;	never-ending joy,
Que brillen sus virtudes	May her virtues shine
Constantes como estrella	constant like a star
Que fluyan a raudales	May her good fortunes flow
Las venturanzas de ella,	in torrents
Y Dios la guarde ilesa,	And may God keep
—¡Perlita angelical!	The pearl angel from all harm!

In 1995, doña Herminia's virtues were bright and animated as she recounted the details of her father's career as a pioneer journalist and as she remembered her own upbringing and life as a frontier schoolteacher in the land of scarcity and want that was rural New Mexico. These underpinnings of her own experiences, for example the years she taught at the small village of Maes, New Mexico, in the late 1920s, had not left her, and she continued to share them. To my surprise, she was still writing short articles about New Mexico and sending them on to Ana Pacheco's *La Herencia del Norte*, a magazine that was just getting started in Santa Fe.

In the moments before completing an interview in which doña Herminia had confirmed so many details in the story of her father's work as a journalist and poet, she turned to me and asked, "Do you have a copy of my father's book?" Before I could answer, she pulled one of the five or six copies that remained in her possession seventy years after publication. "I still have some copies," she remarked, as she handed me the book. Like her father had hoped in his poem, doña Herminia was constant like a star in her concern for disseminating the work of a generation of nuevomexicanos who had committed their energies to the power of la palabra. I treasure my copy of *Poesía y prosa*, and I am humbled by the ways of books and learning, eternally grateful now for the messy workings of querencia and pura chiripada. My father's casual observation that there had been a generation of orators and writers who possessed el don de la palabra would have simply evaporated into empty space had it not been for the four or five books from that time that somehow got handed off to me, and had it not been for my great good fortune, a major de pura chiripada, that gave me the privilege to meet and interview doña Herminia Chacón González while she was still entrusted to us, pure of heart and with a radiant soul. These long shots have finally equipped me to understand and explain the importance of books and other useful things in the land of scarcity and want that typified New Mexico in its beginnings.

The Family Library
of Miguel A. Otero

An Analysis and Inventory

Manuel M. Martín-Rodríguez

The study of private libraries has a significant history as a subfield of literary studies. While different scholars have contributed in their own ways to this type of research, perhaps the two most salient approaches are the cataloging (with or without analysis) of someone's books on one hand, and theoretical speculations on the nature of book collecting on the other. The latter approach is best represented by Walter Benjamin's oft-quoted "Unpacking My Library: A Talk About Book Collecting" (included in his *Illuminations*),[1] while the former embraces such diverse efforts as Timothy W. Ryback's *Hitler's Private Library*[2] and the catalog of Alfred Nobel's books (available online at http://nobelprize.org/alfred_nobel/biographical/library/). For reasons that include socioeconomic status, prominence in public life, scholarly achievements, and similar signs of relevance in a particular society, the owners of private libraries later subjected to scrutiny tend to be famous and/or well-to-do individuals, but there is no reason why the study of smaller libraries assembled by less well known families and individuals should generate less significant information.

Scholarship on Chicano/a private libraries is in its very early stages, as only a handful of analyses have been produced. Two pioneering articles, both published originally in the *New Mexico Historical Review*, are reproduced in this volume, and they explore colonial libraries from the Hispanic period of the present-day U.S. Southwest.[3] In what follows, I will catalog and analyze the private library assembled by New Mexico territorial governor Miguel A. Otero, which, as we will see, contains some legacies from the books owned by his father as well as volumes that in all likelihood belonged to his wife and children.

As I have suggested elsewhere, the study of Mexican American and Chicano/a private libraries is essential to document what Chicanos/as and Mexican Americans have read over the years.[4] Moreover, because of historical processes of disenfranchisement and marginalization, the (literary) history of Chicanos/as is characterized by both lines of continuity and interruptions that result from the disappearance of records and the outright neglect with which official accounts have treated Chicanos/as until recently. Using a metaphor from the 1528 *Manuscrito de Tlatelolco*, I compared that historical process to a net made of holes, in which the strings and the knots represent those lines of connection while the holes in between are a visual rendering of historical discontinuities.[5] I then went on to reflect on the value of documenting private libraries and the transmission of books from generation to generation as a significant way of tracing the permanence of cultural capital among Chicanos/as.[6]

I am fully aware that the mere presence of certain books in someone's library is not a guarantee that those books were read by its owner. Walter Benjamin delights in retelling an anecdote concerning Anatole France that may be illuminating in this regard:

> Suffice it to quote the answer which Anatole France gave to a philistine who admired his library and then finished with the standard question, "And you have read all these books, Monsieur France?" "Not one-tenth of them. I don't suppose you use your Sèvres china every day?"[7]

Benjamin then goes on to tell how during his own "militant age" he would only add to his personal library books he had not read, without bothering to elucidate whether or not he read them later.[8]

And yet, as Benjamin also acknowledges, in the collection, bequest, and inheritance of books or collections of books, there is a feeling of responsibility that transcends the actual reading of the works assembled while stressing the transmissibility of the collection itself.[9] This feeling is of the utmost importance in the case of historically disenfranchised groups in particular, because it becomes a testimony of endurance, cultural continuity, and family and community building. In that sense, governor Otero's book collection is endowed with multiple meanings that include (but exceed) the issue of whether or not he read them, and the same is true of those books collected and transmitted by any other individual or family.[10] Thus, my approach to the Otero family library will explore multiple questions about his collection, including the provenance of the books (whenever known or whenever an educated guess can be formulated), the books that we know for sure he read (or, at least, that he mentioned in his own writings), those he must have acquired for other members of his family, and, finally, the ultimate fate of his collection. In my analysis, I will also comment on genres and types of books he and his family seem to have cherished as well as on their significance for the wider contexts of Mexican American (and, later, Chicano/a) reading tastes and literary history. But first, a brief synopsis of Otero's life and family history is essential, to serve as background for the analysis of his book collection. Otero himself left us a three-volume published autobiography and some autobiographical sketches among his papers,[11] and I will rely on them (as well as on later biographical outlines by Cynthia Secor-Welsh and others).[12]

MIGUEL A. OTERO

Governor Miguel A. Otero was born on October 17, 1859. He was the son of Miguel Antonio Otero and Mary Josephine Blackwood. Of Spanish origin, Otero's grandfather (Vicente) had held offices in Spain prior to relocating to New Mexico sometime before 1800. Miguel A. Otero (father), born in 1829, was educated in his native Valencia County (New Mexico) and then at Saint Louis University (Missouri) and Pingree College (New York). A lawyer by training, Otero I[13] served in both the legislative assembly of the territory of New Mexico and the U.S. House of Representatives. Otero I was also a prominent businessman and a strong supporter of railroad building in New Mexico.

Future governor Miguel A. Otero grew up between Kansas, Colorado, and New Mexico, as the family business of Otero, Sellar & Company (for which he would later serve as bookkeeper and cashier) followed the progress of the transcontinental railroad. Unlike his father, Otero II had some difficulties with formal education, as he seemed to prefer active life to study. After attending one semester of private school in Kansas (an experience he later compared to that of Oliver Twist in Charles Dickens's novel), he went on to enroll in another private school (in Leavenworth, Kansas) for two additional semesters. Following two more years of schooling at Saint Louis University, Otero was back home by 1871. He was then sent to the Naval Academy in Annapolis, Maryland, but he never took the entrance exam. His formal education was then completed with stays at the University of Notre Dame (Indiana) and Saint Louis University.

From 1878 to 1881, Otero was mostly involved with Otero, Sellar & Company. When the company was liquidated, Otero went on to serve as a cashier at San Miguel National Bank. He cofounded the Las Vegas Telephone Company (in which he served as treasurer and secretary), and he pursued other commercial interests. Upon the death of his father in 1882, Otero was named administrator of his father's estate. With these added responsibilities, Otero still found time to stake numerous mining claims and to enter public life as an elected clerk for the city of Las Vegas (New Mexico) in 1883. A letter kept in the Otero papers also confirms that he was a member of the vigilantes in Las Vegas, at least in 1879.

Between 1883 and 1888—when his political career began to take center stage—Otero traveled to the United Kingdom to work on a potential real estate deal. From a business perspective, this trip was a complete failure, since the sale never took place, and Otero's absence from the United States cost him his position as managing director and cashier at San Miguel National Bank. For our purposes, however, the journey becomes memorable, as it provided Otero with the time to reflect on and share with his readers his thinking on literary matters, including his passion for Charles Dickens. In *My Life on the Frontier, 1882–1897*, the author fondly remembers visits to the London theaters and to Westminster Abbey, where he and his companions "viewed the royal tombs and monuments and memorials of English celebrities, Spenser, Milton, Dryden, Handel, Dickens, Thackeray, and several others."[14] His predilection for Dickens is clearly asserted on that same page when Otero continues relating their activities: "The next day, we visited Kensington Museum and the Crystal Palace and back to Cobweb Hall where Dickens frequented occasionally to ponder over some new idea or to refresh his memory." And then, as if to pay the British author an ultimate tribute, Otero concludes: "We sat at the same old table where Dickens often meditated, and took one of his favorite drinks."[15]

To a certain extent, this time away from home and country seems to have been largely regulated by Otero's readings and literary tastes. His mention of

Mark Twain upon visiting the tomb of Abelard and Heloise in Paris suggests that Twain's *The Innocents Abroad* may have served the future governor as a mixture of cautionary tale and travel guide.[16] In the rest of Otero's autobiography references to printed works are abundant, but they tend to identify periodicals, official documents, and historiographic works. On this business/ leisure journey, however, Otero the reader of literature shines through, allowing us a glimpse of his preferences when he read for pleasure.

Back in New Mexico, Otero married Caroline V. Emmett on December 19, 1888. The couple had three children: Miguel A. III (who died in infancy), Elizabeth, and Miguel A. IV. He continued his active life as a businessman and, as mentioned, soon started to intensify his activities in a burgeoning career as a civil servant. The positions he occupied are too numerous to list here, but they include such diverse offices as probate clerk (1888), county clerk (1889), district court clerk (1890–1893), and chairman of the New Mexican delegation to the Republican national conventions of 1900 and 1904. Of course, his most significant position was that of governor of the Territory of New Mexico, an office that he occupied for nine years, starting with his appointment by President William McKinley in 1897. As governor, Otero worked toward statehood for New Mexico and the modernization of the territory. He was also involved in many high-visibility initiatives, including his successes in water law and policy and his participation in recruiting New Mexican volunteers for Theodore Roosevelt's Rough Riders. The Spanish-American War gave New Mexicans an opportunity to rethink and affirm their American identity, as their disproportionate participation in this armed conflict would suggest. For Otero, as Secor-Welsh has explored,[17] this negotiation of identity was necessarily complicated, since he had to downplay his ethnicity, yet seek the Hispanic vote.

At the end of his governorship, Otero went to Europe once again, this time accompanied by his son. Upon his return to the United States, family life was to change dramatically, as he first separated from his wife in 1904, filing for divorce in 1909. Otero occupied several public positions during the following decades, and he remarried in 1913. Otero and his new wife, Maud Pine Frost (widow of Max Frost), had no children.

In 1917, President Woodrow Wilson appointed Otero marshal of the Panama Canal, a position he occupied until 1921. During his stay in Panama, Otero likely became interested in broadening his knowledge of the history of the European presence in the Americas. Six years later, as a result of that interest, Otero finished a manuscript entitled "The Narrative of the

Conquistadores of Spain and the Buccaneers of England, France, and Holland."[18] This historical work contains references to multiple sources, proving Otero's careful research of his topic.[19] Otero's approach to this history of economic expansion, plunder, and violence is rather candid, anticipating the style of his autobiographical works of the following decade:

> The conquistadores and the buccaneers enjoyed the same occupation, the pursuit of gold.— and resorted to the same methods in obtaining it.— seizure, plunder, and murder; but they selected different victims. Under the guise of Christianity, the conquistadores seized, plundered, and murdered the Indians, while the buccaneers openly devoted all their time and attention to seizing, plundering, and murdering the Spaniards.[20]

Otero's interest in the conquistadores continued in the 1930s, as he was a member of the National Advisory Committee of the Coronado Cuarto Centennial. Always a shrewd businessman, Otero took this opportunity to offer to sell Gilberto Espinosa (secretary of the committee) the Old María Josefa bell, allegedly brought to New Mexico by Francisco Vázquez de Coronado.

More importantly, the 1930s saw the publication of three of Otero's works: *My Life on the Frontier, 1864–1882* (1935), *The Real Billy the Kid, with New Light on the Lincoln County War* (1936), and *My Life on the Frontier, 1882–1897: Death Knell of a Territory and Birth of a State* (1939). A third autobiographical volume, *My Nine Years as Governor of the Territory of New Mexico, 1897–1906*, would follow in 1940. While for reasons of space and topic I will not undertake an analysis of these works here, I would like to point out that they are of considerable value for our task of documenting Otero's personal and family library, since they contain numerous references to publications owned by Otero, thus allowing us to determine that he possessed *and* read those titles.[21]

Conversely, the books in his library may serve to illuminate Otero's own writing, as Secor-Welsh has astutely suggested. For Secor-Welsh, Otero's thirty volumes of Charles Dickens, and the twelve by Sir Walter Scott, may explain some of the main traits of his style:

> One could contribute Otero's sentimentality and maybe even his reformist impulses to his close reading of Dickens. . . . Similarly, Sir

Walter Scott's novels may have encouraged Otero to romanticize the Southwest, and more importantly, probably kindled an appreciation of the art of good storytelling and vivid characterization.[22]

Otero spent the 1930s and early 1940s devoted to politics and writing, and enjoying the success of his own books, especially the first two published. During those decades, he contributed numerous articles and stories to local papers, while attempting—without success—to place some of his writings in national publications like the *New Yorker*.[23] On August 7, 1944, Otero died at the age of eighty-three. He had been bedridden for the last three years of his life, which suggests that he must have found comfort and intellectual stimulation in works from the substantial library he amassed over a lifetime. The fact that this library was sent to the University of New Mexico confirms the value that he and his family placed on the collection. Unfortunately, the collection was not kept intact, but at least we have a record of its catalog and some extant volumes.

The following section of this chapter contains a complete listing of the books in Otero's library, as identified in the catalog kept in box 7 of the Otero papers. Throughout that section, I will call attention to those books we know for sure that he read, indicating any other information I have been able to find about them, including what Otero had to say about them in his own publications. The following section will list such items as brochures, periodicals, and ephemera kept in the Otero papers but not listed in the catalog of his library. After that, I will devote some space to books that Otero must have read or consulted (since he mentions them in his own writings), although there is no evidence that he owned copies of them. The inventory of his books and readings ends with a list of periodicals, journalists, and printers cited by Otero. Finally, I will close the chapter with a preliminary analysis of the library.[24]

BOOKS IN THE LIBRARY OF MIGUEL A. OTERO[25]

A. R. N. *Margaret Vere*. New York: Pott, Young, n.d.

Abbott, Jacob. *History of Margaret of Anjou, Queen of Henry VI of England*. New York: Harper, 1871.

Acts of the Legislature Assembly of the Territory of New Mexico. Sessions 13, 26–28, 29, 31, 33, and 35–38.

Address to the Students of Phillips Exeter Academy on the Death of Henry Linn Waldo Jr. of Kansas City, Mo.

Aikman, Duncan. *Calamity Jane and the Lady Wildcats*. New York: Henry Holt, 1927.

American Ballad Collection. Boston: Oliver Ditson, 1885.

Ames, Mary Clemmer. *Life and Scenes in the National Capital*. Cincinnati: Queen City Publishing Company, 1874.

Ancient and Accepted Scottish Rite. Valley of Santa Fe Orient of New Mexico. 21st Reunion. June 19–21, 1916.

Anderson, C. L. *Old Panama and Castilla del Oro*. Washington, D.C.: Press of the Sudwarth Company, 1911.[26]

Arosemena, Justo D., ed. *Panama in 1915*. *Panama Morning Journal*. Panama City: Morales y Rodríguez, 1915.

Bacheller, Irving. *Eben Holden*. Boston: Lothrop, 1900.

Badeau, Adam. *Military History of Ulysses S. Grant, from April, 1861, to April, 1865*. New York: D. Appleton & Company, 1881.

Bailey, Philip A. *Golden Mirages: The Story of the Lost Pegleg Mine, the Legendary Three Gold Buttes, and Yarns of and by Those Who Know the Desert*. New York: Macmillan, 1940.

Bailey, Temple. *The Tin Soldier*. Philadelphia: n.p., 1919.

Bakewell, Paul, Jr. *Past and Present Facts About Money in the United States*. New York: Macmillan, 1936.

Baldwin, James. *Old Greek Stories*. New York: American Book Company, 1895.

Bandelier, Adolph F. A. *The Gilded Man*. New York: D. Appleton & Company, 1893.

Bangs, John Kendrick. *Bikey the Skycicle*. New York: Riggs Publishing Company, 1902.

———. *Coffee and Repartee*. New York: Harper & Brothers, 1893.

Barclay, Florence L. *The Mistress of Shenstone*. New York: G. P. Putnam's Sons, 1911.

Barker, Ruth Laughlin. *Caballeros*. New York: D. Appleton & Company, 1932.

Bartlett, John. *Familiar Quotations*. Boston: Little, Brown, 1904.

Bates, W. H. *The Cure of Imperfect Sight by Treatment Without Glasses*. New York: Central Fixation Publishing Company, 1920.

Beach, Frederick Converse, ed. *The Americana* [*Encyclopedia Americana*]. 16 vols. New York: Scientific America Compiling Department, 1906.

Beach, Rex E. *The Iron Trail*. New York: A. L. Burt, 1913.

Beasley, Norman. *Frank Knox, American*. New York: Doubleday, 1936.

Becke, Louis. *Tom Gerrard*. London: T. Fisher Unwin, 1905.

Beckett, Gilbert Abbott. *The Comic Blackstone*. London: Bradbury, Evans, 1872.

Bede, Cuthbert. *The Adventures of Mr. Verdant Green*. New York: Carleton, 1878.

Belasco, David. *The First Night in David Belasco's Stuyvesant Theatre*. N.p., 1907.

Belcher, Joseph. *Facts for Boys*. New York: Sheldon, 1865.

Bell, William A. *New Tracks in North America*. London: Chapman & Hall, 1869.[27]

Bennett, Estelline. *Old Deadwood Days*. New York: Charles Scribner's Sons, 1935.

Benson, A. R. *General Corporation Laws of the State of Delaware, Passed 1899, Ammended by the Revised Statutes of 1915, and Further Ammended by the 95th, 96th, and 97th General Assemblies*. March 1921.

Blaine, James J. *Twenty Years of Congress from Lincoln to Garfield*. Norwich, CT: Henry Bill Publishing Company, 1884.

Bogardus, Adam H. *Field, Cover, and Trap Shooting*. New York: J. B. Ford & Company, 1874.

Bolanden, Conrad von. *The Progressionists and Angela*. New York: Catholic Publication Society, 1873.

Bolles, Albert S. *Everybody's Legal Adviser*. 5 vols. New York: Doubleday, Page & Company, 1922.

———. *Putnam's Handy Lawbook for the Layman*. New York: G. P. Putnam's Sons, 1921.

Book of Common Prayer. London: Eyre & Spottiswoode, n.d.

Books I Have Read. Norwood, MA: Clippings, n.d.

Bourget, Paul. *A Divorce*. New York: Charles Scribner's Sons, 1904.

———. *The Land of Promise*. Chicago: F. T. Neely, 1895.

Boyce, Neith. *The Eternal Spring*. New York: Fox, Duffield & Company, 1906.

Bradley, Mrs. *Handsome Is That Handsome Does*. Boston: Lothrop, Lee & Shepard, 1868.

Braeme, Charlotte M. *The Squire's Darling*. New York: Optimus, n.d.

Brewerton, George Douglas. *Overland with Kit Carson*. New York: A. L. Burt, 1930.

Brockett, L. P. *The Life and Times of Abraham Lincoln*. Philadelphia: Bradley & Company, 1865.

Brooks, Noah. *The Mediterranean Trip: A Short Guide to the Principal Points on the Shores of the Western Mediterranean and the Levant*. New York: Charles Scribner's Sons, 1902.

Buffum, George T. *Smith of Bear City and Other Frontier Sketches*. New York: Grafton Press, 1906.

Burdett, Charles. *The Life of Kit Carson*. Philadelphia: John E. Potter, 1869.

Burnett, Frances H. *The Shuttle*. New York: Grosset & Dunlap, 1907.

Bush, Richard G. *Reindeer, Dogs and Snow Shoes: A Journal of Siberian Travel and Explorations Made in the Years 1865, 1866, and 1867*. New York: Harper & Brothers, 1871.

Business Corporation Under the Laws of Delaware. 6th ed. 1922.

Cable, George W. *Dr. Sevier*. Boston: Ticknor, 1884.

Caine, Hall. *The Deemster*. Chicago: E. A. Weeks, n.d.

———. *The Eternal City*. New York: D. Appleton & Company, 1905.

———. *The Shadow of a Crime*. New York: Caldwell, n.d.

Carlyle, Thomas. *On Heroes, Hero-Worship, and the Heroic in History*. Chicago: Hill, n.d.

Carroll, Mary Teresa Austin. *Glimpses of Pleasant Homes*. New York: Catholic Publication Society, 1869.

Carter, W. N. *Harry Tracy, the Desperate Western Outlaw*. Chicago: Laird & Lee, 1902.

Casson, Herbert N. *The Romance of the Reaper*. New York: Doubleday, Page & Company, 1908.

Catherwood, Mary H. *Lazarre*. Indianapolis: Bobbs-Merrill, n.d.

Cervantes Saavedra, Miguel de. *The History of Don Quixote de la Mancha*. Boston: Pierce, 1848.

Chambers, Robert W. *The Conspirators*. New York: Harper & Brothers, 1900.

———. *The Girl Philippa*. New York: D. Appleton & Company, 1916.

Chamisso, Adelbert von. *Peter Schlemihl*. New York: G. P. Putnam's Sons, n.d.

Chandler, J. A. C. *Makers of Virginia History*. New York: Silver Burdett, 1904.

Charges Against Benjamin S. Baker of Omaha, Judge of Second Judicial District of the Territory of New Mexico, Made by the Good Government League of the City of Albuquerque.

Chavasse, Pye Henry. *Advice to a Wife*. London: Churchill, 1877.

Cholmondeley, Mary. *Red Pottage*. New York: Harper & Brothers, 1900.

Churchill, Winston. *The Celebrity*. New York: Macmillan, 1905.

Claflin, Tennessee. *Essays on Social Topics*. Westminster, London: Roxburghe Press, n.d.

Clay, Bertha M. *Repented at Leisure*. New York: J. S. Ogilvie, n.d.

Cochran, Thomas. B. *Legislative Handbook and Manual of the State of Pennsylvania, 1888*. Harrisburg, PA: E. K. Meyers, 1888.

———. *Smull's Legislative Handbook, and Manual of the State of Pennsylvania*. Harrisburg, PA: E. K. Meyers, 1887.

Coe, George W. *Frontier Fighter: Autobiography*. Boston: Houghton Mifflin, 1934.

Coleridge, Samuel Taylor. *Ye Rime of Ye Ancient Mariner*. New York: Roycroft Press, 1899.

Compendium of American Genealogy. Vol. 5. Chicago: Institute of American Genealogy, 1933.

Compiled Laws of New Mexico. N.p., 1897.

Comprehensive Standard Dictionary of the English Language. New York: Funk & Wagnalls, 1934.

Conard, Howard L. *'Uncle Dick' Wootton, the Pioneer Frontiersman of the Rocky Mountain Region*. Chicago: W. E. Dibble & Company, 1890.[28]

Connelley, William E. *Wyandot Folk-Lore*. Topeka, KS: Crane & Company, 1899.

Connor, Ralph. *Black Rock: A Tale of the Selkirks*. Chicago: M. A. Donahue, n.d.

———. *The Man from Glengarry: A Tale of the Ottawa*. Chicago: Fleming H. Revell, 1901.

Cook, John W. *Hands Up; or, Twenty Years of Detective Life in the Mountains and on the Plains: Reminiscences, a Condensed Criminal History of the Far West*. Denver: W. F. Robinson, 1897.

Cooke, John Esten. *Out of the Foam: A Novel*. New York: Carleton, 1871.

Corelli, Marie. *God's Good Man: A Simple Love Story*. New York: Dodd, Mead & Company, 1904.

Cox, Samuel S. *Diversions of a Diplomat in Turkey*. New York: Charles L. Webster, 1887.

Cox, William V. *Celebration of the One Hundredth Anniversary of the Establishment of the Seat of Government in the District of Columbia, 1800–1900*. Washington, D.C.: Government Printing Office, 1901.

Craddock, Charles Egbert. *In the Tennessee Mountains*. Boston: Houghton Mifflin, 1885.

———. *The Prophet of the Great Smoky Mountains*. Boston: Houghton Mifflin, 1886.

——— *Where the Battle Was Fought: A Novel*. Boston: Ticknor, 1886.

Crawford, Francis Marion. *Casa Braccio*. New York: Macmillan, 1895.

Cremony, John C. *Life Among the Apaches*. San Francisco: A. Roman & Company, 1868.

Crockett, Samuel R. *The Adventurer in Spain*. New York: Frederick A. Stokes, 1903.

Cross, Victoria. *Paula: A Sketch from Life*. New York: Kensington Press, ca. 1908.

Cullen, Dr. [Edward]. *Isthmus of Darien Ship Canal*. London: E. Wilson, 1853.

Curtis, Francis. *The Republican Party, 1854–1904*. New York: G. P. Putnam's Sons, 1904.

Custer, Elizabeth B. *Tenting on the Plains*. New York: Charles L. Webster, 1887.

Dante. *Dante's Inferno*. New York: Cassell, 1860.

———. *The Divina Commedia and Canzoniere*. 3 vols. Boston: Heath, 1907.

Daudet, Alphonse. *L'arlesienne*. New York: Caldwell, 1894.

Davis, Mrs. Jefferson. *Jefferson Davis: A Memoir by His Wife*. 2 vols. New York: Belford, 1890.

Davitt, Michael. *Within the Pale: The True Story of Anti-Semitic Persecutions in Russia*. New York: A. S. Barnes, 1903.

Dawes, S. E. *Hours with Mamma*. New York: American Tract Society, 1865.

De Goncourt, Edward and Jules. *Germaine Lacerteux*. London: Gibbings & Company, 1892.

De la Ramée, Marie Louise. *Muriella, or Le selve*. Boston: L. C. Page & Company, 1897.

———. *Toxin*. New York: Frederick A. Stokes, 1895.

Dean, Teresa. *White City Chips*. Chicago: Warren, 1895.

Dhu, Helen. *Stanhope Burleigh, the Jesuits in Our Homes: A Novel*. New York: Stringer & Townsend, 1855.

Dick, William B. *Dick's Games of Patience or Solitaire with Cards*. New York: Dick & Fitzgerald, 1883.

Dickens, Charles. *The Works of Charles Dickens*. 30 vols. New York: Collier, n.d.[29]

Dictionary of Select and Popular Quotations. Philadelphia: E. Claxton, 1882.

Doré, Gustave. *The Bible Gallery*. New York: Cassell, 1880.

Dorsey, Anna H. *The Oriental Pearl; or, The Catholic Emigrants*. Baltimore: John Murphy, 1868.

Drage, Geoffrey. *Cyril: A Romantic Novel*. London: W. H. Allen, 1892.

Duchess. *Beauty's Daughters*. Philadelphia: J. B. Lippincott, 1880.

Dyar, Muriel Campbell. *Davie and Elizabeth*. New York: Harper & Brothers, 1908.

Dye, Eva Emery. *The Conquest: The True Story of Lewis and Clark*. Chicago: A. C. McClurg & Company, 1903.

Eames, Jane A. *Sarah Barry's Home*. New York: Protestant Episcopal S. S. Union and Church Book Society, 1870.

Eddy, Mary Baker. *Science and Health with Key to the Scriptures*. Boston: J. Armstrong, 1902.

Edgeworth, Maria. *Edgeworth's Early Lessons: Harry and Lucy Concluded*. 4 vols. Boston: Crosby & Nichols, n.d.

Ellis, Clara Spalding. *What's Next; or, Shall a Man Live Again?* Boston: Gorham Press, 1906.

Ellison, Edith Nicholl. *The Blossoming of the Waste.* New York: Calkins & Company, 1908.

Encyclopaedia Britannica. 9th ed. 24 vols. New York: Charles Scribner's Sons, 1878.

Encyclopaedia of the New West. Marshall, TX: U.S. Biographical Publishing Company, 1881.

Exquemeling, Alexander O. ***History of the Buccaneers of America.*** **London: J. Walker, 1810.**[30]

Farmer, James Eugene. *Essays on French History.* New York: G. P. Putnam's Sons, 1897.

Farmer, Lydia Hoyt. *A Knight of Faith.* New York: J. S. Ogilvie, 1889.

Fern, Fanny. *Folly as It Flies.* New York: Carleton, 1868.

Feuillet, Octave. *A Marriage in High Life.* New York: Munro's Sons, n.d.

Fielding, Henry. *Works of Henry Fielding.* New York: George Routledge, n.d.

Finlay, James Ralph. *Report of Appraisal of Mining Properties of New Mexico, 1921–1922.* Santa Fe: Printer of the Catholic Publishing Company, 1992.

Finley, Martha. *Wanted: A Pedigree.* New York: Dodd, Mead & Company, 1871.

Fisher, Jacob. *The Cradle of the Deep: An Account of the Adventures of Eleanor Channing and John Starbuck.* New York: Grosset & Dunlap, 1912.

Fiske, Dwight. *Why Should Penguins Fly?* New York: McBride, 1936.

Foraker, Joseph Benson. *Notes of a Busy Life.* Vol. 1. Cincinnati: Stewart & Kidd, 1917.

Ford, Paul Leicester. *The Great K. & A. Train Robbery.* New York: Dodd, Mead & Company, 1897.

———. *The Honorable Peter Stirling and What People Thought of Him.* New York: Henry Holt, 1896.

Fothergill, Jessie. *The First Violin: A Novel.* New York: Munro's Sons, n.d.

Fouqué, Friedrich de la Motte. *Undine; or, The Water Spirit.* New York: James Miller, n.d.

France, R. H. *Germs of Mind in Plants.* Chicago: Charles H. Kerr & Company, 1905.

Frost, Max, and Paul A. F. Walter. *Santa Fe County.* Santa Fe, NM: Bureau of Immigration, 1906.

———. *The Land of Sunshine.* Santa Fe: New Mexican Printing Company, 1904.

Frost, William Henry. *The Court of King Arthur: Stories from the Land of the Round Table.* New York: Charles Scribner's Sons, 1902.

———. *The Knights of the Round Table: Stories of King Arthur and the Holy Grail.* New York: Charles Scribner's Sons, 1902.

Fulton, Maurice Garland, ed. ***Pat F. Garrett's Authentic Life of Billy, the Kid.*** **New York: Macmillan, 1927.**[31]

Fulton, Maurice Garland, and Paul Horgan, eds. *New Mexico's Own Chronicle: Three Races in the Writings of Four Hundred Years.* Dallas: Banks Upshaw & Company, 1937.

Galaxy of Song: Popular Songs, with Complete Accompaniments for the Piano or Cabinet Organ, and Their Composers. Philadelphia: Thomas Hunter, 1883.

Gandy, Lewis Cass. *The Tabors: A Footnote of Western History*. New York: Press of the Pioneers, 1934.

Gause, Frank A., and Charles Carl Carr. *The Story of Panama: The New Route to India*. Boston: Silver Burdett, 1912.

General Laws of New Mexico, from the Promulgations of the Kearney Code in 1846 to the End of the Legislative Session in 1880. Albany, NY: W. C. Little, 1880.

Gibbon, Edward. *The History of the Decline and Fall of the Roman Empire*. 5 vols. Philadelphia: Henry T. Coates, n.d.

Gibbons, James Cardinal. *Our Christian Heritage*. Baltimore: John Murphy, 1889.

Giddings, J. Wight. *From Here and There*. New York: Cochrane, 1910.

Gilbert, Clinton W., et al. *The Mirrors of Washington*. New York: G. P. Putnam's Sons, 1921.

Gilder, Jeannette L. *Masterpieces of the World's Best Literature*. New York: Current Literature Publishing Company, 1905.

Glasscock, Carl B. *The War of the Copper Kings*. New York: Grosset & Dunlap, 1935.

Goodwin, Mrs. M. F. *The Golden Rule and Its Fruits*. Boston: American Tract Society, n.d.

Graham, Andrew J. *The Hand-Book of Standard or American Phonography*. New York: Andrew Graham, 1894.

Grant, Blanche C. *When Old Trails Were New: The Story of Taos*. New York: Press of the Pioneers, 1934.

Grant, H. B. *Tactics and Manual for Knight Templars*. Cincinnati: Pettibone, 1882.

Grant, Robert. *Unleavened Bread: A Novel*. New York: Charles Scribner's Sons, 1900.

Grant, Ulysses S. *Personal Memoirs*. 2 vols. New York: Charles L. Webster, 1885.

Graydon, Williams. *Graydon's Forms of Conveyancing*. Philadelphia: Kay, Jun. & Brother, 1852.

Grayson, David. *Adventures in Friendship*. New York: Doubleday, Page & Company, 1910.

Green, Evelyn Everett. *Alwyn Ravendale*. New York: American Tract Society, n.d.

Greene, Francis Vinton. *Report on the Russian Army and Its Campaigns in Turkey in 1877–78*. New York: D. Appleton & Company, 1879.

Greenleaf, Sue. *Wed by Mighty Waves: A Thrilling Romance of Ill-Fated Galveston*. Chicago: Laird & Lee, 1900.

Grey, Maxwell. *The Silence of Dean Maitland: A Novel*. New York: D. Appleton & Company, 1888.

Grinnell, George Bird. *American Duck Shooting*. New York: Forest & Stream, 1901.

Guerber, H. A. *The Story of the Romans*. New York: American Book Company, 1896.

Hadley, Anna R., et al. *Hiram Hadley*. Boston: Little, Brown, 1924.

Hale, Edward E. *His Level Best, and Other Stories*. Boston: J. R. Osgood, 1873.

——. **The Man Without a Country. New York: Platt & Peck, 1910.**[32]

Halévy, Ludovic. *L'abbé Constantin*. New York: Munro's Sons, n.d.

Haley, J. Evetts. *Charles Goodnight, Cowman and Plainsman*. Boston: Houghton Mifflin, 1936.

Half-Hours with Great Novelists: Charles Dickens, Anthony Trollope, William Black, Charles Lever, and Others. Chicago: Donohue, Henneberry & Company, ca. 1884.

Hamilton, C. D. P. *Modern Scientific Whist.* New York: Brentano's, 1894.

Hamilton, M. *The Dishonor of Frank Scott.* New York: Harper, 1900.

Hammerton, John A. *An Outline of English Literature: Being a Chronicle of Great Writers from the Time of Chaucer to the Present Day, with a Casual Commentary.* New York: W. H. Wise & Company, 1938.

Hammerton, John A., and Harry E. Barnes. *The Illustrated World History: A Record of World Events from Earliest Historical Times to the Present Day.* New York: W. H. Wise & Company, 1937.

Hardwicke-Pennybacker, Anna J. *New History of Texas for Schools.* Austin: Percy V. Pennybacker, 1900.

Hardy, Thomas. *A Pair of Blue Eyes.* New York: New York Publishing Company, n.d.

Harte, Bret. *Tales of the Argonauts.* Boston: Houghton Mifflin, 1882.

———. *Thankful Blossom.* Toronto: Belford Brothers, 1877.

Harvard University Catalogue. 1910–1911.

Harvey, Charles M. *Republican National Convention, St. Louis, June 16th to 18th, 1896. With a History of the Republican Party and a Survey of National Politics Since the Party's Foundation, etc., etc.* St. Louis, MO: I. Haas Publishing and Engraving Company, 1896.

Haskins, William C. *Canal Zone Pilot: Guide to the Republic of Panama and Classified Business Directory.* Panama: Star & Herald Company, 1908.

Hatton, Joseph. *The Princess Mazaroff: A Romance of the Day.* New York: Lovell, 1891.

Hauff, Wilhelm. *Arabian Days' Entertainments.* Boston: Ticknor & Fields, 1859.

Hay, John. *Memorial Address on the Life and Character of William McKinley.* Washington, D.C.: Government Printing Office, 1903.

Hay, Mary Cecil. *The Squire's Legacy.* New York: Lovell, n.d.

Hays, Milton D. *My Grandfather's Best Brand; or, No, I Thank You; and, A Parent's Mistake: Two Romances of the Sixties.* Pittsburgh, PA: Milton D. Hays Company, 1908.

Hazelrigg, Clara H. *A New History of Kansas.* Topeka, KS: Crane & Company, 1895.

Headley, Joel Tyler. *The Life and Travels of General Grant.* Philadelphia: Hubbard Brothers, 1879.

Henry, O. *Roads of Destiny.* New York: Doubleday, 1909.

———. *The Voice of the City.* New York: McClure Company, 1908.

Hertz-Garten, Theodor. *Through the Red-Litten Windows; and The Old River House.* New York: Cassell, 1892.

Hildebrand, Samuel S. *Autobiography.* Jefferson City, MO: State Times Books and Job Printing House, 1870.

Hinkle, James F. *Early Days of a Cowboy on the Pecos.* Roswell, NM: printed by author, 1937.

Hollister, Uriah S. *The Navajo and His Blanket*. Denver: U.S. Colortype, 1903.

Holmes, Mary Jane. *What Will the World Say?* Chicago: Belford, Clarke & Company, 1881.

Holy Bible. New York: American Bible Society, 1912.[33]

Holy Bible. New York: Nelson & Sons, n.d.

Hopkins, Rufus C. *Muniments of Title of the Barony of Arizona*. San Francisco: Bancroft Company, 1893.

Hornung, Ernest W. *A Bride from the Bush*. New York: Charles Scribner's Sons, 1897.

Houssaye, Henry. *Cleopatra: A Study*. New York: Duprat & Company, 1890.

Howard, Blanche Willis. *Guenn: A Wave on the Breton Coast*. Boston: Asgood, 1884.

Hubbard, Elbert. *Health and Wealth*. New York: Roycroft Shop, 1908.

———. *The Man of Sorrows*. New York: Roycroft Shop, 1906.

———. *The Mintage, Being Ten Stories and One More*. New York: Roycroft Shop, ca. 1910.

———. *White Hyacinths*. New York: Roycroft Shop, 1907.

Hume, David. *The History of England, from the Invasion of Julius Caesar to the Revolution in 1688. Embellished with Engravings on Copper and Wood, from Original Designs*. London: Printed for J. Wallis, by T. Bensley, 1803.

Hume, Henriette. *Dorothy*. Chicago: Donohue, Henneberry & Company, 1890.

Illustrated History of New Mexico. Chicago: Lewis Publishing Company, 1895.

Ingraham, J. H. *The Pillar of Fire*. Philadelphia: G. G. Evans, 1860.

———. *The Throne of David*. Boston: Roberts Brothers, 1865.

Inman, Henry. *Tales of the Trail: Short Stories of Western Life*. Topeka, KS: Crane & Company, 1898.[34]

Inner Shrine, The. Boston: Grosset & Dunlap, 1909.

Irving, Theodore. *The Conquest of Florida by Hernando de Soto*. New York: Putnam & Sons, 1868.

Jeaffreson, John Cordy. *A Book About Lawyers*. New York: Carleton, 1867.

Jenkins, John S. *The New Clerk's Assistant; or, Book of Practical Forms*. N.p.: n.d.

Jerome, Jerome K. *Iddle Thoughts of an Iddle Fellow*. New York: Caldwell, n.d.

———. *Three Men in a Boat*. Title page missing; no publishing information.

Johnston, Mary. *To Have and to Hold*. Boston: Houghton Mifflin, 1900.

Jones, Fayette Alexander. *New Mexico Mines and Minerals*. Santa Fe: New Mexican Printing Company, 1904.

Kaler, James Otis. *Toby Tyler*. New York: Harper & Brothers, 1903.

Kavanagh, Julia. *Adèle*. New York: D. Appleton & Company, 1858.

———. *Grace Lee*. New York: D. Appleton & Company, 1868.

———. *Queen Mab*. New York: D. Appleton & Company, 1864.

———. *Silvia*. New York: D. Appleton & Company, 1867.

Kellogg, Margaret Augusta. *Leo Dayne: A Novel*. Boston: J. H. West, 1899.

Kelly, Charles. *Outlaw Trail*. Salt Lake City: printed by author, 1938.

Kelly, Fanny. *Narrative of My Captivity Among the Sioux Indians*. Cincinnati: Wilstach, Baldwin & Company, 1871.

Kelly, Florence Finch. *With Hoops of Steel*. Indianapolis: Bowen-Merrill, 1900.

Kelsey, D. M. *History of Our Wild West*. Chicago: Thompson & Thomas, 1901.

Kendall, George W. *Narrative of the Texan Santa Fe Expedition*. 2 vols. New York: Harper & Brothers, 1844.

Kent, Rockwell. *World-Famous Paintings*. New York: W. H. Wise & Company, 1939.

King, Charles. *Kitty's Conquest*. Philadelphia: J. B. Lippincott, 1891.

———. *The Story of Fort Frayne*. Chicago: F. T. Neely, 1895.

———. *Trooper Ross, and Signal Butte*. Philadelphia: J. B. Lippincott, 1895.

Kingsley, Charles. *Hypatia*. New York: Caldwell, n.d.

———. *Hypatia*. New York: Macmillan, 1878.

Kingsley, Florence Morse. *The Transfiguration of Miss Philura: A Comedy in Four Acts*. New York: Funk & Wagnalls, 1901.

Kingsley, Henry. *Austin Elliot: A Novel*. New York: Dodd, Mead & Company, n.d.

———. *The Recollections of Geoffrey Hamlyn*. New York: Dodd, Mead & Company, n.d.

Kipling, Rudyard. *Stalky & Co*. New York: Doubleday & McClure, 1899.

Kirby, Mary and Elizabeth. *The World at Home; or, Pictures and Scenes from Far-Off Lands*. London: Nelson & Sons, 1873.

Kirby, William. *The Golden Dog: A Romance of the Days of Louis XV in Quebec*. Boston: J. Knight, 1896.

Knickerbocker, Diedrich. *A History of New York*. New York: G. P. Putnam's Sons, 1880.

Koger, Sam A., comp. *State of Oregon Election Laws*.

Korolenko, Vladimir G. *The Vagrant and Other Tales*. New York: T. Y. Crowell & Company, 1887.

Kyne, Peter B. *The Pride of Palomar*. New York: Cosmopolitan Book Corporation, 1921.

Laboulaye, Edouard. *Laboulaye's Fairy Book*. New York: Harper, 1867.

Ladd, Horatio Oliver. *Chunda: A Story of the Navajos*. New York: Eaton & Mains, 1906.

———. *History of the War with Mexico*. New York: Dodd, Mead & Company, 1883.

———. *The Story of New Mexico*. Boston: Lothrop, 1891.

Langford, Nathaniel Pitt. *Vigilante Days and Ways*. Chicago: A. C. McClurg & Company, 1912.

Lanman, Charles. *Dictionary of the United States Congress*. Washington, D.C.: Government Printing Office, 1864.

Lardner, Dionysius. *Popular Lectures on Science and Art*. New York: Greeley & McElrath, 1850.

Lasserre, Henry. *Our Lady of Lourdes*. New York: D. & J. Sadlier, 1872.

Laws of the State of New Mexico. Passed at sessions 1, 6, and 10–11.

Le Queux, William. *Zoraida: A Romance of the Harem and the Great Sahara*. New York: Frederick A. Stokes, 1895.

Lee, Minnie Mary. *The Brown House at Duffield: A Story of Life Without and Within the Fold*. Baltimore: Kelly, Piet, 1876.

———. *The Heart of Myrrha Lake*. New York: Catholic Publication Society, 1872.

Legislative Blue Book of the Territory of New Mexico. Santa Fe, NM: C. W. Greene, 1882.

Lehr, Elizabeth D. *"King Lehr" and the Gilded Age*. Philadelphia: J. B. Lippincott, 1935.

Lengyel, Emil. *The Danube*. New York: Random House, 1939.

Lent, Edward B. *Being Done Good*. New York: Brooklyn Eagle Press, 1904.

Lever, Charles J. *Tales of the Trains*. London: Ward, Lock & Company, n.d.

Lewis, Alfred Henry. *Wolfville*. New York: Frederick A. Stokes, 1897.

Lewis, Sinclair. *Mantrap*. New York: Harcourt Brace, 1926.

Light of the World; or, Our Saviour in Art. London: British-American Company, 1899.

Light of the World; or, Our Saviour in Art. London: British-American Company, 1900.

Lindsay, Anna R. *The Warriors*. New York: T. Y. Crowell & Company, 1903.

Linthicum, Richard. *A Book of the Rocky Mountain Tales*. Denver: W. F. Robinson, 1892.

Little, Frances. *The Lady of the Decoration*. New York: Century, 1907.

Lloyd, John Uri. *Stringtown on the Pike: A Tale of Northernmost Kentucky*. New York: Dodd, Mead & Company, 1901.

Local and Special Laws of New Mexico. N.p., 1884.

Long, John L. *Miss Cherry-Blossom of Tokyo*. Philadelphia: J. B. Lippincott, 1900.

Long, Joseph R. *Outline of the Jurisdiction and Procedure of the Federal Courts*. Charlottesville, VA: Michie, 1911.

Long, Joseph W. *American Wild-Fowl Shooting*. New York: J. B. Ford & Company, 1874.

Longfellow, Henry Wadsworth. *Evangeline*. New York: Maynard, Merritt & Company, 1893.

Lord, Eliot, et al. *The Italian in America*. New York: B. F. Buck, 1905.

Lynch, Lawrence L. *Shadowed by Three*. Chicago: Donnelley, Gassette & Loyd, 1882.

Lyons, Joseph A. *The American Elocutionist and Dramatic Reader for the Use of Colleges, Academies, and Schools*. Philadelphia: E. H. Butler & Company, 1874.

———. *Silver Jubilee of the University of Notre Dame, June 23, 1869*. Chicago: Myers, 1869.

Lytton, Edward Bulwer. *Leila; or, The Siege of Granada, Calderon the Courtier, and the Pilgrims of the Rhine*. London: Routledge, 1875.

———. *A Strange Story, and The Haunted and the Haunters*. New York: Mershon, n.d.

MacDonald, George. *Warlock O'Glenwarlock: A Homely Romance*. Boston: Lothrop, Lee & Shepard, 1881.

Mackie, John. *Sinners Twain: A Romance of the Great Lone Land*. New York: Frederick A. Stokes, 1895.

MacLaren, Ian. *Our Neighbors*. New York: Dodd, Mead & Company, 1903.

Maeterlinck, Maurice. *Wisdom and Destiny*. New York: Dodd, Mead & Company, 1906.

Mahan, Bruce E., and Ruth A. Gallaher. *Stories of Iowa for Boys and Girls*. New York: Macmillan, 1929.

Mallock, William H. *The Old Order Changes*. New York: G. P. Putnam's Sons, 1888.

Marlitt, E. *Gold Elsie*. New York: Allison, 1895.

———. *In the Schillingscourt*. Chicago: M. A. Donohue, n.d.

———. *The Old Man'selle's Secret*. New York: Lovell, Coryell, n.d.

Martin, Charles A. *Catholic Religion: A Statement of Christian Teaching and History*. Cleveland, OH: Apostolate Publishing, 1910.

Massett, Stephen C. *Drifting About*. New York: Carleton, 1863.

Masson, Gustave. *French Classics*. 5 vols. Oxford: Clarendon Press, 1876.

Maxim, Hudson. *Defenseless America*. New York: Hearst's International Library, 1915.

May, E. J. *Bertram Noel: A Story for Youth*. New York: D. Appleton & Company, 1870.

———. *Mortimer's College Life*. New York: D. Appleton & Company, 1870.

McCarthy, Justin. *Lady Judith: A Tale of Two Continents*. New York: Sheldon, 1871.

McClure, Alexander K. *Recollections of Half a Century*. Salem, MA: Salem Press, 1902.

McClure, J. B. *Abraham Lincoln's Stories and Speeches*. Chicago: Rhodes & McClure, 1896.

McCutcheon, George Barr. *Graustark: The Story of a Love Behind a Throne*. Chicago: H. S. Stone, 1901.

———. *The Husbands of Edith*. New York: A. L. Burt, 1908.

———. *Nedra*. New York: Dodd, Mead & Company, 1905.

McDougal, Henry Clay. *Recollections, 1844–1909*. Kansas City, MO: Franklin Hudson, 1910.

McElroy, John. *The Red Acorn: A Novel*. Chicago: H. A. Sumner, 1883.

McGowan, Jonas H. *The Lawyer's Hand-Book of Federal Practice*. Washington, D.C.: Brodix, 1891.

Mee, Arthur, J. A. Hammerton, and S. S. McClure. *The World's Greatest Books*. 20 vols. New York: W. H. Wise & Company, 1910.

Memorial Addresses Delivered in the Senate and House of Representatives of the United States in Memory of Andrew A. Jones, a Senator from New Mexico. Washington, D.C.: Government Printing Office, 1929.

Memorial Services Held in the House of Representatives of the United States, Together with Remarks in Eulogy of Bronson Cutting, Late Senator from New Mexico. Washington, D.C.: Government Printing Office, 1935.

Merimée, Prosper. *Colomba*. New York: T. Y. Crowell & Company, 1897.

Michelson, Miriam. *In the Bishop's Carriage*. Indianapolis: Bobbs-Merrill, 1903.

Miller, Alice. *The Blue Arch*. New York: Charles Scribner's Sons, 1910.

Miller, Hettie E. *The Quill-Driver*. Chicago: E. A. Weeks, 1895.

Mills, Mabel Louise. *Moulding Public Opinion to Help Save Our Trees*. Los Angeles: American Reforestation Association, 1927.

Mills, W. W. *Forty Years at El Paso, 1858–1898*. El Paso, TX: printed by author, 1901.

Milton, John. *Paradise Lost*. Edited by Robert Vaughan. New York: Cassell, n.d.

Mitchell, John Ames. *Amos Judd*. New York: Charles Scribner's Sons, 1901.

Monette, John W. *History of the Discovery and Settlement of the Valley of the Mississippi*. New York: Harper & Brothers, 1848.

Montague, Margaret P. *Uncle Sam of Freedom Ridge*. New York: Doubleday, Page & Company, 1920.

Moore, Frank Frankfort. *The Sale of a Soul*. New York: Frederick A. Stokes, 1895.

Morals and Dogma of the Ancient and Accepted Scottish Rite of Freemasonry. Charleston, SC: Supreme Council of the Southern Jurisdiction, 1871.

Morell, Parker. *Diamond Jim: The Life and Times of James Buchanan Brady.* New York: Simon & Schuster, 1934.

Morris, Robert. *Freemasonry in the Holy Land.* New York: Masonic Publishing Company, 1872.

Morris, Mrs. Robert C. *Dragons and Cherry Blossoms.* New York: Dodd, Mead & Company, 1896.

Museum of Foreign Literature and Science. Vols. 11, 4 (n.s.). Philadelphia: E. Littell, 1827.

Musick, John R. *Stories of Missouri.* New York: American Book Company, 1897.

National Cyclopedia of American Biography. New York: J. T. White, n.d.

New Mexico State Penitentiary. *Report of Board of Commissioners and Superintendent for the 63rd Fiscal Year.* 1916.

New Mexico Statutes. Denver: Courtright, 1929.

New Testament. New York: Christian Herald Bible House, 1900.

New Thought Annual. Chicago: Psychic Research Company, 1902.

Nicholson, Meredith. *The Lords of High Decision.* New York: Doubleday, Page & Company, 1909.

———. *Rosalind at Redgate.* Indianapolis: Bobbs-Merrill, 1907.

Oliphant, Mrs. *The Makers of Venice.* New York: Caldwell, n.d.

Ollivant, Alfred. *Danny.* New York: Doubleday, Page & Company, 1902.

Orcutt, William Dana. *The Moth: A Novel.* New York: Harper & Brothers, 1912.

Orsini, Abbé. *Life of the Blessed Virgin Mary, Mother of God.* New York: D. & J. Sadlier, 1856.

Osborne, William Hamilton. *The Red Mouse: A Mystery Romance.* New York: A. L. Burt, 1909.

Otero, Miguel A. *Message of Miguel A. Otero, Governor of New Mexico, to the 36th Legislative Assembly.* 1899, 1901, 1903, and 1905.

Otero, Nina. *Old Spain in Our Southwest.* New York: Harcourt, Brace, 1936.

Ouida [Maria Louise Ramé]. *Puck.* Philadelphia: J. B. Lippincott, 1890.

———. *Ruffino.* New York: F. M. Lupton, n.d.

Overton, Gwendolen. *The Heritage of Unrest.* New York: Macmillan, 1901.

Page, Thomas Nelson. *Gordon Keith.* New York: Charles Scribner's Sons, 1903.

———. *Red Rock.* New York: Charles Scribner's Sons, 1899.

Palmer, Mrs. Potter. *Address and Reports of Mrs. Potter Palmer, President of the Board of Lady Managers, World's Columbian Commission.* Chicago: Rand McNally, 1899.

Parker, Richard Green. *Aids to English Composition: Prepared for Students of All Grades. Embracing Specimens and Examples of School and College Exercises and Most of the Higher Departments of English Composition, Both in Prose and Verse.* New York: Harper & Brothers, 1854.

Parks, Samuel C. *The Great Trial of the Nineteenth Century.* Kansas City, MO: Hudson-Kimberly, 1900.

Parley, Peter. *Peter Parley's Merry Stories.* New York, James Miller, n.d.

Patterson, Joseph Medill. *A Little Brother of the Rich.* New York: Grosset & Dunlap, 1908.

Peters, George William. *American Whist.* Boston: Houghton Mifflin, 1890.

Peterson, C. S. *Representative New Mexicans.* Denver: printed by author, 1912.

Phillips, David Graham. *The Fashionable Adventures of Joshua Craig.* New York: Grosset & Dunlap, 1909.

Pinkerton, Allan. *Claude Melnotte as a Detective, and Other Stories.* Chicago: W. B. Keen, Cooke, 1875.

Poe, John W. *The True Story of the Killing of Billy the Kid.* Los Angeles: E. A. Brininstool, 1919.[35]

Pope, Charles Henry. *Solar Heat: Its Practical Applications.* Boston: printed by author, 1903.

Prince, L. Bradford. *Historical Sketches of New Mexico.* Kansas City, MO: Ramsey, Millett & Hudson, 1883.

Pritchard, Martin J. *Without Sin: A Novel.* Chicago: H. S. Stone, 1896.

Proceedings of the House of Representatives of the Territory of New Mexico, 34th Session. 1901.

Prudden, T. Mitchell. *On the Great American Plateau: Wanderings Among Canyons and Buttes, in the Land of the Cliff-Dweller, and the Indian of To-Day.* New York: G. P. Putnam's Sons, 1906.

Putnam's Handy Map Book. New York: G. P. Putnam's Sons, n.d.

Raine, William MacLeod. *Famous Sheriffs and Western Outlaws.* New York: Garden City Publishing Company, 1929.

Rathborne, George. *Miss Fairfax of Virginia: A Romance of Love and Adventure Under the Palmettos.* New York: Street & Smith, 1899.

Rayne, Mrs. M. L. *Against Fate: A True Story.* Chicago: Railroad News Company, 1879.

Read, Opie P., and Frank Pixley. *The Carpetbagger: A Novel.* Chicago: Laird & Lee, 1899.

Reade, Charles. *A Terrible Temptation: A Story of the Day.* Detroit: Craig & Taylor, n.d.

Redding, M. Walcott. *Ecce Orienti!* New York: printed by author, 1870.

Reichenbach, Moritz von. *The Eichhofs: A Romance.* Philadelphia: J. B. Lippincott, 1888.

Renan, Ernest. *The Life of Jesus.* New York: Carleton, 1870.

Report of the Governor of New Mexico for Fiscal Year Ended June 30. 1897–1898, 1900–1901, and 1903.

Report of the Governor of New Mexico to the Secretary of the Interior. Washington, D.C.: Government Printing Office, 1897–1905.

Report of the Secretary of the Interior for the Fiscal Year Ended June 30, 1903. Washington, D.C.: Government Printing Office, 1903.

Report of the Secretary of the Interior for the Fiscal Year Ended June 30, 1904. Washington, D.C.: Government Printing Office, 1904.

Report of the Secretary of the Interior for the Fiscal Year Ended June 30, 1905. Washington, D.C.: Government Printing Office, 1905.

Report of the Secretary of the Interior for the Fiscal Year Ended June 30, 1906. Washington, D.C.: Government Printing Office, 1906.

Report of the Secretary of the Territory of New Mexico (1905–06) and Legislative Manual, 1907.

Report of the Secretary of the Territory of New Mexico (1907–08) and Legislative Manual, 1909.

Retzsch, Moritz. *Illustrations to Goethe's Faust.* Boston: Estes & Lauriat, 1877. Contains selections of Goethe's text.

Richardson, James D. *A Compilation of the Messages and Papers of the Confederacy.* 2 vols. Nashville: United States Publishing Company, 1905.

Ridpath, John Clark. *The Life and Works of James G. Blaine.* Denver: World Publishing Company, 1893.

Ritch, William G. *Illustrated New Mexico: Historical and Industrial.* Santa Fe, NM: Bureau of Immigration, 1885.

Rives, Amélie. *A Brother to Dragons, and Other Old-Time Tales.* New York: Harper & Brothers, 1888.

Roe, A. S. *The Star and the Cloud; or, A Daughter's Love.* New York: Carleton, 1853.

Rollins, Montgomery. *Tables Showing the Net Returns from Bonds and Other Redeemable Securities.* London: Routledge, n.d.

Rules of the Supreme Court for the Territory of New Mexico. 1897.

Russell, Charles Wells. *The Fall of Damascus: An Historical Novel.* Boston: Lee & Shepard, 1878.

Russell, Mary Annette. *Elizabeth and Her German Garden.* New York: Charles Scribner's Sons, 1907.

Ryan, Marah Ellis. *The Flute of the Gods.* New York: Frederick A. Stokes, 1909.

———. *For the Soul of Rafael.* Chicago: A. C. McClurg, 1906.

Saint-Pierre, Bernardin de. *Paul and Virginia.* Philadelphia: J. B. Lippincott, 1860.

Salisbury, William. *The Career of a Journalist.* New York: B. W. Dodge & Company, 1908.

Saltus, Edgar. *Imperial Purple.* Chicago: Morrill, Higgins & Company, 1892.

Sánchez, Pedro. *Memorias sobre la vida del presbítero don Antonio José Martínez.* Santa Fe: Compañía Impresora del Nuevo Mexicano, 1903.

Saunders, Marshall. *Beautiful Joe.* Philadelphia: C. H. Bones, 1899.

Saxton, Robert. *Mental Photographs: An Album for Confession of Tastes, Habits and Convictions.* New York: Henry Holt, 1884.

Scenes and Narrations from German History. New York: Pott, Young, n.d.

Scott, Walter. *The Heart of Midlothian.* New York: John B. Alden, 1885.

———. *The Waverly Novels (Guy Mannering, The Monastery, Anne of Geierstein, The Pirate, Kenilworth, The Fair Maid of Perth, The Abbot, Woodstock, Waverley, St. Ronan's Well, Old Mortality, The Heart of Midlothian, Ivanhoe, Rob Roy,*

Peveril of the Peak, The Bride of Lammermoor). New York: T. Y. Crowell & Company, n.d.

———. *The Waverly Novels (Red Gauntlett, Quentin Durward, The Antiquary, The Betrothed, The Black Dwarf, Count Robert of Paris, The Fortunes of Nigel, The Talisman)*. N.p.: n.d.

Scribner's Monthly. Vol. 20 (May–October 1880).

Scoullar, William J. *El "Libro azul" de Panamá*. Panama City: Latin American Publicity Bureau, 1916–1917.

Seabrook, William B. *The Magic Island*. New York: Blue Ribbon Books, 1929.

Seawell, Molly Elliot. *The Marriage of Theodora*. New York: A. L. Burt, 1910.

Senate Manual Containing the Standing Rules and Orders of the United States Senate. Washington, D.C.: Government Printing Office, 1918.

Serrano, Mary J. *Marie Bashkirtseff: The Journal of a Young Artist, 1860–1884*. New York: Cassell, 1889.

Seton, Ernest Thompson. *The Biography of a Grizzly*. New York: Century, 1902.

———. *Lives of the Hunted*. New York: Charles Scribner's Sons, 1901.

———. *Monarch: The Big Bear of Tallac*. New York: Charles Scribner's Sons, 1904.

———. *The Trail of the Sandhill Stag*. New York: Charles Scribner's Sons, 1901.

———. *Wild Animals I Have Known*. New York: Charles Scribner's Sons, 1900.

Shakespeare, William. *The Complete Works of Shakespeare*. 3 vols. New York: Johnson, Fry & Company, n.d.[36]

———. *The Gilbert Shakespeare*. London: Routledge, n.d. [ca. 1883].

———. *Shakespeare Illustrated*.[37]

Shelley, Mary. *Frankenstein*. New York: Home Book Company, n.d.

Sidney, Margaret. *The Pettibone Name: A New England Story*. Boston: Lothrop, 1882.

Sienkiewicz, Henryk. *Quo Vadis*. Boston: Little, Brown, 1897.

Skinner, Hubert M. *Readings in Folk-lore: Short Studies in the Mythology of America, Great Britain, the Norse Countries, India, Syria, Egypt, and Persia*. New York: American Book Company, 1893.

Smiles, Samuel. *Happy Homes and the Hearts That Make Them*. Chicago: United States Publishing House, 1889.

Smith, Arthur D. H. *John Jacob Astor: Landlord of New York*. New York: Blue Ribbon Books, 1929.

Smith, William Henry. *The Life and Speeches of Hon. Charles Warren Fairbanks*. Indianapolis: W. B. Burford, 1904.

Smollett, Tobias G. *The History of England from the Revolution to the Death of George the Second*. London: Paternoster Row, 1804.

———. *Works of Tobias Smollett*. New York: Routledge, n.d.

Song Album. Vol. 1. New York: Richard A. Saalfield, n.d.

Southworth, Emma D. *India: The Pearl of the Pearl River*. Philadelphia: T. B. Peterson & Brothers, 1875.

———. *Retribution*. Philadelphia: T. B. Peterson & Brothers, 1875.

Spalding, John L. *Education and the Higher Life*. Chicago: A. C. McClurg & Company, 1903.

Spalding, M. J. *The History of the Protestant Reformation*. Baltimore: John Murphy, 1866.

Spanish and Mexican Land Laws in New Spain and Mexico. St. Louis, MO: Buxton & Skinner, 1895.

Standish, Burt L. *Frank Merriwell's Courage*. Philadelphia: David McKay, 1903.

Statehood for New Mexico. 1900–1904.

Stephens, James. *The Crock of Gold*. New York: Macmillan, 1919.

Stevens, Isaac N. *The Liberators: A Story of Future American Politics*. New York: B. W. Dodge & Company, 1908.

Stockton, Frank R. *The Casting Away of Mrs. Lecks and Mrs. Aleshine*. New York: Century, 1892.

———. *The Young Master of Hyson Hall*. Philadelphia: J. B. Lippincott, 1889.

Sue, Eugène. *The Mysteries of Paris*. N.p.: Routledge, n.d.

Supreme Court of the Territory of New Mexico Record (New Mexico Mining Co. Defendants). 1891.

Swift, Jonathan. *Travels into Several Remote Nations of the World*. Chicago: Belford, Clarke & Company, 1889.[38]

Swinton, William. *Campaigns of the Army of the Potomac: A Critical History of Operations in Virginia, Maryland and Pennsylvania, from the Commencement to the Close of the War*. New York: C. B. Richardson, 1866.

Synon, Mary. *McAdoo, the Man and His Times: A Panorama in Democracy*. Indianapolis: Bobbs-Merrill, 1924.

Table of Distances, Territory of New Mexico. Santa Fe, NM: Adjutant General's Office, 1881.

Tales from McClure's: Adventure. New York: Doubleday & McClure, 1895.

Tales from McClure's: Humor. New York: Doubleday & McClure, 1899.

Tales from McClure's: Romance. New York: Doubleday & McClure, 1899.

Tales from McClure's: The West. New York: Doubleday & McClure, 1898.

Tales from McClure's: War. New York: Doubleday & McClure, 1898.

Tarkington, Booth. *The Magnificent Ambersons*. New York: Doubleday, Doran & Company, 1929.

Taylor, Bayard. *Picturesque Europe*. New York: D. Appleton & Company, 1877.

Taylor, Benjamin F. *The World on Wheels, and Other Sketches*. Chicago: S. C. Griggs, 1878.

Taylor, Charles M. *The British Isles Through an Opera Glass*. Philadelphia: G. W. Jacobs, 1899.

Tennyson, Alfred Lord. *Queen Mary*. Boston: J. R. Osgood, 1875.[39]

Thackeray, William M., et al. *Half-Hours with Great Authors*. Chicago: Donohue, Henneberry & Company, n.d.

Tolstoi, Alexis. *Prince Serebryani*. New York: Dodd, Mead & Company, 1892.

Tompkins, Juliet Wilbor. *Dr. Ellen*. New York: Grosset & Dunlap, 1908.

Tourgée, Albion W. *Bricks Without Straw: A Novel*. New York: Fords, Howard & Hulbert, 1880.

———. *A Fool's Errand*. New York: Fords, Howard & Hulbert, 1880.

Townley, Houghton. *The Gay Lord Waring*. New York: Grosset & Dunlap, 1910.

Townsend, George Alfred. *Tales of the Chesapeake*. New York: American Book Company, 1880.

Tracy, Louis. *The Final War*. New York: G. W. Dillingham, 1896.

———. *The Pillar of Light*. New York: E. J. Clode, 1904.

Train, Elizabeth P. *Madam of the Ivies*. Philadelphia: J. B. Lippincott, 1898.

Training of Rachel Haller, The. Philadelphia: American Baptist Society, 1900.

Trebor. *As It May Happen: A Story of American Life and Character*. Philadelphia: Porter & Coates, 1879.

Trollope, Anthony. *The Prime Minister*. New York: American Book Company, n.d.

Tucker, Ray, and Frederick R. Barkley. *Sons of the Wild Jackass*. Boston: L. C. Page & Company, 1932.

Twain, Mark. *The Innocents Abroad*. Hartford, CT: American Publishing Company, 1872.[40]

Twain, Mark, and Charles Dudley Warner. *The Gilded Age*. Hartford, CT: American Publishing Company, 1874.

Twitchell, Ralph Emerson. *The History of the Military Occupation of the Territory of New Mexico from 1846 to 1851*. Denver: Smith-Brooks Company, 1909.

———. ***The Leading Facts of New Mexican History*. 2 vols. Cedar Rapids, IA: Torch Press, 1911.**[41]

Tyrrell, Charles A. *The Royal Road to Health; or, The Secret of Health Without Drugs*. New York: Tyrrell's Hygienic Institute, 1901.

Underhill, Ruth M. *First Penthouse Dwellers of America*. New York: J. J. Augustin, 1938.

United States Bankruptcy Law of July 1, 1898, and Ammendments Thereto of Feb. 5, 1903. Washington, D.C.: Government Printing Office, 1903.

United States Congress. *Obituary Addresses on the Occasion of the Death of Hon. William R. King of Alabama, Vice-President of the United States, Delivered in the Senate and House of Representatives, and in the Supreme Court of the United States, Dec. 8–9, 1853*. Washington, D.C.: Armstrong, 1854.

———. *Obituary Addresses on the Occasion of the Death of Hon. Henry Clay, a Senator of the U.S. from the State of Kentucky, Delivered in the Senate and in the House of Representatives of the U.S., June 30, 1852*. Washington, D.C.: Armstrong, 1852.

———. *Obituary Addresses on the Occasion of the Death of Hon. Daniel Webster of Massachusetts, Secretary of State for the United States, Delivered in the Senate and in the House of Representatives of the U.S., Dec. 14–15, 1852*. Washington, D.C.: Armstrong, 1853.

United States Congress, House. *Speech of Hon. William A. Oldfield of Arkansas in the House of Representatives, March 4, 1925*.

United States Congress, Senate. *Japanese Immigration Legislation Hearings Before the Committee on Immigration. 68th Congress, 1st Session, March 11–15, 1924.*

United States Senate. Document no. 603. *The Code of the People's Rule. 61st Congress, 2nd Session, May 31, 1910.*

United States Department of State. *Documentary History of the Constitution of the United States of America, 1787–1870.* Washington, D.C.: Department of State, 1894.

Vance, Louis Joseph. *The Brass Bowl.* Indianapolis: Bobbs-Merrill, 1907.

Vasili, Paul. *Berlin Society.* New York: S. W. Green's Son, 1884.

Viljoen, Ben J. *An Exiled General.* St. Louis, MO: A. Noble, 1906.

Vizetelly, Frank H. *A Desk-Book of Errors in English.* New York: Funk & Wagnalls, 1906.

———. *New Standard Encyclopedia.* 25 vols. New York: Funk & Wagnalls, 1931.

———. *New Standard Encyclopedia Year Book (1932–36).* New York: Funk & Wagnalls, n.d.

Volney, C. F. *The Ruins; or, Meditation on the Revolution of Empires.* New York: Isaac H. Blanchard, n.d.

Wack, Henry Wellington. *The Story of the Congo Free State.* New York: G. P. Putnam's Sons, 1905.

Wagner, Charles. *The Simple Life.* New York: J. S. Ogilvie, 1904.

Walcott, Earle Ashley. *Blindfolded.* Indianapolis: Bobbs-Merrill, 1906.

Walford, Lucy B. *A Bubble.* New York: Frederick A. Stokes, 1895.

Ward, Elizabeth Stuart [formerly Phelps]. *The Gates Ajar.* Boston: Fields, Osgood & Company, 1869.

Ward, Mrs. Humphry. *Lady Rose's Daughter: A Novel.* New York: Harper & Brothers, 1903.

Warden, Florence. *The House on the Marsh.* New York: Munro's Sons, n.d.

Watanna, Onoto. *The Wooing of Wistaria.* New York: Harper, 1902.

Watts, Mary S. *Nathan Burke.* New York: Grosset & Dunlap, 1910.

Weaver, George S. *The Lives and Graves of Our Presidents.* Chicago: National Book Concern, 1896.

Webster, Noah. *An American Dictionary of the English Language.* Chicago: Hill, n.d.

Wetherell, Elizabeth. *Queechy.* Philadelphia: J. B. Lippincott, 1866.

Weyman, Stanley J. *The Abbess of Vlaye.* New York: Longmans, Green & Company, 1904.

———. *The House of the Wolf.* New York: Munro's Sons, n.d.

White, C. A. *The Student's Mythology: A Compendium of Greek, Roman, Egyptian, Assyrian, Persian, Hindoo, Chinese, Thibetian, Scandinavian, Celtic, Aztec, and Peruvian Mythologies, in Accordance with Standard Authorities. Arranged for the Use of Schools and Academies.* New York: W. J. Widdleton, 1879.

White, Stewart E. *The Blazed Trail.* New York: McClure, Phillips & Company, 1903.

Whitehill, Dorothy. *Mary Cinderella Brown: A Novel.* New York: D. Appleton & Company, 1923.

Whiteing, Richard. *No. 5 John Street*. New York: Century, 1899.

Whiting, Lilian. *From Dream to Vision of Life*. Boston: Little, Brown, 1906.

Whitford, William C. *Colorado Volunteers in the Civil War: The New Mexico Campaign of 1862*. Denver: State Historical and Natural History Society, 1906.

Whittier, John Greenleaf. *The Tent on the Beach and Other Poems*. Boston: Ticknor & Fields, 1867.

Wiggin, Kate Douglas. *Rebecca of Sunnybrook Farm*. Boston: Houghton Mifflin, 1904.

Wilde, Oscar. *The Ballad of Reading Gaol*. New York: Roycroft Shop, 1905.

Williams, Henry Smith. *The Book of Marvels*. New York: Funk & Wagnalls, 1931.

Wilson, Harry Leon. *The Spenders: A Tale of the Third Generation*. New York: Grosset & Dunlap, 1902.

Wilson, Rufus R. *Lincoln in Portraiture*. New York: Press of the Pioneers, 1935.

Wilstach, Frank J. *Wild Bill Hickok*. New York: Doubleday, Page & Company, 1926.

Winchester, Dean E. *New Mexico School of Mines, Bulletin no. 9: The Oil and Gas Resources of New Mexico*. Socorro: New Mexico School of Mines, 1933.

Winter, John Strange. *The Truth-Tellers: A Novel*. Philadelphia: J. B. Lippincott, 1896.

Wiseman, Cardinal Nicholas P. *Fabiola*. New York: D. & J. Sadlier, 1875.

Wister, Mrs. A. L.[42] *The Alpine Fay: A Romance*. Philadelphia: J. B. Lippincott, 1895.

———. *Banned and Blessed*. Philadelphia: J. B. Lippincott, 1895.

———. *Countess Erika's Apprenticeship*. Philadelphia: J. B. Lippincott, 1891.

Wister, Owen. *The Virginian*. New York: Macmillan, 1902.

Woods, Katharine Pearson. *Metzerott, Shoemaker*. New York: T. Y. Crowell & Company, 1889.

Wright, Harold Bell. *The Calling of Dan Matthews*. New York: A. L. Burt, 1909.

———. *The Shepherd of the Hills*. New York: A. L. Burt, 1907.

Zweig, Stefan. *Mary Queen of Scotland and the Isles*. New York: Viking Press, 1935.

OTHER PRINTED MATTER IN THE OTERO PAPERS

American Kennel Gazette. April 1, 1936, issue.

Bismarck Hotel. "Song Folder." [Music]

Coronado Cuarto Centennial First Annual Report. 1935.

Coronado Magazine. 1935.

De Valera Wheelright, Catherine. *A Mother's Appeal for Her Son. Delivered in Washington, D.C., on May 4, 1924, at a Mass Meeting of Protest Against the Imprisonment of President De Valera and Over 1000 Irish Patriots*. Published by the American Association for the Recognition of the Irish Republic.

Love Affairs of King Henry VIII. Ten-Cent Pocket Series, no. 286. Girard, KS: Haldeman-Julius Company, n.d.

McGarry, William Rutledge. *Our Submerged and Paramount Issues: Being the Concluding Letter in the Correspondence upon the Cost and Danger of Religious Bigotry in Our Politics*. Silver Spring, MD: Press of the Maryland Publishing Company, 1928.

Monitor. June 1940 issue.

National Geographic. No issues kept, but there is record of his subscription from 1935, which means he would have received issues of the magazine for at least that year.

New Mexico Scottish Rite Bulletin, 22:3 (May–June 1940).

Panama Canal Record, 13:23 (1920).

Sambusco Talks, December 1938.

Taylor, Tell. "Down by the Old Millstream." [Music sheet, autographed]

OTHER BOOKS, PLAYS, AND AUTHORS
MENTIONED BY OTERO[43]

Addison, Joseph. "The Campaign."[44]

Anghiera, Pietro Martire. *The Decades of the New World.**

Archenholz, Wilhelm von.*

Bancroft, Hubert H. *History of Arizona and New Mexico.**

Banim, John. *Damon and Pythias.*[45]

Barrie, James M. *Peter Pan.*[46]

Brininstool, E. A.[47]

Burney, James.*

Burns, Robert. "To a Mouse."[48]

Burns, Walter N. *The Saga of Billy the Kid.*[49]

Burton, Richard. *The English Heroe; or, Sir Francis Drake Revived.**

Camden, William.*

Charlevoix, Pierre François Xavier de. *History of Santo Domingo.**

Colón, Cristóbal. *Diario de a bordo.* Translated by Bartolomé de las Casas.*

Conway, Jay T. *A Brief Community History of Raton, New Mexico, 1880–1930: Commemorating Her Fiftieth Birthday.*[50]

Cooper, James Fenimore. *The Last of the Mohicans.*[51]

Dampier, William.*

Dryden, John.[52]

Dumas, Alexandre, *père. The Three Musketeers.*[53]

Evelyn, John.*

Fernández de Oviedo, Gonzalo. *Historia general y natural de las Indias.**

Fletcher, Francis. *The World Encompassed by Sir Francis Drake.**

Full Relation of Another Voyage into the West Indies Made by Sir Francis Drake from Plimouth, 28 Aug, 1595, A. London, 1652.*

Gay, John. *Fables.*[54]

Gilbert, William S. *H.M.S. Pinafore.*

———. *The Mikado.*[55]

Grosvenor, Charles Henry, ed. *William McKinley: His Life and Work.*[56]

Hakluyt, Richard.*

Halleck, Fitz-Greene. "On the Death of Joseph Rodman Drake."[57]

Hammond, George P., and Thomas Donnelly. *The Story of New Mexico.*[58]

Hay, John Milton. "Jim Bludso of the Prairie Belle," in *Pike County Ballads and Other Pieces.*[59]

Herrera y Tordesillas, Antonio de. *Historia generalde los hechos de los castellanos en las islas i tierra firme del mar oceano.**

Hervé [Florimond Ronger]. *Chilpéric.*[60]

Jaramillo, Juan. *Relación.**

L., H. W. "Ode to the Governor."[61]

Lanier, Sydney. "Psalm of the West: V."*

Laughton, John Knox. *Dictionary of National Biography.**

Mahony, Francis. "The Sweet Bells of Chandon."[62]

Markham, Clements R.*

Meek, Sam Cary. "We Are Coming Governor Otero!"[63]

Montgomery, James. "The West Indies."*

Nichols, Philip. *Sir Francis Drake Revived.**

Núñez Cabeza de Vaca, Álvar.[64]

Pepys, Samuel. *Diary.*[65]

Prescott, William H. *The Conquest of Peru.**

Prince, LeBaron Bradford.[66]

Raynal, Abbé.*

Read, Benjamin M. *Illustrated History of New Mexico.*[67]

Robertson, William. *The History of America.**

Rowe, Nicholas. *The Fair Penitent.*[68]

Sharp, Bartholomew. *The Voyages and Adventures of Capt. Barth. Sharp.**

Siringo, Charles A. *The History of Billy the Kid.*[69]

Spenser, Edmund.[70]

Spenser, Willard. *The Little Tycoon.*[71]

Stedman, Edmund C. "Oh, What a Set of Vagabundos."*

Stephens, Henry P. *Billee Taylor.*[72]

Volmöller, Karl. *The Miracle.*[73]

Walker, J. *History of the Buccaneers of America.* London, 1810.*

Wallace, Lewis.[74]

PERIODICALS, PUBLISHERS, EDITORS, AND PRINTERS MENTIONED BY OTERO

Alamogordo News.[75]

Albuquerque American.[76]

Albuquerque Citizen.[77]

Albuquerque Journal.[78]

Albuquerque Review.[79]

American Mercury.[80]

Arizona Gazette.[81]

Arizona Republican.[82]

Associated Press.[83]

Bandera Americana, La.[84]

Berger, William M.[85]
Blackwood, James.[86]
Blackwood's Magazine.[87]
Burns, Walter N.[88]
Carlsbad Argus.[89]
Chama Tribune.[90]
Chicago Journal.[91]
Chicago Times-Herald.[92]
Chicago Tribune.[93]
Clayton Enterprise.[94]
Collier, T. W.[95]
Collier's.[96]
Daily New Mexican.[97]
Daily Optic.[98]
Deming Headlight.[99]
Denver News.[100]
Denver Press.[101]
Denver Republican.[102]
Denver Times.[103]
Doña Ana County Republican.[104]
Elizabeth Town Miner.[105]
El Paso Times.[106]
Farmington Hustler.[107]
Fergusson, Harvey.[108]
Field and Farm.[109]
Fort Sumner Review.[110]
Friend, Edward.[111]
Frontier.[112]
Frost, Max.[113]
Globe-Democrat (St. Louis).[114]
Gringo and Greaser.[115]
Holmes, J. C.[116]
Hubbell, Frank.[117]
Hughes, J. D.[118]
Hyde, Albert E.[119]
Independiente, El (Las Vegas).[120]
Inter Ocean.[121]
Kistler, Russ A.[122]
Kusz, Charles G.[123]

Las Vegas Examiner.[124]
Las Vegas Record.[125]
Las Vegas Republican.[126]
Lordsburg Liberal.[127]
Los Angeles Times.[128]
Martin.[129]
McKinley County Republican.[130]
Montoya, Néstor.[131]
New Mexican (Santa Fe).[132]
New Mexico Review.[133]
New York Clipper.[134]
New York World.[135]
Otero County Advertiser.[136]
Otero Optic.[137]
Pecos Valley Stockgrower.[138]
Pecos Valley Stockman.[139]
Porter, Guy.[140]
Prescott Mining Courier.[141]
Pueblo Chieftain.[142]
Raton Independent.[143]
Raton Range.[144]
Red River Prospector.[145]
Rio Grande Republican.[146]
Rocky Mountain News.[147]
San Marcial Bee.[148]
Santa Fe Capital.[149]
Sheridan, Joe J.[150]
Sol de Mayo, El.[151]
Springer Sentinel.[152]
Stockman.[153]
Taos Cresset.[154]
Tribune.[155]
Trinidad News.[156]
Trinidad Times.[157]
United States Journal for Investors.[158]
Upson, Ash.[159]
Washington Post.[160]
Washington Star.[161]
Wilcox. Lute.[162]

A BRIEF ANALYSIS OF THE OTERO FAMILY LIBRARY

The Legacy of Miguel A. Otero I

I have found no records detailing which books in Otero's family library were inherited from his father. The only title that we know for sure belonged to Otero I is William A. Bell's *New Tracks in North America*, since Otero II tells us as much in *My Life on the Frontier, 1882–1897*.[163] But Otero I, an educated man who taught Greek and Latin at Fishkill on the Hudson,[164] must have assembled his own book collection during his lifetime. As his son, and as the executor of his estate, Miguel A. Otero II may have had privileged access to that collection, and he may have kept some volumes for himself and his family.

An area where these legacies are likely to have occurred is that of books on Freemasonry, since both father and son were masons. It is possible that the oldest titles in this area in Otero's library might have belonged to his father. These would include such volumes as M. Walcott Redding's *Ecce Orienti!* (1870), *Morals and Dogma of the Ancient and Accepted Scottish Rite of Freemasonry* (1871), and Robert Morris's *Freemasonry in the Holy Land* (1872). By contrast, more recent titles like *Ancient and Accepted Scottish Rite* (1916) doubtless belonged to Otero II.

Following a similar chronological line of reasoning, one could be tempted to ascribe all books published before the 1880 to the library of Miguel A. Otero I, but the possibility that Otero II might have acquired them at a later date (as old books) cannot be discounted and, in fact, is quite likely in many cases. A few titles, however, give us additional reasons to think that they could have belonged to Otero I, or, at least, that he could have bought them for his then-young children. One of them is Joseph Belcher's *Facts for Boys* (1865), a book printed when Otero II was only six years old, which his father could have purchased for his benefit and/or that of his siblings. The same can be said of Mrs. Bradley's *Handsome Is That Handsome Does* (1868), another book for children with a strong emphasis on moral education. It is unlikely that Otero II would have bought such old books for his own children in the 1890s, and so it seems reasonable to think that they might have been purchased by his father. In this same category of children's books we could add to the list of potential legacies S. E. Dawes's *Hours with Mamma* (1865) and Edouard Laboulaye's *Fairy Book* (1867), to which I will return later. Juvenile books like Mary and Elizabeth Kirby's *The World at Home* (1873), E. J. May's *Bertram Noel: A Story for Youth* and *Mortimer's College Life* (both from 1870), and school-oriented tomes like Joseph A. Lyons's *The American Elocutionist and Dramatic Reader for the Use of Colleges, Academies, and Schools* (1874) are also good candidates to be considered possible gifts of the senior Otero to his adolescent son(s). It is also possible that the twenty-four-volume set of the *Encyclopaedia Britannica* from 1878 might have belonged to Otero I, perhaps for his own use or, most likely, for the benefit of his offspring.

Mary T. A. Carroll's *Glimpses of Pleasant Homes* (1869) is also likely to be a legacy from the paternal library. Otero II would not marry until two decades later, and it is unlikely that he would buy this type of household-oriented book before then. The same could be said about Pye H. Chavasse's *Advice to a Wife* (1877), a book that might have been intended for Otero's sister, Mamie Josephine.

In addition to domestic, school, and children's books, it would be reasonable to think that some of the older literature books in Otero II's library could have belonged to his father, especially given the latter's expertise in classical literature. Candidates in this category would be Dante's *Inferno* in an edition from 1860; perhaps Bernardin de Saint-Pierre's *Paul and Virginia* (an 1860 edition); and the five-volume set of *French Classics* edited by Gustave Masson (1876).

I am aware of the speculative nature of this section and, in consequence, of its potential pitfalls. However, I would find it strange if Bell's *New Tracks in North America* were the only book belonging to Miguel A. Otero I that his son would have kept. In the absence of records that would permit us to trace the provenance of the books one way or the other, educated guesses like the ones above may well be all we can offer.

Main Features of the Otero Family Library

The inheritance of some of Otero I's books, and the presence of books for different members of Otero II's household, suggest the convenience of referring to the Otero library as a *family* library rather than a *personal* library. The collection as a whole paints the portrait of a well-educated family for whom reading must have been a pleasurable and regular occupation involving all of its members. In this final section, I will discuss library holdings by thematic categories, analyzing what they tell us about the reading tastes of one of territorial New Mexico's most influential households.

Creative Literature

The largest section of the Otero family library is composed of novels, poetry, collections of short stories, anthologies, and other literary works. As a group, these texts satisfied the very different tastes of several family members, although determining who in the household liked what remains difficult beyond what we know from comments on some of these books made by Otero II. With that reservation in mind, several general parameters can be safely established.

The presence of ancient and modern classics indicates an appreciation for quality literature and/or a desire to furnish the library with time-sanctioned and critically acclaimed books. As mentioned above, some of these titles might have belonged to Otero I, but there is no reason to suppose that readers in the younger Otero's household could not enjoy Dante's poetry or Shakespeare's plays. A conscious desire to stock the shelves with this type of literature is evident from the presence of several compendia of masterpieces, such as Gustave Masson's *French Classics*, Mee, Hammerton, and McClure's *The World's Greatest Books*, the *Museum of Foreign Literature and Science*, Jeannette Gilder's *Masterpieces of the World's Best Literature*, and even *Half-Hours with Great Novelists* and James Baldwin's *Old Greek Stories*. The slight educational bent of these titles is complemented by John Hammerton's *An Outline of English Literature: Being a Chronicle of Great Writers from the Time of Chaucer to the Present Day, with a Casual Commentary*, the only literary history/criticism title in the collection, which must have guided the family's appreciation for the English classics. But, beyond those compilations, the Otero library reveals its depth with titles by American and foreign authors like Adelbert von Chamisso, the de Goncourt brothers, Alphonse Daudet, Henry Fielding, Thomas Hardy, Samuel Taylor Coleridge, Bret Harte, O. Henry, Vladimir Korolenko, Henry Wadsworth Longfellow, Maurice Maeterlinck, John Milton, Bernardin de Saint-Pierre, Jonathan Swift, Alfred Tennyson, William Makepeace Thackeray, John Greenleaf Whittier, and Oscar Wilde, among others.

Some titles in this category deserve special commentary because of their added value as we attempt to reconstruct what they may have meant for their owners and what they may tell us about literary tastes at the time. Cervantes's *Don Quixote*, for instance, is the only book from the Spanish-language literary tradition in the Otero library. This is somewhat surprising, considering that Otero's grandfather was born in Spain, but it may be indicative of the Otero family's firm allegiance to the United States; in fact, as far as the Otero library is concerned, *Don Quixote* may not even be representative of the Hispanic literary tradition at all, and its presence may be due to its status as a universal classic, not unlike that of Shakespeare's plays.

The *Works of Tobias Smollett*, likewise, may merit closer scrutiny considering Smollett's influence on Dickens. As mentioned earlier, Dickens was Otero's favorite author, and the acquisition of Smollett's works may signal Otero's desire to better understand that influence. Alongside Walter Scott's novels, Mark Twain's books, and Moritz Retzsch's *Illustrations to Goethe's Faust*, it is probably safe to say that *The Works of Tobias Smollett* and *Don Quixote* were read by Otero himself, and other family members may have enjoyed them as well.

By contrast, more than forty books in the Otero library belong to the romance genre or to the domestic fiction subgenre. In all likelihood, these must have been books favored by the female members of the Otero household, even if other readers may have found them of interest as well. The list of titles in this category is too long to explore in detail, but included are Florence L. Barclay's *The Mistress of Shenstone*, Charlotte M. Braeme's *The Squire's Darling*, Duchess's *Beauty's Daughters*, and Geoffrey Drage's *Cyril: a Romantic Novel*. Class status ensured all members of the Otero family leisure time to read, and books of this type must have provided numerous hours of entertainment for them.

Somewhat related to the domestic narratives but much more didactic in purpose are literary works that played a formative role as far as religious, moral, and spiritual matters were concerned. More than a dozen titles can be considered part of this group, including Marie Corelli's *God's Good Man*, Jane A. Eames's *Sarah Barry's Home*, the very popular *Unleavened Bread* by Robert Grant, and several books by J. H. Ingraham and by Minnie Mary Lee. Many of these texts were printed by religious presses such as the Catholic Publication Society, the Protestant Episcopal S. S. Union and Church Book Society, the American Baptist Society, and the American Tract Society, which reveals a continuous (although apparently somewhat diverse) involvement with faith in the Otero family.

Also didactic, to a certain extent, are the close to thirty children's and young adult books in the library. In keeping with publishing trends at the time, moral lessons and norms of behavior were commonly introduced to young readers through otherwise entertaining books.[165] Titles such as E. J. May's *Bertram Noel: A Story for Youth*, for example, do little to disguise their utilitarian intention, as the author acknowledges in the preface: "If the views intended to be set forth in a story do not plainly declare themselves in the body of the work, it is to be feared that no prefatory elucidation will do much to improve matters."[166] The same could be said of Mrs. Bradley's *Handsome Is That Handsome Does* (part of the Proverb Series published by Lee & Shepard), whose ending suggests a precise role for the reader, who is expected to deliberate along with the protagonist: "She sat silent, pondering with sudden conviction the truth that had come home to her in these chance words,—*Handsome Is That Handsome Does*."[167]

But other books for young readers in the library openly exceed their moral and conventional roles, as they deal in more ambivalent and progressive terms with such issues as gender roles (as is the case with the books by Julia Kavanagh) or sex and school (as in Rudyard Kipling's *Stalky & Co.*). Others fall into the reference or textbook category, best exemplified by Richard Green Parker's *Aids to English Composition* and C. A. White's *The Student Mythology*. Others, in turn, partake in the general interest in geography and society that I will discuss in more detail below, as with Bruce E. Mahan and Ruth A. Gallaher's *Stories of Iowa for Boys and Girls* and Mary and Elizabeth Kirby's *The World at Home*.

Still, for me, the most interesting title in this area of the collection is Edouard Laboulaye's *Fairy Book*. A few years ago, in an article entitled "Chicano/a Children's Literature: A *Transaztlantic* Reader's History" (2006), I advocated an approach to Chicano/a children's literature from a framework that transcended nationalism and that accounted for children's books *read* by Chicanos/as (in addition to those authored by them).[168] A history written from that kind of perspective, I suggested, would emphasize the rhizomatic connections beyond and across national and cultural traditions that allow us to map what texts people from a certain group read and valued, regardless of their authors' national origins. As a small example of this process, I discussed José Martí's *La Edad de Oro*, considered by many the first U.S. Latino/a children's magazine. While analyzing the contents of *La Edad de Oro*, I suggested the inclusion of texts by non-Hispanic authors, Laboulaye among them: "And if Martí did not hesitate to incorporate fantastic tales by French writer [Edouard] René Lefebvre de Laboulaye (1811–1883) in the pages of *La Edad de Oro* it is, no doubt, because French children's literature already enjoyed a degree of success in Spain and Latin America."[169] Finding Laboulaye's tales among the books owned by this prominent New Mexican family (of Spanish descent) not only confirms the popularity of the Frenchman but also strengthens my call for empirical research to trace the actual presence of books in public and private libraries, as it is only through evidence of this kind that we will be able to paint an accurate picture of the reading practices and preferences of Chicanos/as and Hispanic Americans in general.

Well represented as well in the Otero library (within the creative literature category) is historical fiction, with books ranging from ancient Rome (e.g., Wiseman's *Fabiola*, Sienkiewicz's *Quo Vadis*, and Saltus's *Imperial Purple*) to the very contemporary, as in Peter B. Kyne's *The Pride of Palomar*, a 1921 California hacienda novel in which one of the characters dies in Siberia fighting the Bolsheviks.[170] In between those two poles, we find books about many other historical periods and events, including World War I (Bailey's *The Tin Soldier*), the so-called Indian Wars in Arizona (Overton's *The Heritage of Unrest*), and the Franco-Prussian War of 1870 (in Halévy's *L'abbé Constantin*), among others.

Alongside this interest in history of the Oteros as readers, I have already mentioned their curiosity for books about other places, both domestic and foreign. Many of the novels in their library stand out precisely for the variety of locales in which they are set and for the role that those geographical settings play in their plots and/or in the society they represent. Included in this subgroup are tales of the woods in Michigan (White, *The Blazed Trail*), high society in Indiana (Tarkington, *The Magnificent Ambersons*), the Great Plains (Mackie's *Sinners Twain* and the very popular *The Virginian* by Owen Wister), New England (Sidney's *The Pettibone Name*), Alaska (Beach, *The Iron Trail*), Canada (Connor's *Black Rock* and *The Man from Glengarry*), and, of course, New Mexico and the rest of the Southwest, in novels such as Edith Nicholl Ellison's *The Blossoming of the Waste*, Sue Greenleaf's *Wed by Mighty Waves*, and Alfred Henry Lewis's *Wolfville*. The South is also well represented in the two books by Albion W. Tourgée, both focused on Reconstruction (and therefore also relevant as historical fiction), and in the works by Thomas Nelson Page, a chief champion of the Lost Cause.

The Otero library was also well stocked with fiction that dwelled upon contested social issues such as prison reform (as in *Dr. Sevier* by George W. Cable—an author who shared public readings with Mark Twain), divorce (fiercely opposed by Paul Bourget in his *roman à thèse* of that title), animal cruelty (Marshall Saunders's *Beautiful Joe*), and industrial conflict (Meredith Nicholson's *The Lords of High Decision*). Social critique is likewise at the heart of Ouida's *Puck*, a novel told from the perspective of the dog whose name provides the book's title.

Poetry books, although not particularly abundant in the Otero library, are nonetheless present with some influential books by Coleridge, Dante, Longfellow, Milton, Whittier, and Wilde, indicating—at least—an occasional engagement with verse in this family's reading habits.

Finally, I would be remiss not to point out that there are many other authors and genres represented in the creative literature section of the library (e.g., humor, detective fiction, and theater), but space constraints do not permit me to discuss them here.

Western Americana

Moving on to the nonfiction side of the collection, it comes as no surprise that one of the strongest areas would be that of Western Americana. Because of Otero's interest in the figure of Billy the Kid and because of his family's role in the development of the American West, more than fifty volumes in the collection are devoted to Western history, biography, and general reference (e.g., the *Encyclopedia of the New West*) about the lands then still recently conquered by the United States. Among these books, we can appreciate an interest for Native American peoples, represented by titles such as William E. Connelley's *Wyandot Folk-Lore*, John C. Cremony's *Life Among the Apaches*, Uriah S. Hollister's *The Navajo and His Blanket*, Fanny Kelly's *Narrative of My Captivity Among the Sioux Indians*, Horatio Oliver Ladd's *Chunda: A Story of the Navajos*, T. Mitchell Prudden's *On the Great American Plateau*, Ruth M. Underhill's *First Penthouse Dwellers of America*, and Adolph F. A. Bandelier's *The Gilded Man*. The same is true for books about Spanish exploration and settlement of the Southwest, including the Bandelier text just mentioned, Nina Otero's *Old Spain in Our Southwest*, and Ruth L. Barker's *Caballeros*.

But the strength for this section is in the so-called Wild West that young Otero knew firsthand, and that clearly fascinated him, as is evident in his autobiography and in his book about Billy the Kid. Some of the Western characters in Otero's library include Calamity Jane (see Duncan Aikman), Kit Carson (in books by George D. Brewerton, Charles Burdett, and Maurice G. Fulton), Harry Tracy (see W. N. Carter), George W. Coe (through his autobiography), "Uncle Dick" Wootton (see Howard L. Conard), H. A. W. Tabor (see Lewis Cass Gandy's *The Tabors*), Charles Goodnight (see J. Evetts Haley's book of that title), Butch Cassidy (see Charles Kelly's *Outlaw Trail*), and Wild Bill Hickok (see Frank J. Wilstach). William M. Raine's *Famous Sheriffs and Western Outlaws* also provides a vivid representation of many Wild West characters. To this roster of legendary historical figures we should add General George Armstrong Custer, the subject of Elizabeth B. Custer's *Tenting on the Plains*, and the general portrait of the land and selected individuals in the short stories of Henry Inman (*Tales of the Trail*). Although technically literature, the cowboy novels of Florence Finch Kelly (*With Hoops of Steel*) and Paul L. Ford's *The Great K. & A. Train Robbery* fit here as well, as does D. M. Kelsey's *History of Our Wild West*.

Plentiful as well are books about the pioneering experiences of settlers in all parts of the West, from Estelline Bennett's South Dakota (as portrayed in her *Old Deadwood Days*), Nathaniel Pitt Langford's Montana (*Vigilante Days and Ways*), and W. W. Mills's *Forty Years at El Paso*, to the most immediate Colorado–New Mexico narratives of Philip A. Bailey (*Golden Mirages*), Blanche C. Grant (*When Old Trails Were New*), and James F. Hinkle (*Early Days of a Cowboy on the Pecos*).

Exploration and the description of natural resources, an area of particular interest to Otero, are represented by William A. Bell's *New Tracks in North America* (which also contributed a railroad topic that the Otero family must have appreciated as part of their own experience), Rufus C. Hopkins's *Muniments of Title of the Barony of Arizona*, Fayette Alexander Jones's *New Mexico Mines and Minerals*, Dean E. Winchester's *New Mexico School of Mines*, and, of course, Eva Emery Dye's book about Lewis and Clark.

Last but not least, New Mexico and its history received a special place in the collection, whether through acquisition or, perhaps, through the presentation of certain volumes to Otero as governor and public figure. Likely gifts are Max Frost and Paul A. F. Walter's *The Land of Sunshine* and *Santa Fe County*, especially given Otero's friendship with Frost.[171] Maurice Fulton and Paul Horgan's edited volume, *New Mexico's Own Chronicle*, is one of the library's several history books about the state, to which we could add George W. Kendall's *Narrative of the Texan Santa Fe Expedition*, Horatio

Oliver Ladd's *The Story of New Mexico*, L. Bradford Prince's *Historical Sketches of New Mexico*, and Ralph Emerson Twitchell's *The Leading Facts of New Mexican History* and *The History of the Military Occupation of the Territory of New Mexico*, among others.

History and Biography[172]

Otero's penchant for books of a historical nature makes this one of the richest subdivisions of his family library. Foreign and classical histories and biographies include Henry Houssaye's *Cleopatra*, the acclaimed *History of the Decline and Fall of the Roman Empire* by Edward Gibbon, H. A. Guerber's *The Story of the Romans*, Jacob Abbott's *History of Margaret of Anjou*, James Eugene Farmer's *Essays on French History*, David Hume's *The History of England*, Tobias Smollett's *The History of England from the Revolution to the Death of George the Second*, *Scenes and Narrations from German History*, Francis Greene's *Report on the Russian Army and Its Campaigns in Turkey*, and Henry Wellington Wack's *The Story of the Congo Free State*, as well as general titles such as C. F. Volney's *The Ruins; or, Meditations on the Revolutions of Empires*, Thomas Carlyle's *On Heroes*, and *The Illustrated World History* by John Hammerton and Harry Barnes.

In this category, I have set apart those books focused on Latin(o) America, since the "foreign" label may not convey the rapport that Otero might have felt for them. These titles include studies on the Spanish conquest of present-day U.S. territory (Irving's *The Conquest of Florida by Hernando de Soto*), several books on Panama that must have been of special value for a man who lived in that country for years (Anderson's *Old Panama and Castilla del Oro*, Arosemena's *Panama in 1915*, Gause and Carr's *The Story of Panama*, and Scoullar's *El "Libro azul" de Panamá*—a bilingual book), and others on Mexico (Ladd's *History of the War with Mexico*) and Hispanic New Mexico (Sánchez's *Memorias sobre la vida del presbítero don Antonio José Martínez*, a rare Spanish-language title in the collection).

More numerous are books on U.S. history and biography, and they range from very specific (the biography of one individual, the story of a state) to panoramic approaches to life and history. Among the former, we could cite L. P. Brockett's *The Life and Times of Abraham Lincoln*, Joel Tyler Headley's *The Life and Travels of General Grant*, and Mary Synon's *McAdoo, the Man and His Times*. There are also some autobiographies, including Alexander K.

McClure's *Recollections of Half a Century*, Henry Clay McDougal's *Recollections, 1844–1909*, and Ulysses S. Grant's *Personal Memoirs*. Among the histories of individual states we find J. A. C. Chandler's *Makers of Virginia History*, Clara Hazelrigg's *A New History of Kansas*, and Anna J. Hardwicke-Pennybacker's *New History of Texas for Schools*. More general titles range from reference volumes (*The Compendium of American Genealogy*, *The National Cyclopedia of American Biography*) to national histories (Hudson Maxim's *Defenseless America*, George Weaver's *The Lives and Graves of Our Presidents*), and even transnational titles like Alexander Exquemeling's already cited *History of the Buccaneers of America*.

Government, Law, and Politics

The titles I am grouping in this section share an emphasis on the historical record with those discussed in the preceding two but, in this case, they are more directly associated with legislative, executive, and judicial powers and activities. Many of these books are compilations of documents and records (e.g., *Acts of the Legislature Assembly of the Territory of New Mexico* and Thomas Cochran's *Legislative Handbook and Manual of the State of Pennsylvania*) that Otero obviously kept for reference. Others are devoted to individual and group experiences in politics, such as James J. Blaine's *Twenty Years of Congress* and Francis Curtis's *The Republican Party, 1854–1904*. Otero's interest in law is also seen in practical titles that, rather than compiling legislative records, serve as self-help introductions to the workings of the law. Such books include Albert S. Bolles's *Everybody's Legal Adviser* and *Putnam's Handy Lawbook for the Layman*.

General Reference

As in any other private library, reference books in this collection satisfy diverse needs for different family members. For the benefit of the entire family we find the sixteen-volume *Encyclopedia Americana* edited by Frederick Converse Beach, the *Encyclopaedia Britannica*, and Frank H. Vizetelly's *New Standard Encyclopedia*. The library is also well equipped with writing tools, including a *Comprehensive Standard Dictionary of the English Language*, Noah Webster's *American Dictionary of the English Language*, and such useful tools as a *Dictionary of Select and Popular Quotations*, John Bartlett's *Familiar Quotations*, and Vizetelly's *Desk-Book of Errors in English*. A different type of writing is the subject of John Jenkins's *The New Clerk's Assistant; or, Book of Practical Forms*. Writing properly and effectively was much appreciated in the society to which the Oteros belonged, and we can see in titles like these a deliberate attempt to improve the family's communicative skills on paper.

Religious Books

The Otero library contains a considerable number of titles on religion and spirituality. In addition to two copies of the Holy Bible, the New Testament, and *The Book of Common Prayer*, titles in this area include Henry Lasserre's *Our Lady of Lourdes*, Charles Martin's *Catholic Religion*, Abbé Orsini's *Life of the Blessed Virgin Mary*, Ernest Renan's *The Life of Jesus*, James Cardinal Gibbons's *Our Christian Heritage*, and *The History of the Protestant Reformation* by M. J. Spalding, plus religious art books such as Gustave Doré's *The Bible Gallery*. From our present context, perhaps the most curious title among these is Mary Baker Eddy's *Science and Health with Key to the Scriptures*. The majority of works in this category belong to the Roman Catholic faith, but *The History of the Protestant Reformation* must have served to familiarize the Otero family with other ways of understanding Christianity.

Other Books in the Library

Smaller groupings of books that reflect other (reading) interests of the Otero family complete our panorama of the collection. Music, for instance, is represented by titles such as *American Ballad Collection*, *Galaxy of Song*, and Andrew Graham's *The Hand-Book of Standard or American Phonography*. Hunting, one of Otero's passions since his youth, also makes its way into the shelves with works such as Joseph Long's *American Wild-Fowl Shooting*, Adam Bogardus's *Field, Cover, and Trap Shooting*, George Bird Grinnell's *American Duck Shooting*, and the five books by Ernest Thompson Seton. Card games are the subject of several volumes, including C. D. P. Hamilton's *Modern Scientific Whist* and George William Peters's *American Whist*.

Art books in the Otero library reflect, once more, a balance between formative works (e.g., Dionysius Lardner's *Popular Lectures on Science and Art* and Rockwell Kent's *World-Famous Paintings*) and those that indicate a specific interest such as *The Light of the World; or, Our Saviour in Art* (of which the library contains two editions), the already mentioned *Illustrations to Goethe's Faust* by Moritz Retzsch, and Mary J. Serrano's *Marie Bashkirtseff.*

Of these other thematic interests, travel contributes the largest number of volumes to the library, demonstrating, once more, the family's passion for other lands and other peoples. Significant titles in this category include Noah Brooks's *The Mediterranean Trip*, Samuel Crockett's *The Adventurer in Spain*, Bayard Taylor's *Picturesque Europe*, and Charles Taylor's *The British Isles Through an Opera Glass*. As mentioned, Mark Twain's *The Innocents Abroad* is also credited in Otero's writings as a most useful reading for his own travels to the United Kingdom.

Finally, miscellaneous books provide us with a fascinating glimpse into diverse family activities and concerns. W. H. Bates's *The Cure of Imperfect Sight by Treatment Without Glasses*, for instance, reveals how the Oteros coped with loss of vision. Charles Tyrrell's *The Royal Road to Health*, likewise, signals this family's interest in medical alternatives (the book is subtitled *The Secret of Health Without Drugs*). Intriguing, to say the least, is the presence among the shelves of Charles H. Pope's *Solar Heat: Its Practical Applications*, a book that considers the industrial applications of solar energy while identifying the "Western Highland" of the United States as an exceptional region for exploring this alternative source of energy.

But, by far, the most fascinating volume in the entire catalog of the collection is the one identified in its card as *Books I Have Read* (Clippings, n.d.). My attempts to locate this item at the University of New Mexico have been unsuccessful, even with the help of the appropriate librarians, which suggests that this tome was not kept when the collection was processed. The "Clippings" books (printed in Norwood, Massachusetts) were blank volumes to use as scrapbooks or, as the title of one of them suggested, as "Hobby Book[s] for Your Favorite Subject." The one in the Otero library contained, without a doubt, a record of readings by (at least) one member of the family, perhaps Otero himself. Without that information, we cannot know for sure what other books Otero may have read, but, at least, this analysis of his family library allows us to get a better picture of the intellectual life of one of New Mexico's most prominent Hispanic families.

Notes

I would like to express my gratitude to the staff of the Southwest Studies Library (Center for Southwest Research, University of New Mexico) for their assistance during my work with the Otero papers in their collection.

1. Walter Benjamin, *Illuminations* (New York: Schocken Books, 2007).
2. Timothy W. Ryback, *Hitler's Private Library: The Books That Shaped His Life* (New York: Alfred A. Knopf, 2008).
3. For the end of the nineteenth century, see also Francisco A. Lomelí, "A Literary Portrait of Hispanic New Mexico," in *Pasó por aquí: Critical Essays on the New Mexican Literary Tradition, 1542–1988*, ed. Erlinda Gonzales-Berry (Albuquerque: University of New Mexico Press, 1989), 131–48.
4. Manuel M. Martín-Rodríguez, *Life in Search of Readers: Reading (in) Chicano/a Literature* (Albuquerque: University of New Mexico Press, 2003), esp. chapter 5.
5. Manuel M. Martín-Rodríguez, "'A Net Made of Holes': Towards a Cultural History of Chicano Literature," *Modern Language Quarterly* 62:1 (March 2001): 1–18.
6. Martín-Rodríguez, *Life in Search of Readers*, 156.
7. Benjamin, *Illuminations*, 62.
8. Ibid.
9. Ibid., 66.
10. See A. Gabriel Meléndez's essay in this volume for an additional example.
11. Currently housed at the Southwest Studies Library (Center for Southwest Research, University of New Mexico).
12. Cynthia Secor-Welsh, introduction to *My Life on the Frontier, 1864–1882*, by Miguel A. Otero (Albuquerque: University of New Mexico Press, 1987), vii–lxxix.
13. Miguel A. Otero never used the suffix "Sr." to refer to his father or "Jr." to refer to himself; instead, he used roman numerals to distinguish between members of the family with the same name. I have followed that practice here. Whenever I use Otero without a roman numeral, it should be understood that I refer to Governor Otero.
14. Miguel A. Otero, *My Life on the Frontier, 1882–1897* (1939; repr., Santa Fe, NM: Sunstone Press, 2007), 69. Citations refer to the reprint edition.
15. Ibid.
16. Ibid., 76.
17. Secor-Welsh, introduction to *My Life on the Frontier, 1864–1882*, xxx–xxxi.
18. In a 1933 autobiographical sketch kept in box 7 of the Otero papers, Otero says that he finished this work in 1925. The manuscript that I have consulted, in box 5 of the papers, is dated 1927.
19. These references are included below, under the heading "Other Books, Plays, and Authors Mentioned by Otero."

20. Miguel A. Otero, "The Narrative of the Conquistadores of Spain and the Buccaneers of England, France, and Holland" (unpublished manuscript, Otero papers, box 5, folder 14), n.p.

21. I have catalogued all those references in my ongoing Chicano/a Literature Intertextual Database (http://faculty.ucmerced.edu/mmartin-rodriguez/index_ files/CLID.htm), a research work in progress that currently includes more than thirty-one thousand references to print culture in works by Chicanos/as.

22. Secor-Welsh, introduction to *My Life on the Frontier, 1864–1882*, lx.

23. Ibid., lxiii.

24. Space constraints prevent me from engaging in a deeper analysis of the Otero library, which I reserve for a future publication.

25. Many of the authors' names are pseudonyms. Books and/or author names in bold are those that Otero mentions in his publications or manuscripts.

26. Cited in Otero's unpublished manuscripts.

27. In *My Life on the Frontier, 1882–1897*, Otero says the following about this title: "After arranging for our transportation we stepped into the bar of the Westminster Hotel, and, to our great surprise, who should we run into but Dr. P. A. Ames, of Las Vegas, New Mexico; Dr. William A. Bell, M.A.; and M. B. Cantab, who edited 'New Tracks in North America,' in two volumes, 1869. Dr. Bell was a great friend of my father and presented to him the two volumes, which I still have in my library" (72).

28. Otero quotes from this book in his *My Life on the Frontier, 1864–1882* (Albuquerque: University of New Mexico Press, 1987), 147.

29. As mentioned, Dickens was Otero's favorite author, and he cites him and his books several times. In *My Life on the Frontier, 1864–1882*, we read: "I can only compare my experiences at this frontier boarding school with those of which Dickens relates in Oliver Twist" (5). Later in the same book, Otero mentions a different novel by Dickens: "Somehow the name 'Dolly Varden' had been fixed upon her by the frequenters of the dance hall, because in those days a style of dress with a loud pattern of bright colors and flowers was called 'Dolly Varden' after the young lady in Dickens' Barnaby Rudge" (72). The second volume of Otero's autobiography contains the three Dickens references mentioned above in the discussion of his trip to London.

30. Cited by Otero in his unpublished "The Narrative of the Conquistadores of Spain and the Buccaneers of England, France, and Holland."

31. This is what Otero had to say about the book in his own *The Real Billy the Kid* (Houston, TX: Arte Público Press, 1998): "Garrett presented the writer with an autographed copy of his book, The Authentic Life of Billy the Kid. When he did so, he said: 'Much of it was gathered from hearsay and "made out of whole cloth."' This book, written by Garrett in 1882, is nevertheless unquestionably the most authentic account of the life and adventures of Billy the Kid ever issued" (5–6).

Some pages later, Otero is much more critical: "When the reader reaches the exact statements made by Garrett after his capture and later, his killing of Billy the Kid, he can judge for himself. Throughout Garrett's own recital one may read between the lines and note the apologies and laudations. All in all, Garrett wants one to believe that duty called him. All of which to the author's mind, is unadulterated rot" (71–73). Otero later quotes Garrett on pages 77–84 of the same book, and then on pages 135–42.

32. From his mention of Edward E. Hale in *My Nine Years as Governor of the Territory of New Mexico, 1897–1906* (1940; repr., Santa Fe, NM: Sunstone Press, 2007), it is unclear whether or not Otero read *The Man Without a Country*, but, considering that he owned a copy of the book and that he held Mr. Hale in great esteem, it is safe to assume that he did. Here is the relevant quotation from Otero: "And the other because I was seated just across from the President at a table with Edward Everett Hale, author of The Man Without a Country. I enjoyed being with Mr. Hale, and loved to hear him talk. He was so interesting and pleasant I can never forget him" (300).

33. Otero cites the Bible several times in his works, in ways that leave no doubt that he was familiar with its texts. References include the following from *My Life on the Frontier, 1864–1882*: "It was received in such condition as to remind him of the passage in the Bible about the crumbs that fell from the table" (6), and "It was as somber and gloomy as were the secrets of Enoch, and the tragedies of that gruesome trail will never be written for the reason that the most of them never came to light" (239). Other quotations, in *My Nine Years as Governor of the Territory of New Mexico* for example, reference the Bible in ways that do not involve Otero directly, as on page 168 (where a Bible is presented as a gift to someone else), or on page 244 (where a telegram received by Otero includes a biblical quotation). In *The Real Billy the Kid*, Otero mentions several people as reading the Bible (55, 57).

34. Otero makes several critical references to Inman's *Tales* in *My Life on the Frontier, 1864–1882*: "Inman, for example, in his *The Old Santa Fé Trail*, adds his bit of embroidery when he writes of the old Indian chief, Two Lance, and his ability to shoot an arrow entirely through a buffalo when running on horseback, that 'he accomplished this remarkable feat in the presence of the Grand Duke Alexis of Russia, who was under the care of Buffalo Bill near Fort Hays, Kans'" (55). Immediately afterward, Otero continues elaborating on the *Tales*: "In another account it states: 'General Sheridan called out from the carriage to Buffalo Bill: "Cody, get in here and show the Duke how you can drive. Reed will exchange places with you and ride your horse." Later, as they approached Medicine Lodge Creek, the General said: "Shake them up a little, Bill, and give us some old-time stage driving." No more was needed. On the horses bounded, faster and faster, until they came to a steep hill which led down into the Valley of the Medicine; straight down the hill they went, bounding along over the ruts, while both General and Prince were kept busy holding on to their seats. In fine old style they

dashed into the camp where they were to obtain a fresh relay, but the Grand Duke begged to be excused from any more of the same kind (of driving)'" (55–56). In his concluding remarks on the subject, Otero clearly states his skepticism about Inman's account: "I am positive that the Grand Duke Alexis and his party never hunted either there or near Fort Hays, as Inman asserts" (56).

35. The first time Otero mentions this book in his *The Real Billy the Kid*, it is someone else who claims having read it: "Mr. Chavez began by commenting on some of the accounts he had read: 'Most of the accounts of the Lincoln County War are far from true. The stories I have read were written by Pat Garrett, Charlie Siringo, Harvey Fergusson and Walter Noble Burns. I have also read the account of the killing of The Kid, published by E. A. Brininstool, which is correct. It was written by John W. Poe, who was with Garrett. All the other accounts are filled with inaccuracies and discrepancies, and do no justice to The Kid'" (121). Otero read the book as well, as the following quotation from *The Real Billy the Kid* demonstrates: "In John W. Poe's *Billy the Kid*, privately printed by E. A. Brininstool of Los Angeles, California, Mr. Poe states that Billy the Kid had both a pistol and the butcher knife, and at one time had the drop on Garrett, but for some reason did not fire. Poe further states: 'I was forcibly impressed with the idea that a Higher Power controls and rules the destinies of men. To me it seemed that what occurred in Fort Sumner that night had been foreordained'" (142).

36. Otero's knowledge of Shakespeare came both from his readings and from attending live performances, like the one he recalls in *My Life on the Frontier, 1864–1882*: "The Frederick Ward Theatrical Company happened to be playing in Las Vegas for a week's engagement at the Rosenthal Theater on Railroad Avenue. The repertoire, as I remember, was made up entirely of Shakespearian tragedies— *Hamlet, King Lear, Macbeth, Julius Caesar* and *Romeo and Juliet*. The theater was crowded every night, and in addition we had a great time entertaining the troupe" (243). Of more significance for our purposes is the following quotation from *Hamlet* from *My Nine Years as Governor of the Territory of New Mexico*: "He was a man, take him for all in all, / I shall not look upon his like again" (178). Later in the same book, Otero mentions Iago (377).

37. No other data recorded for this book. Probably Charles Lamb and Mary Seymour, *Shakespeare Illustrated, with the History of Each Drama* (Chicago: M. A. Donohue, 1889).

38. The only reference to Swift's *Gulliver's Travels* in Otero's writings occurs in *My Life on the Frontier, 1864–1882*: "Before concluding my recollections of Otero, I must relate a good story connected with our old Brobdingnagian denizen of the dance halls referred to in a preceding chapter as Steamboat" (134). While the word "Brobdingnagian" was used in common speech, the fact that Otero owned Swift's *Travels* suggests that, in his case, his characterization of the "Steamboat" comes from a direct reading of the British satirist.

39. Otero quotes from Tennyson's "Locksley Hall" in *My Life on the Frontier, 1882–1897*: "That is truth the poet sings, / That a sorrow's crown is remembering happier things" (72). The quotation may have come from one of the "great books" collections in Otero's library.

40. As mentioned above, Otero had Twain's work in mind during his own travels in London. In *My Life on the Frontier, 1882–1897*, he says: "The following day we visited the great cemetery of Pere la Chaise to find the celebrated tomb of Abelard and Heloise, with its effigies of the lovers lying, at last, side by side in their long sleep. An elaborate story of their love affair is told by Mark Twain in his 'Innocents Abroad, or the New Pilgrims Progress'" (76).

41. Otero quotes from Twitchell's book in *My Nine Years as Governor of the Territory of New Mexico*, 34, 142–43, 226 (where the quotation refers to Twitchell's assessment of Otero as governor), 314, 333, 334. Otero's complicated relationship with Twitchell is best exemplified by the following quotation from *My Nine Years*: "Ralph Emerson Twitchell was anything but an impartial on-looker at the time. He was very bitter against Andrews and heaped abuse on all who did not agree with him. He left the hall without voting, and his account on this convention in the *Leading Facts of New Mexican History* is unjust, unfair, and absolutely false. Yet, he admitted that my candidate proved an excellent man for the place. He says in the book just referred to, volume II, page 545: 'Laboring day and night for his constituents, Mr. Andrews, in his capacity as delegate, has no superior in the Congress of the United States'" (239).

42. Translator, given credit as author in the catalog of the library.

43. I include here books that Otero mentions either in his published works or in his manuscripts but that are not part of the catalogued collection. Otero may have owned copies of these publications at some time prior to the bequest of his books to the University of New Mexico, but there are no records to that effect. The only thing we know for sure is that he read or consulted them. An asterisk (*) after an entry means that Otero cited that particular book in his manuscript "The Narrative of the Conquistadores of Spain and the Buccaneers of England, France, and Holland," dated 1927. Since no record of ownership is available, I list only authors and titles, without other bibliographical information. I have not included names of public figures (e.g., Eleuterio Baca) or relatives (e.g., Nina Otero Warren) who became published authors but are not mentioned by Otero as such.

44. Quoted partially in *My Nine Years as Governor*, 178.

45. This is one of several plays mentioned by Otero in *My Life on the Frontier, 1864–1882*: "Frederick Ward, noticing the great amount of interest taken in the Knights of Pythias, offered to have his troup produce *Damon and Pythias* for the following Saturday-night performance" (243). Otero also mentions operas in his works (*Faust*, for instance, although Otero does not indicate the composer, which makes it difficult to guess which of the several versions was presented; Bizet's *Carmen* and Lecocq's *Giroflé-Girofla* are also mentioned).

46. Otero attended the opening of this play: "On the opening night at the National Theater. Maude Adams was to present *Peter Pan* for the first time, and I secured one of the large private boxes and had the pleasure of taking Mrs. Max Frost, Mrs. Brown, and the three daughters of my good friend, W. Scott Smith. We occupied the upper box on the left side facing the stage. Of course, we had an excellent view of the large crowd in attendance" (303).

47. Cited in *The Real Billy the Kid*, 6.

48. Otero quotes part of the poem in *My Nine Years as Governor*, 172.

49. Mentioned in *The Real Billy the Kid*, 6, 85, 94.

50. In *My Life on the Frontier, 1882–1897*, Otero makes it clear that he read this book: "My friend Mr. William A. Chapman, an old resident of Raton, has materially helped me to present the facts in the bloody encounter, by furnishing me with a copy of *A Brief Community History of Raton, New Mexico*, by Jay T. Conway, covering the period from 1880" (14).

51. The following quotation from *My Life on the Frontier, 1864–1882*, suggests that Otero was at least familiar with Cooper's book: "The last of the pulmonary Mohicans was Jack Crawford, who died only a few years ago" (173).

52. If Otero did not read him, at least he was familiar with his name, as the following quotation from *My Life on the Frontier, 1882–1897*, demonstrates: "We then took in Westminster Abbey and viewed the royal tombs and monuments and memorials of English celebrities, Spenser, Milton, Dryden, Handel, Dickens, Thackeray, and several others" (69).

53. Otero uses Dumas's title as a header for a section of *My Life on the Frontier, 1882–1897*. He then explains why: "My very close associates, in those days, were Fabian and Arthur W. Conger; in fact, we were known as the 'Three Musketeers'" (189).

54. Otero quotes from the *Fables* in *My Life on the Frontier, 1864–1882*: "Look 'round, the wrecks of play behold, / Estates dismembered, mortgaged and sold" (265).

55. For both plays by Gilbert, see note 60.

56. Otero contributed to this book and cites it in *My Nine Years as Governor*, 178.

57. Quoted in *My Life on the Frontier, 1882–1897*, 194.

58. Cited as reference in *My Nine Years as Governor*, 218.

59. Mentioned in *My Nine Years as Governor*, 243.

60. One of the several plays presented by the Las Vegas theatrical company to which Otero belonged, as he reminisced in *My Life on the Frontier, 1882–1897*: "Las Vegas was very busy during these early days, organizing many social clubs and a good sized theatrical company, the principal members of which were: Page B. Otero, D. H. Rust,. Harry J. O'Bryan, Ed Knickerbocker, Ned Groos, and myself; Mrs. Jacob Gross, Hattie Knickerbocker, May G. Dunlop, Mary Dold, Mamie J. Otero, Carrie V. Emmett, Emilie Tetard, Emma Dale Bradsby, besides many other girls and boys to swell the chorus. Our instructor was John D. Hand, from Chicago, a very high class musician, who was also the leader of Hand's Orchestra.

Some of the plays were: *Chilperic, Pinafore, Little Tycoon, Mikado, Billee Taylor,* and two or three others which I am unable to name" (32).

61. This poem, whose author is only identified by initials, is included in *My Nine Years as Governor,* 25–27.

62. Otero quotes this poem in *My Life on the Frontier, 1882–1897,* as he talks about his travels: "The trip was so regulated as to allow us to hear the Bells of Shandon, as we passed close to the Church of Shandon, made famous by the poem of the Rev. Francis Mahony—'The Sweet Bells of Shandon'" (followed by the quotation).

63. This poem is included in *My Nine Years as Governor,* 37–38.

64. Otero mentions him citing a secondary source in *My Nine Years as Governor,* 309.

65. In *My Life on the Frontier, 1864–1882,* Otero quotes from a newspaper article by Lute Wilcox in which Wilcox makes the reference to Pepys. There is no other indication that Otero may have read Pepys.

66. Governor Prince was the author of several books of historical nature. Otero mentions him several times, but only on one occasion is his name associated with writing (see note 74).

67. Otero was very critical of Read's book: "However, what could one expect from a man who wrote a history of New Mexico and left my father out of the book simply because I declined to pay him $300 to put him in?" (*My Nine Years as Governor,* 76).

68. Alluded to indirectly in *My Life on the Frontier, 1864–1882,* 216.

69. Mentioned in *The Real Billy the Kid,* 73.

70. See note 52.

71. See note 60.

72. See note 60.

73. The reference to this play in *My Life on the Frontier, 1864–1882,* reads as follows: "During their visit Mrs. Manners gave birth to a daughter, an elder sister of the much admired Lady Diana [Cooper], who proved such a success in the play, *The Miracle*" (267).

74. Otero mentions him several times in *My Nine Years as Governor.* On two occasions, there is an acknowledgment of Wallace's writing career, most celebrated for his *Ben-Hur.* On page 180, Otero refers to Wallace as "a celebrated author, like President Roosevelt," and on the same page, he has a guest at his table say (referring to Wallace and LeBaron Bradford Prince): "You know, these literary fellows all stand together, so we will surely oust Otero now!"

75. *My Nine Years as Governor,* 163.

76. Ibid., 163, 205.

77. Ibid., 107, 141, 142, 156, 157, 169, 204, 219, 226, 265.

78. *My Life on the Frontier, 1882–1897,* 7, 135; *My Nine Years as Governor,* 204, 219, 234.

79. *My Life on the Frontier, 1882–1897,* 180, 181.

80. *The Real Billy the Kid,* 6.

81. *My Nine Years as Governor*, 211.

82. Ibid., 220.

83. Ibid., 296.

84. Ibid., 244.

85. Ibid., 148, 160, 183, 184, 185, 238.

86. *My Life on the Frontier, 1864–1882*, 283.

87. Ibid.

88. *The Real Billy the Kid*, 6.

89. *My Nine Years as Governor*, 141.

90. Ibid., 138, 155, 163.

91. Ibid., 254.

92. Ibid., 65.

93. Ibid., 298, 315.

94. Ibid., 199, 203.

95. Ibid., 63, 106, 147.

96. Ibid., 63.

97. *The Real Billy the Kid*, 7.

98. *My Life on the Frontier, 1864–1882*, 132, 153, 154, 155, 165, 166, 167, 176, 181, 202, 207, 208, 233, 241, 246, 251, 252, 254, 256, 257, 258, 260, 267, 268, 269, 274, 279, 280; *My Life on the Frontier, 1882–1897*, 2, 4, 6, 7, 25, 40, 41, 46, 108, 138, 140, 180, 188, 194, 195, 196, 223, 236, 244; *My Nine Years as Governor*, 14, 15, 19, 82, 83, 135.

99. *My Nine Years as Governor*, 20.

100. Ibid., 296.

101. *My Life on the Frontier, 1864–1882*, 279.

102. Ibid., 257, 280; *My Nine Years as Governor*, 20, 165.

103. *My Life on the Frontier, 1882–1897*, 188, 189.

104. *My Nine Years as Governor*, 14, 199, 211.

105. Ibid., 295.

106. Ibid., 286.

107. Ibid., 163.

108. *The Real Billy the Kid*, 6, 121.

109. *My Life on the Frontier, 1864–1882*, 167.

110. *My Nine Years as Governor*, 339.

111. *My Life on the Frontier, 1864–1882*, 251.

112. *The Real Billy the Kid*, 6.

113. *My Nine Years as Governor*, 2, 164, 189, 194, 262, 329, 375, 377, 379, 383.

114. *My Life on the Frontier, 1882–1897*, 196.

115. Ibid., 140, 141.

116. Ibid., 152.

117. Ibid., 148; *My Nine Years as Governor*, 83, 107, 139, 211, 216, 219, 226, 227, 228, 229, 230, 231, 232, 233, 239, 240, 241, 242, 243, 244, 245, 265, 296, 369.

118. *My Nine Years as Governor*, 375.

119. *My Life on the Frontier, 1864–1882*, 201–11; *The Real Billy the Kid*, 130.

120. *My Nine Years as Governor*, 20.

121. Ibid., 200.

122. *My Life on the Frontier, 1864–1882*, 131, 202, 246.

123. Ibid., 140, 141.

124. *My Nine Years as Governor*, 4.

125. Ibid., 157, 225.

126. Ibid., 140.

127. Ibid., 19, 157.

128. Ibid., 165.

129. Otero never gives a first name. He was the editor of the *Stockman*. *My Life on the Frontier, 1882–1897*, 155, 160.

130. *My Nine Years as Governor*, 163.

131. Ibid., 244.

132. *My Life on the Frontier, 1882–1897*, 91, 118, 222, 276, 295, 296; *My Nine Years as Governor*, 2, 19, 29, 33, 39, 40, 81, 82, 83, 84, 85, 86, 89, 104, 105, 121, 136, 141, 154, 155, 160, 162, 164, 166, 167, 168, 169, 175, 186, 187, 200, 202, 207, 211, 219, 223, 225, 229, 234, 243, 247, 249, 256, 259, 260, 261, 262, 324, 325, 332, 333, 334, 336, 340, 341, 369, 377.

133. *My Life on the Frontier, 1882–1897*, 105.

134. Ibid., 45.

135. *My Nine Years as Governor*, 35, 36.

136. Ibid., 163.

137. *My Life on the Frontier, 1864–1882*, 131.

138. *My Nine Years as Governor*, 163.

139. Ibid., 223.

140. *My Life on the Frontier, 1882–1897*, 91.

141. *My Nine Years as Governor*, 210, 211.

142. *My Life on the Frontier, 1882–1897*, 295.

143. Ibid., 152.

144. *My Nine Years as Governor*, 50, 163.

145. Ibid., 163.

146. Ibid., 333.

147. *My Life on the Frontier, 1864–1882*, 280; *My Nine Years as Governor*, 246, 328.

148. *My Nine Years as Governor*, 163.

149. Ibid., 184, 185.

150. Ibid., 244, 378.

151. *My Life on the Frontier, 1882–1897*, 172.

152. *My Nine Years as Governor*, 166.

153. *My Life on the Frontier, 1882–1897*, 160.

154. *My Nine Years as Governor*, 163.

155. *My Life on the Frontier, 1864–1882*, 256.

156. Ibid., 166, 167, 257; *My Life on the Frontier, 1882–1897,* 158.

157. *My Life on the Frontier, 1864–1882,* 255.

158. *My Nine Years as Governor,* 332.

159. *The Real Billy the Kid,* 7, 41.

160. *My Nine Years as Governor,* 160, 289, 293, 298, 334.

161. Ibid., 200.

162. *My Life on the Frontier, 1864–1882,* 167, 246, 247.

163. Otero, *My Life on the Frontier, 1882–1897,* 72.

164. Otero papers, box 7, folder 11.

165. As discussed in more detail above, some of these children's books might have belonged to M. A. Otero II as a child rather than his own offspring.

166. Edith J. May, preface to *Bertram Noel: A Story for Youth* (New York: D. Appleton & Company, 1870), 3.

167. Mrs. Bradley [Mary Emily Bradley], *Handsome Is That Handsome Does,* Proverb Series (Boston: Lothrop, Lee & Shepard, 1868), 323.

168. Manuel M. Martín-Rodríguez, "Chicano/a Children's Literature: A *Transaztlantic* Reader's History," *Journal of American Studies of Turkey* 23 (2006): 15–35.

169. Ibid., 18.

170. This is one of the few books in the Otero library featuring Hispanic characters.

171. It is also possible that these volumes were contributed to the library by Otero's second wife, the widow of Max Frost.

172. Other than Western Americana titles, explored in the preceding section.

Two Colonial New Mexico Libraries

1704, 1776

Eleanor B. Adams

I n an earlier article, written in collaboration with France V. Scholes,[1] we discussed the information available concerning books current in New Mexico prior to the Pueblo Revolt of 1680. Data about this phase of the intellectual life of the frontier of New Spain are scanty, and the sources for the eighteenth century contain very few references to books. No evidence has been found with regard to books owned by colonists. In general, of course, there would have been little occasion to record the books belonging to private individuals, but it is doubtful that the majority of the Spanish settlers had many. The lack of education among the colonists appears to have been still greater than in the preceding century, and, as before, the friars and the provincial governors were almost the only persons who had received the benefit of any formal academic training. Despite the gradual growth of permanent settlement, life in New Mexico in the eighteenth century continued to be that of an isolated frontier outpost, and the chief contact with the intellectual progress of the outside world necessarily came through the Franciscan missionaries and the governors of the province.

Two lists dated more than seventy years apart must serve as examples of the kind of books imported by these secular and ecclesiastical leaders. The first is taken from an inventory of the property of don Diego de Vargas, the reconqueror of New Mexico, made at Santa Fe, April 20, 1704, shortly after his sudden and mysterious death.[2] The second is a catalogue of the library of the Custody of New Mexico remitted in 1777 to the provincial of the Franciscan province of the Holy Gospel, Fray Isidro Murillo, by Fray Francisco Atanasio Domínguez as part of his report on his tour of inspection of the New Mexico missions.[3]

Don Diego José de Vargas Zapata y Luján Ponce de León y Contreras, Marqués de la Nava de Brazinas, was born in Spain in 1643. He belonged to an illustrious and ancient family whose members included many great soldiers, churchmen, and administrators prominent in Spanish affairs over a period of several centuries. It is natural that men of such an energetic and enterprising heritage should have turned to the New World in search of even greater opportunities to exercise their talents and fulfill their ambitions. Don Diego was not the first of the Vargas line to come to America, and on his mother's side he was descended from some of the early conquerors. His career in New Spain began in 1673 when he arrived in Mexico City as a royal courier carrying dispatches to the viceroy. For several years thereafter he served in various administrative posts in New Spain. In 1688 the Crown appointed him governor and captain general of New Mexico with instructions to undertake the reconquest. He reached El Paso in February 1691 and began the difficult task of restoring the rebellious province to the Spanish Crown. After a successful military expedition in 1692, a second expedition entered the province in the autumn of 1693 to resettle it and establish a presidio at Santa Fe. The following three years were spent in subduing the natives by force of arms, refounding the missions, and establishing the colonists in their new homes. Vargas's appointment as governor expired in 1696, and his successor, don Pedro Rodríguez Cubero, arrived in Santa Fe in July 1697. The new governor turned the colonists against the reconqueror, who spent the next three years in prison. Meanwhile the Crown acknowledged Vargas's achievements by granting him the title of Marqués de la Nava de Brazinas and an encomienda in New Mexico. Vargas was released from prison in the summer of 1700 and went to Mexico City to defend himself against the charges preferred by Cubero and the citizens of Santa Fe. The authorities in Spain remained unaware of the whole unhappy situation until 1700, and, after reviewing the case, they ordered the viceroy and audiencia to settle it as soon as possible. As a matter of fact, steps had already been taken in this direction, and in 1703 Vargas was completely exonerated. In 1697 he had been reappointed to the governorship of New Mexico to succeed Cubero, and he was now authorized to resume the office. He reached Santa Fe late in 1703 and lost no time in reestablishing his authority. The problem of hostile Indians was as acute as ever, and late in March of the following year Vargas led an expedition against the Faraon Apaches in the Sandia Mountains. He was not destined to carry it through to a successful conclusion, for he fell ill while pursuing the enemy and died at Bernalillo on April 8, 1704.[4]

The day before he died, Vargas made a will at Bernalillo,[5] leaving in force an earlier will drawn up in Mexico City in 1703. The latter has not been found. Although he made a number of specific bequests of his clothing and personal effects, his books are not mentioned.

There are thirty-three books listed in the inventory of Vargas's property made after his death. In view of conditions on the frontier at that time, however, and the length and dangers of the journey to Santa Fe, it seems a comparatively large number. On the whole it is a curious collection for a frontier library.

The largest group of works concerns the history of the rulers and noble families of Spain and includes Alonso López de Haro's *Nobiliario*; *Ilustraciones Genealógicas de los Cathólicos Reyes* by Esteban de Garibay y Zamalloa; Pedro Salazar de Mendoza's *Origen de las dignidades seglares de Castilla y León*; and Bernabé Moreno de Vargas's *Discursos de la nobleza de España*. Fernando Pizarro y Orellana's *Varones ilustres del Nuevo Mundo* carries the story to the New World. Other historical writings deal with the lives of Charles V and Philip IV. The large proportion of such works clearly reflects Vargas's aristocratic origin and his pride in it. Still other titles (*Grandezas de Madrid, Menosprecio de Corte, Tesoro militar de caballería*, a chronicle of the province of Soria, *Solo Madrid es corte*, etc.) increase the impression that this active soldier and frontiersman was not immune from nostalgia for the things he had left behind in order to win new glory for himself and his king at one of the outposts of the Spanish empire. Even his cookbook may have had its origin at court. It is a temptation to believe that these books were important to him chiefly as a symbol of a way of life.

Like those of his pre-Revolt predecessors,[6] Vargas's library contained a few items of politico-moralistic character and a number of standard works on law. There are also a half a dozen of the devotional writings found in almost any collection of this kind. Perhaps the inclusion of the *Regla de las cinco órdenes de Arquitectura* arose from practical motives.

Six items deal specifically with America. Juan de Solórzano Pereira's *Política Indiana* needs no comment, and we should be surprised if it had been omitted. Gil González Dávila's *Teatro eclesiástico* and Alonso de la Peña Rivas y Montenegro's *Itinerario* relate to the history and practice of the Church in the Indies and would have been of utilitarian value in a mission province. Bernardo de Vargas Machuca's *Milicia y descripción de las Indias* is a learned and comprehensive work in three distinct parts, which include a treatise on military science as well as a detailed description of the Indies. *Varones ilustres del Nuevo Mundo* and the life of Gregorio López describe the achievements of outstanding personalities in the New World. It is also interesting to note that Vargas owned a copy of the *Mística Ciudad de Dios*. Its author, the Spanish mystic Sor María Jesús de Agreda, was identified as the famous "Lady in Blue" of southwestern legend who was miraculously transported to that region in the early seventeenth century and prepared the way for the conversion of certain tribes. Apparently Vargas had no great interest in the lighter forms of literature such as novels or the drama, for there is not one book of this nature listed. He undoubtedly had little time or inclination to read purely for pleasure, and his library is that of a man of action interested in books mainly for their usefulness to him in carrying forward an old tradition in new fields of endeavor.

Fray Francisco Atanasio Domínguez,[7] who arrived in New Mexico in March 1776, where he had been sent as *comisario visitador* of the Custody of the Conversion of Saint Paul by order of his provincial, Fray Isidro Murillo, divides the "kingdom of New Mexico" and its Custody into two branches. He refers to them as the El Paso branch, consisting of a Spanish villa and four Indian pueblos, and the more important New Mexico branch in the interior, which included three Spanish villas (Santa Fe, Albuquerque, and La Cañada) and twenty-two Indian pueblos. Between the time of his arrival and June 10, 1776, Fray Francisco inspected all but three of the missions belonging to the latter group. A letter which he wrote to the provincial after he returned to El Paso in May 1777 and other documents indicate that he was also acting as custodian.

In June 1776, he made plans for an expedition to Monterey with Fray Francisco Vélez de Escalante, then missionary at Zuñi. After various delays they set out on July 29 with eight citizens who had volunteered to accompany them. After traveling a considerable distance into Utah, they abandoned the idea of reaching Monterey and turned back early in October, despite the protests of some of the soldiers. They reached Zuñi on November 24, and, after resting there until December 13, proceeded to Santa Fe, making several stops on the way. Apparently it was during the return journey to Santa Fe that

Domínguez made an informal inspection of three missions he had failed to visit in the spring, Laguna, Acoma, and Zuñi. He reached Santa Fe on January 2, 1777.

Although the Vélez de Escalante–Domínguez expedition into Utah did not accomplish the results they had hoped for, it was the first important exploration of that region. The two friars recorded their experiences in a detailed diary full of significant descriptive material about the country and its inhabitants.[8]

In May Domínguez returned to El Paso, leaving Vélez de Escalante as vice-custodian. On May 27 he forwarded his report on the interior missions, together with various documents relating to mission affairs, to the provincial in Mexico City. He had not yet begun his visitation of the missions belonging to the El Paso branch of the Custody but intended to do so immediately, and on June 26 he wrote that the inspection had been finished and that he was drawing up his report.

Domínguez's activities and reports clearly indicate that he was a man of zeal and intelligence. Nevertheless, the letters and report sent from El Paso reveal great weariness and discouragement. He begged the provincial to allow him to renounce the office of custodian because he felt unable to cope with the problems he had found in the Custody. This unhappy frame of mind may have been partly due to the aftereffects of the hardships he had undergone during the journey into Utah, but there is no doubt that he had found conditions in both the New Mexico and the El Paso districts far from satisfactory and that it had been impossible for him to fulfill certain of the instructions given him by the provincial. The parish records were incomplete and in bad shape, and, because of their ignorance and lack of interest, he was unable to make use of the testimony of the citizens with regard to births, marriages, etc. He was even informed by the Indians that certain *alcaldes mayores* and lieutenants of the New Mexico pueblos had removed the "libros de administración" from the missions "cuyas hojas se han chupado."[9] Moreover, after an outbreak in 1764, Governor Tomás Vélez Cachupín, with the consent of some of the friars, had shut up a number of culprits "en la celda destinada entonces para librería y archivo de esta Custodia, y por su desesperación, o que sé yo, se chuparon muchos libros y quemaron cuantos había de la administración." Some of the missionaries, especially the friar stationed at La Cañada, were suffering extreme poverty, while others were getting comparatively rich by engaging in commercial activities forbidden to them as members of the Order. The necessity of avoiding public scandal

prevented Domínguez from dealing with irregularities in an uncompromis-
ing fashion, and this caused him some uneasiness about the milder course of
action he was forced to take. To add to his difficulties, he had to defend himself against the complaints made by some of the discontented friars, who
attempted to stir up trouble for him in various quarters.

He was also deeply shocked to find how little progress had been made in
civilizing the Indians after so many years of Christian teaching. To use his
own words:

> Even at the end of so many years since their reconquest, the specious
> title or name of neophytes is still applied to them. This is the reason
> why their condition now is almost the same as it was in the beginning,
> for generally speaking they have preserved some very indecent, and
> perhaps superstitious, customs. . . . Most of them do not know their
> saints' names and those who know them do not use them, and when
> we call them by their saints' names they usually have their joke among
> themselves, repeating the saint's name to each other as if in ridi-
> cule. . . . Their repugnance and resistance to most Christian acts is evi-
> dent, for they perform the duties pertaining to the Church under
> compulsion, and there are usually many omissions. They are not in the
> habit of praying or crossing themselves when they rise or go to bed,
> and consequently they have no devotion for certain saints as is cus-
> tomary among us. And if they sometimes invoke God and His saints
> or pray or pay for masses, it is in a confused manner. . . . They do not
> confess annually. If the fathers find some who know how to make a
> proper confession, and these are few, there is rarely anyone capable of
> receiving communion. When in danger of death they do indeed con-
> fess, most of them through an interpreter, since out of all the pueblos
> only those of Isleta, Nambe, San Juan, and Abiquiu (except at Abiquiu
> the interpreters are Spanish) do not make use of one, with very rare
> exceptions, for the fathers find it necessary for clearer explanation.
> They are exceedingly fond of pretty reliquaries, medals, crosses, and
> rosaries, but this does not arise from Christian devoutness (except in a
> few cases) but from love of ornament. And these objects are always
> kept for special occasions, and only when the friars admonish them for
> not wearing them all the time do they wear them until that little scold-
> ing has been forgotten. Then they put them away again until another
> reproof, and so it goes.

After a description of the personal habits of the Indians, Domínguez goes on to discuss the use of the estufas and then the various dances. He divides the latter into two groups: those resembling the contredanses or minuets as danced in Spain, and the "bailes de cabellera." He considered the first a fairly harmless social dance, but was strongly opposed to the second:

> The fathers have been very zealous in their opposition to this "baile de cabellera," but they have only received rebuffs, and so the fathers are unable to abolish this custom and many others, because excuses are immediately made on the ground that [the Indians] are neophytes, minors, etc. Under such pretexts they will always be neophytes and minors with the result that our Holy Faith will not take root and their malice will increase. May God our Lord destroy these pretexts so completely that these wretches may become old Catholics and the greatest saints of the Church.

In spite of his feeling at this time, Domínguez apparently spent most of the next twenty years laboring in the frontier missions. On May 1, 1795, he wrote from Janos to the provincial, Fray Francisco de Cruzealegui,[10] asking him to use his influence at the chapter meeting of 1796 to obtain for him the title of *definidor*. He stated that he had been serving for twenty years as a missionary in New Mexico and as chaplain in presidios of Nueva Vizcaya and that he had documents to prove his merits and services.

Although the report made by Domínguez in 1777 is rather clumsily organized, it is very detailed and conscientious. After a short general statement about New Mexico, each mission is described separately, beginning with that of Santa Fe. In each case there is a careful description of the church, convent, and any other religious edifice, with inventories of their furnishings, equipment, and supplies, statements of income and expenses, services rendered by the Indians, calendar of feasts, and notes concerning the history and organization of the *cofradías*, etc. He also includes data about the location of the pueblos, the physical characteristics and products of the land, the language and customs of the inhabitants, and the number of families living in the mission pueblo and the surrounding area. He gives the name, age, birthplace, and years in the Order of the friars in residence at the time of his *visita* (most of them were natives of New Spain), and a short summary of their careers as missionaries.

This information is followed by an account of the administration of the mission, which varied little throughout the province. Mass was said on Sundays and feast days, after which the congregation often recited the Christian doctrine. In addition, the young unmarried people were summoned to recite the doctrine every morning, and sometimes in the afternoon as well. On these occasions the father devoted more or less time to expounding various points. This seems to have been the extent of the instruction given to the Indians. The obstacles in the way of further teaching were great, for in many pueblos the Indians either did not speak Spanish at all, or spoke little and understood less. Moreover, as Domínguez's general statement about the Indians, quoted above, shows, they had little real interest in matters pertaining to the Faith. The results obtained depended largely on the ability and energy of the friar in charge. It is interesting to note that Father Domínguez was very favorably impressed by the regime at Jémez under Fray Joaquín Ruiz. Here certain of the choirboys were taught to speak Spanish well and also to read, in order that they might serve as teachers and interpreters for the other Indians:

> The system here is different, for one of the little choirboys . . . takes the catechism and with it in his hand recites the doctrine with the others. In addition, he (Ruiz) persuades many married people, who do not know it and are very backward in it, to come to recite the doctrine, although this requires repeated efforts.

In his *auto de visita*, Domínguez warmly expressed his thanks to Father Ruiz for the good order he had found at the mission:

> His Reverence was most gratified and pleased to see the little teachers of the doctrine so learned and well instructed in Christian doctrine, reading, singing, and the manner of assisting at mass, as well as [to observe] their decorum and modesty, for they resemble novices. For all this he gave many thanks to God and charged Father Ruiz to persevere and to continue the fine regime which he has observed up to now.

In fact he was so impressed by the good friar's methods, which he considered those best suited to the spiritual direction and instruction of the Indians, that he gave strict orders that Ruiz's successors should follow them. In order that there might be no excuse, he ordered Father Ruiz to write a detailed account and post it in the convent. This case is unique, for in general Domínguez had a low opinion of the instruction given to the Indians.

Only one other school is mentioned in the report. This was a "muy corta escuela de niños," presumably for Spanish children, conducted by the father at the villa of La Cañada. In return the parents of the children made a small annual payment in kind for the maintenance of the priest. Unfortunately this school was already disintegrating because of the mortal illness of the minister.

At the end of the appendix to this article[11] there is a list of the books found at each mission as shown in the inventories of the sacristies and convents included in Domínguez's report. The number is very small indeed, and, except at Santo Domingo, represents only the essential items for the celebration of the divine offices. Since Domínguez exercised extreme care in recording everything belonging to the missions, we must assume that if there were any other books at the missions, they must have been the property of the friar in charge or borrowed from the library of the Custody. Probably they had their own breviaries. Acoma is the only place where a bookcase is listed among the convent furnishings. The scarcity of books at the missions seems significant in relation to the small amount of formal instruction given to the Indians.

The library and archive of the Custody were kept at the convent of Santo Domingo. The books belonging to the convent itself, including some left behind or donated by various friars, are mentioned in the section of the report which concerns that mission. The catalogues of the library and archive of the Custody are appended at the end of the report. It is not clear whether the prisoners in 1764, already referred to, destroyed any of the library or whether they confined their mischief to the mission records. It will be noted that many of the books were in bad shape when Domínguez saw them.

The catalogue of the library as it existed in 1776 shows 256 items, including a number of duplicates. The actual number of volumes, including sets and duplicate copies listed under a single heading, is somewhat larger. Up to the time of Domínguez's visitation it had apparently been the custom for the friars to borrow books from the collections at the Santo Domingo convent without formality. Certain titles were missing from the convent library, and Domínguez therefore issued an order to the resident missionary and his successors not to allow any friar to take books from the mission without leaving a signed memorandum.

We have no information as to how the books were accumulated. Some may have been donated by friars and laymen of the province. Probably a larger number was supplied by the Order. The Crown evidently provided liturgical books and other things in special cases; for a few items it is specifically stated that the articles are "del Rey."

There are very few works of nonreligious character. Virgil and Ovid are the only Latin classics mentioned by name. Two Greek grammars are listed, as well as Antonio de Nebrija's dictionary and a few other items of this nature. The laws and history of the Indies are represented by Juan de Solórzano Pereira and Antonio de Solís y Rivadeneyra. Francisco Jiménez's translation of Francisco Hernández's important work, *Naturaleza y virtudes de las plantas*, is the only medical publication. Finally, there was a copy of Philipp Clüver's geography.

The largest group of writings are of devotional character and include a large and varied assortment of sermons, prayers, etc., a few lives of saints and religious [figures], and some of the works of the Spanish mystics. Then come the theological treatises of various kinds, among which the scholastics are well represented. The collection is rather weak as far as canon law is concerned. The Decretals, the Council of Trent, and the Mexican councils are listed, but Fray Manuel Rodríguez, whose works had long enjoyed great popularity in New Spain, is one of the few outstanding canonists mentioned. On the other hand, the history and regulations of the Franciscan Order seem to be fairly well covered. The Custody also possessed a number of Bibles and exegetical writings. In addition to the liturgical books in use at the missions, the library of the Custody had quite a few.

Because of the insufficient data given in the catalogue, it is impossible to determine the exact number of American imprints. In some cases where it is possible to identify author and title, we have no way of knowing whether an American or European edition is referred to. Although most of the books must have been imported from Spain, between twenty and thirty at least are almost certainly of American origin. These fall into several categories and include some of the most famous products of the Mexican press.

Among the first books published in Mexico were grammars and vocabularies of the Indian languages, especially Nahuatl. These, together with a number of *doctrinas*, catechisms, and devotional works in Indian languages, were written to aid the clergy in their great task of converting and teaching the natives. The Custodial library at Santo Domingo lists a vocabulary and three grammars. Other items of this nature are the Dominican fray Martín de León's *Camino del cielo en lengua mexicana*, which had wide circulation, and two volumes of sermons in Mexican. The Franciscan fray Juan Bautista's

Advertencias para los confesores de indios was composed for the same general purpose.

At least four of the liturgical books in the library of the Custody were published in Mexico. These are the manuals of Juan de Palafox y Mendoza, Pedro de Contreras Gallardo, and Fray Ángel Serra, and the *Ceremonial* of the Franciscan province of the Holy Gospel. The manuals in use at the mission pueblos (by Augustín de Vetancurt and Diego Osorio) were also of Mexican origin.

The author who appears most frequently is Fray Clemente de Ledesma. Ledesma was a prominent Mexican Franciscan of the late seventeenth century who wrote many religious books of various kinds. He served as provincial of the province of the Holy Gospel during 1694–1696.[12]

Devotional works published in Mexico include José de Barcia y Zambrana's *Epístola exhortatoria*, Pedro Muñoz de Castro's *Exaltación de La Betlemítica Rosa*, Diego López de Andrade's "tomo quaresmal," and the fine sermons of the Jesuit Juan Martínez de la Parra, who was a native of Puebla. There are many editions of the *Luz de Verdades*, which was printed in Spain after the first edition appeared in Mexico in 1691–1692.

Other Mexican imprints listed are Francisco Hernández's *Naturaleza y virtudes de las plantas*; works by Fray Antonio Escoto, Andrés de Borda, Alonso Alberto de Velasco, and Francisco Larraga; the "Chrónica de Dieguinos"; and the *Concilio Mexicano*. The life of Father Margil, listed as missing from the convent library at Santo Domingo, was also probably a Mexican publication. The dates of the first editions of these American books range from the early days of the Mexican press to the 1760s.

Although the library of the Custody seems a rather haphazard collection in some ways, very weak in certain fields, it covers a wide range of religious thought. Presumably it was reasonably adequate for the needs of the friars it served.

Notes

This essay originally appeared as "Two Colonial New Mexico Libraries, 1704, 1776," *New Mexico Historical Review* 19 (April 1944): 135–67. © 1942 by the Historical Society of New Mexico and the University of New Mexico Board of Regents. All rights reserved. Reprinted by permission. Minor stylistic changes have been made to the essay for the current publication, and, where possible, full names and other identifying information for the writers and works mentioned in the essay have been added for the convenience of present-day readers.

1. *New Mexico Historical Review* 17 (1942): 226–70.

2. *Ymbentario de los vienes que se hallaron del señor Marqués de la naba de Brazinas ya difunto gouernador y capitan general que fue deste Reino de la nueua mexico. . .* Santa Fe Archives, sec. 100. Historical Society of New Mexico, Santa Fe.

3. Biblioteca Nacional, Mexico City (cited hereafter as BNM), leg. 10, doc. 43.

4. See J. M. Espinosa, *First Expedition of Vargas into New Mexico, 1692* (Albuquerque: University of New Mexico Press, 1940); J. M. Espinosa, *Crusaders of the Rio Grande: The Story of Don Diego de Vargas* (Chicago: Institute of Jesuit History, 1942); and Lansing B. Bloom, "The Vargas Encomienda," *New Mexico Historical Review* 14 (1939): 366–417.

5. There is a translation of this will in Ralph Emerson Twitchell, *The Spanish Archives of New Mexico*, vol. 1 (Cedar Rapids, IA: Torch Press, 1914), 301–10.

6. See Adams and Scholes, "Books in New Mexico."

7. Unless otherwise indicated in the notes, the following account is based on BNM, leg. 10, docs. 42–49, which include letters from Domínguez to the provincial, the report of the *visita* of the New Mexico missions in 1776, and other letters and papers concerning the New Mexico and El Paso missions.

8. *Diario* in *Documentos para la historia de México*, 2nd ser., vol. 1 (Mexico, 1854), 275–558; P. Otto Maas, *Viajes de misioneros franciscanos á la conquista del Nuevo México* (Seville: Imprenta de San Antonio, 1915), 89–133; and Hubert Howe Bancroft, *Works*, vol. 26, *History of Utah* (San Francisco: History Company, 1889), 7–17.

9. This may mean that they used the paper to make cigarettes.

10. Museo Nacional, Mexico City, asuntos 238.

11. [Note from the editor] Upon the advice of external reviewers, the appendix is not reproduced here. I urge the interested reader to consult the original *New Mexico Historical Review* publication for details. Throughout this chapter, I have also removed from the text all references to the catalog of books in the appendix.

12. Fray Francisco Antonio de la Rosa Figueroa, "Becerro general" (unpublished manuscript, Newberry Library, Chicago).

Books in New Mexico,
1598–1680

Eleanor B. Adams and France V. Scholes

D uring the past few years, interest in the intellectual history of the Spanish colonies has grown rapidly. One manifestation of this interest is the increasing number of studies on the book trade and the importation and distribution of books, especially in the major colonies and centers of population such as Mexico and Peru. These have already refuted the conventional notion that the scientific, philosophical, and literary works current in Spain and Europe during the sixteenth and seventeenth centuries were seldom available in or even permitted to enter the colonies.[1] But it is equally important, perhaps even more important, to know what books reached the outlying areas, which did not enjoy the same facilities for formal academic training as were to be found in the richer and more populous districts. On the frontier the dissemination of ideas and the degree of intellectual enlightenment necessarily depended in great measure upon the kind of books imported and circulated and their influence upon the people who owned them, and through them, upon others. The unlettered, of course, formed the major part of the population. Those who owned books in large or small numbers were few, but what books there were reached the people in some form, by loan to those who could read, or, more indirectly, by the conversation and discussions of those who had read them, colored inevitably by their personal reactions and interpretations.

This was the case in New Mexico in the seventeenth century. As the northernmost outpost of Spain in North America, it was an isolated frontier colony cut off from the rest of New Spain by vast stretches of territory inhabited by hostile Indian tribes. Since it possessed but few easily exploitable resources, its economic importance was small and it attracted relatively few colonists. Not many of those who came had enjoyed much, if any, academic training. A certain number of mission schools were founded within the province, especially during the first three or four decades after the establishment of the colony, for the purpose of teaching the elements of Christian doctrine and rudiments of reading and writing. No formal education beyond this existed.

Information concerning books that were brought to New Mexico prior to the Pueblo Revolt of 1680 consists of scattered incidental references in various contemporary sources, citations of works which are found in documents dealing with the never-ending Church-State controversy, and a few lists of volumes in the possession of certain provincial governors. Additional data may have been recorded in private papers and in the local Franciscan archives as part of inventories of church and convent furnishings, but these records, along with the provincial governmental archive, were destroyed in 1680. As might be expected, most of the books were in the possession of the Franciscan friars and the provincial governors. Undoubtedly the colonists owned more books than are noted in the contemporary sources that have been preserved, but the number was not large in any case.[2]

The Franciscan friars constituted the most learned group in the province. A considerable number had been educated in Spain, where they had entered the Order before going out to the New World. Most of the others had been trained in the colleges and seminaries of Mexico City, Puebla, or other educational centers of New Spain. Several had achieved some prominence in the Order before entering the New Mexico mission field; others were rewarded by promotion or preferment after their years of service in the province. Fray Tomás Manso, who served for years as director of the mission supply caravans, was elevated to the see of Nicaragua, and according to tradition Fray Alonso de Benavides became archbishop of Goa. Fray Francisco de Ayeta, who played such a prominent role in local affairs both before and after the Pueblo Revolt, was appointed special representative of all the Franciscan provinces of New Spain at the royal court. But no less worthy of mention as intellectual leaders in New Mexico are men like Fray Esteban de Perea, Fray Juan de Salas, Fray Cristóbal de Quirós, and Fray Antonio de Ibargaray—to note only a few—who spent the best years of their lives in the province.

The friars who accompanied the Oñate expedition were undoubtedly the owners of most of the books taken to New Mexico when the province was founded, but unfortunately the documents relating to the expedition contain no lists describing the kind of books they had. It may be assumed that most of the books were Bibles, breviaries, missals, and ecclesiastical treatises of various descriptions, but the inventories, if we had them, would probably reveal that some of the friars brought with them classics of Latin and Spanish literature and a few volumes on medicine, science or pseudoscience, and other mundane subjects. The earliest documentary evidence concerning books imported by the Franciscans is found in the treasury accounts of the first three decades of the seventeenth century, which sometimes record in considerable detail the kind of supplies purchased at royal expense for friars sent out to the province and for those already serving in the missions. The book items refer, however, only to the purchase of breviaries, missals, and choir books of various kinds. Works of nonliturgical character were apparently privately owned, or were supplied at the expense of the Order for convent libraries.

It would be interesting to know what books were brought to New Mexico by Fray Esteban de Perea, Fray Juan de Salas, Fray Alonso de Benavides, and other leaders in the early missionary history of the province, but the documents record no information on this point. The only reference we have to a book owned by one of the early friars relates to a work on astrology said to be the property of the lay brother Fray Alonso de San Juan, who came to New Mexico before the end of the Oñate period and took an active part in mission affairs for some thirty years. In 1626, when Benavides was investigating conditions in the province, a certain Lucas de Figueroa gave the following testimony:[3]

> He states and solemnly declares that about a year ago, having entered the house of a Mexican Indian called Pancho Bolon, a smith in this Villa [of Santa Fe], he found there a book of astrology and secrets of nature and of other strange things. Since the aforesaid Indian did not know how to read, this declarant asked for the loan of it and took it from him. He kept it about five or six months, at the end of which time Fray Alonso de San Juan, lay brother of St. Francis in this Custody, carried it off, saying that it was his. During the time that this declarant had it, he found in it the account of the planets at all hours, prognosticating according to the nature of each planet the aspect and character of the persons who

were born under each planet, foretelling how long they might live and certain future events in the course of their lives. He did this once on the basis of the time of her birth as told to him by a woman of this Villa called Ana Ortiz, and he informed her that apparently she had had an illness, according to what the influences of her sign indicated for her. She replied that this was true and that she had had it at the time he named. He also told her that she would be very fecund. In the same way he prophesied the birth of a child, daughter of Francisco de Almazán, a resident of this place, foretelling several events which were to befall him, and other similar things. And although it is true that this seemed to him to be proper curiosity and he manifested it as such, he always believed and understood that everything was subject to the will of God and made this clear to all those with whom he dealt.

These remarks illustrate the influence that a book of esoteric character might have on a relatively unlettered colonist. Figueroa's confession was undoubtedly prompted by knowledge that Benavides, who was acting under authority as commissary of the Holy Office, was inquiring into the prevalence of superstition, and it was this factor that was responsible for the witness's final affirmation that all things were subject to God's will and that he had emphasized this point in the prognostications he had made.

The convent libraries, made up of books received or inherited from private owners and works purchased at the expense of the Order for general use, constituted the most important collections at the disposal of the friars. Each mission must have had a few books, but the most extensive collections were undoubtedly those kept at the convent of Santo Domingo, ecclesiastical capital of the province, and at the convent of Santa Fe. The inventories of these collections, which once comprised part of the Franciscan archives, are irretrievably lost, but fortunately we have other records which provide considerable evidence concerning their contents.

The most important source of information is a series of opinions and letters written by Fray Juan de Vidania ca. 1640–1641 at the time of a bitter controversy between Governor Luis de Rosas and the Franciscans. This controversy was precipitated by numerous incidents involving the authority of the custodian as local head of the church, questions of ecclesiastical immunity and privilege, and similar problems. At the height of the dispute the province was divided into two hostile camps. The convent at Santa Fe was closed, and all of the friars in residence there, except Vidania and a lay brother, who were staunch supporters of the governor, were expelled from the villa. Most of the friars and a group of colonists who espoused their cause assembled at Santo Domingo, whence the custodian, Fray Juan de Salas, fulminated excommunications against Rosas and his Franciscan allies. In a series of opinions, drafted at the request of the governor, Vidania formulated arguments to support Rosas's actions and to challenge the validity of the prelate's edicts. These views were also reiterated in letters to Salas and other friars.[4]

In these papers Vidania cited numerous authorities in such a way that it may be inferred that in most cases he had their writings at hand for reference. The documents not only contain many verbatim quotations but have numerous marginal notes giving author, brief title, or both, and frequently the volume, chapter, section, or other appropriate subdivisions of works cited to support arguments in the text. Some of the books that he used may have been in the library or archive of the Casa Real, but most of them are of such character that they probably belonged to the library of the Santa Fe convent.

Among the works quoted or cited we find Aristotle's *Topics*, Caesar's *Gallic Wars*, and Ovid's *Metamorphoses*. The Church fathers are represented by Saint Augustine's work, *Contra Faustum Manichaeum*. The documents also contain references to Saint Ambrose and Saint Gregory, but it is difficult to determine whether Vidania had their writings at hand, or used references to them in other works. Saint Thomas Aquinas's *Summa Theologica* is cited several times.

Justinian appears two or three times, and there are numerous references to the *Nueva recopilación* and to special royal cedulas and ordinances. Alonso de Villadiego's *Instrucción política* and Juan de Hevia Bolaños's *Curia philipica*, which deal with Spanish civil procedure and administration, are cited, but it is interesting to note that Juan de Solórzano Pereira and Jerónimo Castillo de Bobadilla are not mentioned. Politico-moralistic writing is represented by Fray Juan Márquez's *Gobernador christiano*.

There are numerous citations to the Decretals and other parts of the *Corpus juris canonici*, the decrees of the Council of Trent, and various papal bulls. The references to jurists and canonists cover a rather wide range. The Italians are represented by P. Baldo, Bartolus de Saxoferrato, Robert Bellarmine, Thomas Cajetan, Nicolás de Tudeschis Panormitanus, and Silvestro Mazzolini. Among the Spaniards we find Domingo de Soto, Francisco Suárez, Diego de Covarrubias y Leiva, the celebrated Martín de Azpilcueta Navarro, and others of lesser renown. The *Quaestiones regulares* of the Portuguese Franciscan fray Manuel Rodríguez and his *adiciones* to his treatise on the Bull of the Crusade are referred to again and again. Finally, we have several citations to Fray Juan Focher, Fray Alonso de la Veracruz, and Fray Juan Bautista, well known for their services in Mexico in the sixteenth century.

This is not the place to analyze Vidania's interpretations of canon law and his use or misuse of the authorities he quoted or cited. Only a trained canonist would be qualified for such a task. It will be interesting, however, to note what his brother Franciscans thought of his learning, and what he, in turn, thought of his critics. In a letter to the Franciscan commissary general of New Spain, one of the friars wrote:

> This said Fray Juan de Vidania was the fountain head and teacher of this conspiracy. He is false in everything, and for the Latin solecisms in the letter he wrote Your Reverence alone, he deserved to be deprived of the service of the altar and divine office. And for the falseness with which he cites the sacred canons and holy scripture, he should be deprived forever of the opportunity to read sacred canons and holy scripture, since he has so falsely applied what he reads.[5]

Vidania's contempt for his critics is reflected in all of his writings, but especially in one of his letters which illustrates his power of sarcasm, and, incidentally, provides interesting sidelights on his acquaintance with books and authors. Referring to a certain friar who was especially active in challenging the validity of his propositions, he said:

> This grammarian . . . is so ignorant that he has not even read the *Categories* or *Predicaments* of Aristotle, or the *Perihermenias* and *Topics*, or even the common-places of Cicero. And so he frequents the haunts of the vulgar and unlettered . . . composing syllogisms to make it seem that what I have done was fallacious and sophistries of little substance. . . . What an ignoramus I am, for I believed that one could not know these things without knowing the philosophers! . . . In vain I pondered the commentaries of the philosophers, and without reason did my teacher guide me through the categories of Porphyry[6] to the logic of Aristotle! And, leaving aside these humane branches of study, in vain and without cause did I have for my masters in holy theology the most learned Valencia[7] and the greatly renowned Leiva,[8] not to mention others! The erudition of my teachers and continual meditation from my early youth

up to my present age upon the lesson to be found in various branches of moral and scholastic learning and evangelical discourse has availed me nothing. There, indeed, have we found a perfect and whole man without his having been taught by anyone. This must be some divine spirit or fantastic deity who surpasses and conquers Tully in eloquence, Aristotle in arguments, Plato in wisdom, and Aristarchus in erudition.

This outburst illustrates the invective power of Vidania's pen and explains, in part, why Governor Rosas valued him as an ally.

In the end Vidania suffered disgrace for his defense of Rosas and his disobedience to the custodian's decrees. A formal investigation of his conduct was made in 1641, after Rosas had been removed from office, and he was sent to Mexico City for trial by the Holy Office. One source states that he escaped during the journey to New Spain;[9] another records that he was finally punished (*penitenciado*).[10]

The documents relating to the Church-State controversies of the 1660s also contain some information concerning books in the possession of the friars, but it adds very little to the data found in the Vidania papers. We find numerous references to the decrees of the Council of Trent and to various papal bulls, especially the *Omnimoda* of Pope Adrian VI on which the custodians based their authority as ecclesiastical judges ordinary, but citations to canonists are rare. In a petition defending his jurisdiction as ecclesiastical judge, the vice-custodian, Fray García de San Francisco, cited Baldo, Navarro, and Panormitanus.[11] We also have an account of a theological dispute at the Santa Fe convent during which a volume by the canonist Fray Manuel Rodríguez was taken down and consulted to settle a point at issue.[12] All of these writers are cited in the Vidania papers, and these later references to them serve as additional evidence that Rosas's advocate had his authorities at hand. The only references to works not previously mentioned relate to three books apparently owned by Fray Nicolás de Freitas, director of the Santa Fe convent in 1622–1663, and Fray Felipe de la Cruz, a lay brother resident at the convent of Santo Domingo in 1662.[13]

Finally, the journal of Governor Diego de Vargas concerning the reconquest of New Mexico records the discovery of certain books that had undoubtedly been kept in the convents of the Zuñi area. On November 10, 1692, he arrived at Corn Mountain, on the top of which the Indians of the pueblo of Alona then were living. The following day he ascended the rock, and in one of the rooms of the pueblo he found various ecclesiastical ornaments and seventeen books. With one exception, a volume of Francisco de Quevedo's works, they were of religious character.[14]

In the documentary sources for the period prior to 1659, we have noted only three references to books in the possession of provincial governors. The first tells of a work entitled *Práctica criminal eclesiástica* owned by Governor Pedro de Peralta (1610–1614).[15] His possession of a book of this kind fits in with statements made by Vidania in his opinions in defense of Rosas to the effect that Peralta was a *bachiller* and that he had been trained in canon law ("bien entendido y graduado en canones").[16] Peralta's term of office was characterized by a violent controversy with the Franciscan prelate Fray Isidro Ordóñez, who was bold enough to arrest the governor and hold him in jail for several months.[17] Subsequent to the arrest, Ordóñez and Fray Luis de Tirado, minister at the Santa Fe convent, ransacked Peralta's papers and personal effects, and Tirado kept the book noted above.

The second reference relates to books in the hands of Governor Juan de Eulate (1618–1625). Governor Eulate, like Peralta, was involved in controversy with the friars, who accused him, among other things, of asserting authority over the local prelate, even in spiritual affairs, and of propositions contrary to the Faith. Eulate's attitude toward ecclesiastical authority was inspired in part by an exaggerated notion of his authority as representative of the king, and by disputes with the friars concerning the general direction of Indian affairs. The erroneous propositions ascribed to him were the result of his fondness for theological dispute and his delight in shocking his listeners by proclaiming scandalous and unorthodox views.[18] It is obvious that he had more than ordinary interest in doctrinal matters and politico-ecclesiastical problems, and it is not surprising, therefore, to find references to his ownership of ecclesiastical books. Unfortunately, the sources do not record their titles, and only one author is noted—the Portuguese canonist, Fray Manuel Rodríguez.[19]

In 1656 Juan Manso de Contreras, brother of Fray Tomás Manso who successfully directed the mission supply service for a quarter century, became governor, and he served the average three-year term. His successor, Governor Bernardo López de Mendizábal, conducted his residencia with considerable severity and held him in jail until the summer of 1660 when he was able to escape to Mexico City. Among the effects which he left behind in his cell in the Casa de Cabildo in Santa Fe was a book entitled *Jornadas para el cielo*,[20] one of the numerous devotional works of the popular Franciscan preacher, Fray Cristóbal de Moreno.

Such is the information at hand concerning books owned by governors who served prior to 1659. The paucity of the data is undoubtedly explained by the character of the available documentary sources for this period, which deal mostly with special incidents or special phases of administration, in which references to books in the possession of provincial governors would be only incidental. Except for Manso, we have no inventories or lists of the property and personal effects of the dozen or more persons who held office, and even in Manso's case the list is obviously incomplete.

The two immediate successors of Manso were Bernardo López de Mendizábal (1659–1661) and Diego de Peñalosa (1661–1664). These men became involved in prolonged controversy with the friars and were eventually tried by the Holy Office of the Inquisition. López's wife, doña Teresa de Aguilera y Roche, also stood trial before the tribunal.[21] The records of these cases and the prolonged litigation over the property of the defendants constitute the most important block of sources at present available on the history of New Mexico prior to the Pueblo Revolt, and they throw a flood of light on every phase of social life in the province. The papers contain detailed inventories of the property and personal effects of the two governors, including numerous books of various kinds.

Bernardo López de Mendizábal was a native of the province of Chietla in New Spain. He received an academic education in the Jesuit colleges of Mexico City and Puebla, and in the Royal University where he studied arts and canon law. After spending a few years in the galleon service, he went to Cartagena where one of his cousins was bishop. At the latter's request he prepared to enter the priesthood, but finally abandoned this vocation and married the daughter of the local governor. His wife, doña Teresa de Aguilera y Roche, was a native of Italy, where her father had held an administrative post before his transfer to Cartagena. Her mother was an Irishwoman who had been reared in the household of the Marqués de Santa Cruz in Spain. Eventually López returned to Mexico where he held office as alcalde mayor, first in the province of San Juan de los Llanos, and later at Guaiacocotla. In 1658 the viceroy, Duque de Alburquerque, named him governor and captain general of New Mexico.

From the beginning of his term of office López antagonized both the Franciscan friars and many of the soldier-colonists. He introduced innovations in the system of Indian labor, increasing the wage scale for household servants and farm laborers and reducing the number of Indians in service at the missions. Instead of supporting the friars in their campaign against

Indian ceremonial dances, he authorized the public performance of these pagan ceremonies in all of the pueblos. He also called into question the authority of the custodian as ecclesiastical judge ordinary, and in the summer of 1660 actually forbade the prelate to exercise such authority pending a decision by the viceroy on the subject. Resentment against López's governmental policies was accentuated by his personal conduct, negligence in the observance of his religious obligations, and by tactless remarks which many persons regarded as bordering on unorthodoxy and heresy. The gossip-mongering servants at the Casa Real made things worse by reporting incidents which many persons professed to regard as evidence that both the governor and his wife were practicing Jews.

The friars sent lengthy reports to Mexico City, and in 1661 López was replaced as governor by Diego de Peñalosa. The residencia proceedings which Peñalosa conducted were unduly severe, and at times were characterized by fraud. In the midst of the trial ex-governor Manso returned bearing edicts of the audiencia calling for a review of his own residencia and settlement of claims he had made against López. To satisfy these claims, part of López's property was embargoed, and in the inventories made at the time we find the first references to books in his possession. The books and other property were placed in deposit with a local citizen, and there is evidence that part of these goods, including most of the books, were later taken over by Peñalosa.[22]

The complaints against López filed by the friars had also been referred to the Holy Office, and in the spring of 1662 the tribunal issued orders to arrest him and his wife, doña Teresa. Execution of these decrees was carried out on August 26, 1662, by Fray Alonso de Posada, the local prelate and commissary of the Inquisition. The property remaining in López's hands was embargoed in the name of the Inquisition, and elaborate inventories were made preparatory to shipment of the property to Mexico City. In these lists and in copies later filed during litigation in the viceregal capital, we have additional lists of books belonging to the governor and doña Teresa.[23] Additional evidence concerning their book holdings is also found in the lists of personal effects in their possession when they entered the jail of the Inquisition, and in numerous incidental references and passages in the trial proceedings.[24]

The lists of their books show an extremely large proportion of religious and didactic works. In spite of the accusations that they neglected their religious duties and were even suspect in the Faith, doña Teresa, at least, seems to have been devout enough after her own fashion. She excused their irregularity in attendance at Mass on the grounds of illness and the fact that she was unaccustomed to the severity of the New Mexico climate. Their critics made a particular point of an incident which took place while the procession was passing the Casa Real on Good Friday, 1661, accusing them of disrespect for the religious ceremony. Their replies are in essential agreement. Both state that they were ill, and she adds that she was reading aloud to him "the passion of Our Lord," while he identifies the book as Cristóbal de Fonseca, *Discursos morales para las ferias de la Cuaresma*. They alleged the same reason for their absence from the reading of an Edict of the Faith, and in reply to the criticism on this point and to the charge that she had never been known to show particular devotion to any saint, doña Teresa more than once went into considerable detail on the subject of her favorite devotions, the cofradías to which she belonged, and the devotions and bulls pertaining to them which she used. She listed among her favorite prayers those in the *Perfecto Cristiano*, and this book was one of the three she had with her when she was admitted to the jail of the Inquisition in April 1663. In November of the same year, at one of her audiences before the tribunal, she asked to be allowed to have this work.

It is interesting to note that an edict of the Holy Office to withdraw from circulation certain litanies, books, and other things was read in Santa Fe during López's stay in New Mexico. He and his wife were present, and she testifies as follows:

And in addition, when Fray Diego de Santander read the first edicts, I handed over to him the Office of the Pure and Immaculate Conception of Our Lady and that of the Glorious Patriarch St. Joseph, and some Litanies of the Most Sweet and Lovely Mother of God, and the Memorial of the five greatest sorrows of the Most Holy Virgin, because all these were among those which the edict of this Holy Tribunal ordered taken up; and as a faithful and Catholic Christian, obedient to its commands, I was the first to give them up, although they had been among my particular devotions.

She also claimed that she had been in the habit of reading devotions to her attendants and presented them with extra copies of certain ones which she happened to have. Apparently they had also brought almanacs with them, for doña Teresa remarked that in case of doubt as to whether a certain day was a Church feast, the guardian would send to ask them to look at their *calendarios*.

In his testimony concerning López's conduct on the way to Mexico City, Fray Salvador de Guerra says that he was told by a certain lay brother, Fray Felipe de la Cruz, who had the task of bringing food to the prisoners during their stay at the convent of Santo Domingo, that don Bernardo had asked him for a spiritual book to read. Fray Felipe brought him Antonio de Molina's *De oración*, but said that López was not satisfied with it and asked him to find a *libro de romances* because Molina was too spiritual for him. In his defense López contradicted this, saying that he read the book two or three times and kept it until the day he left Santo Domingo without asking for another, "nor did he scorn it; indeed he loved it because it affected him deeply."

Although the number of secular books listed as the property of don Bernardo and doña Teresa is not large, they had some of the outstanding and most influential works current at the time. In general there was no occasion to cite them in the controversies, accusations, and replies recorded in the documents, but it seems likely that they were read and enjoyed, for unless they suited the needs and taste of their owners, there would have been little point in carrying them on the long and arduous journey to New Mexico.

The practical usefulness of certain items, such as a book on surgery and Antonio de Argüello's treatise on public documents, makes further comment on them unnecessary; and since there is evidence that the works of Antonio de Nebrija, especially the grammar and vocabularies, were popular among educated persons in the colonies and were imported in large numbers, it is not surprising to find that López owned his Latin vocabulary. The possession of such historical works as a life of Philip the Prudent and the chronicle of the Augustinian Order in New Spain is in keeping with López's interests as a widely traveled man who had held military and administrative posts of various kinds. The same is true of a book in Latin called *The Prince*. Although other books, including Machiavelli's famous work, fit the description given, it may have been Diego de Saavedra Fajardo's *Empresas políticas*. A copy of this turns up later in Peñalosa's possession, and there is ample evidence that he kept such of López's books as took his fancy. In fact he probably acquired some of the volumes which are listed only among his property when he ransacked López's residence on different occasions, and he may even have taken books kept for reference in the library or archive of the Casa Real at the time when he carried off a large part of the local archive. Saavedra Fajardo's brilliant work enjoyed great popularity, and in view of Peñalosa's literary tastes, as shown by the inventories of his books, especially his predilection for Gracián, it is likely that this book would have appealed to him if he found it among López's belongings. López owned another book dealing with the same general subject, which was among his personal effects when he was brought to the jail of the Holy Office in Mexico City. This was Fray Juan Márquez's *Gobernador Christiano,* one of the many Spanish works written to refute Machiavelli's *The Prince* by setting forth the virtues of the ideal Christian monarch.

The López inventories show only four books designed more for amusement than instruction. One of these was Cervantes's *Don Quixote.* Unfortunately, we have only the single reference to it at the time it was embargoed by Peñalosa's order in July 1662. There is no further record of what happened to it, but it is likely that it remained in New Mexico. Vicente Espinel's *Marcos de Obregón* and a book of *comedias* by different authors were taken to Mexico City with the rest of the property embargoed by order of the Holy Office, and they were eventually returned to doña Teresa.

Only one of the four, Ariosto's *Orlando furioso,* is mentioned other than in the inventories. Doña Teresa had a copy of this in Italian, which had been given to her by her father, and her reading of it gave rise to much speculation and suspicion. It is unlikely that her fondness for it would have aroused so much comment if her critics in their ignorance had not seized the opportunity to ascribe the worst possible motives to her obvious enjoyment of a book concerning the contents of which they had only her word to go on. Although she told at least one of her accusers that it was in Italian and concerned love, they professed to believe that because of her character and conduct it was sure to contain "English heresies" and that she must be a heretic too. It is not difficult to understand why doña Teresa inspired suspicion and dislike on the part of the citizens of Santa Fe, for in that rough and isolated frontier community she must have seemed a very exotic personality. A fine lady by birth and upbringing, well traveled, apparently educated above the average according to the standard of the time, she made no attempt to conceal her impatience with the follies and ignorance of her servants and neighbors. They, in turn, could hardly have been expected not to resent her superiority and strange ways, especially since she used little tact in her relationships with them. Many of the accusations against her and her husband were based on modes of life so foreign to local custom that they were believed to be Jewish rites. Her reading of a book in a tongue unknown to them was merely one item in a long list of actions misunderstood and criticized because they were out of the common in that place and time. Nevertheless these accusations were incorporated in the formal charges against her, and her replies not only throw light upon conditions in New Mexico but reflect her own knowledge and opinions concerning the value and standing of what she read.

Her principal reason for reading Ariosto was to practice the Italian language, which she had learned as a child, and her father had given her the book so that she would not forget it.

> But the said book contains nothing against our Holy Faith but only what the books called romances of chivalry usually contain: enchantments and wars. And sometimes she could not help laughing when she was reading those things.

On another occasion she wrote:

> If the book had been evil, [my father] would not have permitted me to read it, nor would he have done so, for he was a very good Christian. And this book, according to what I heard from him and other persons, has been translated into our Castilian language, like the Petrarch, of which it is a companion volume although the style is different.

It is quite clear that it never entered her head that the book in itself might be frowned upon as improper reading for good Catholics, let alone that it might actually be forbidden. This may serve as some commentary on how dead the letter of the laws forbidding the exportation to the New World of romances of chivalry and similar fiction was, even though clerical opinion in Spain itself tended to consider such works dangerous to the morals of the majority because of inability to distinguish facts from fiction. Moreover, this aspect of the matter did not come up in her hearings before the tribunal of the Inquisition. The fiscal's charge was founded, not upon the identity of the book as the *Orlando furioso*, but upon the statements of witnesses concerning the probable heretical nature of a book in an unknown tongue which they had seen doña Teresa read. He added that the charge could not be dismissed until "it is proved what the book is and it is examined and found to contain no tainted doctrines condemned by our Mother the Church." To this she replied as follows:

> She said that the book referred to in the charge can only be the one she has already mentioned . . . , that it is current and widely read in both Italy and Spain by persons who understand it, for at the beginning of each chapter there is a statement called the allegory which says that only

the good is to be taken from it and not the bad; and it inculcates great morality and good doctrine; and God help the witness who had such suspicions.

Later on, written statements which she made in her defense show the influence of her lawyer. In them she reiterates her declaration that the book was "the works of Ariosto, which are not condemned," and qualifies the testimony of her accusers as "not testifying but jumping to a rash conclusion and injuring me." Then she goes on to say:

But the chief thing is that in order to be able to proceed with this charge, it was absolutely necessary to prove what this book was and that it was heretical or condemned, because owning and reading books, even though they may be in a foreign language, for the Italian, or Tuscan, language is not unintelligible or unknown as the charge says, are not prohibited but regularly allowed and permitted. The witness was under obligation to say that it was a forbidden book and the charge should have been based on this condition and proof of it, for to presume such a thing is a violation of law, which regularly allows books. And no book is assumed to be forbidden unless proof is offered, especially in this kingdom where the vigilance of this Holy Tribunal is so astute in the examination and expurgation of books and in withdrawing from circulation those which should not be current. . . . And it is not the obligation of the accused, but of the plaintiff, who is the fiscal, to prove that it is forbidden, because even if forbidden books are found in anyone's possession, it is necessary to prove two things in order to give origin to presumption of heresy: first, that the books are by a heretical author; second, that the person who has them knows this. Moreover, there is still a dispute among the doctors as to whether the presumption which arises from this is valid. But in this case there can be none, nor any motive for suspicion or surprise that, knowing the Italian language, I should have a book in it, nor is it my fault that the servants who saw me read are ignorant.

Here the matter rested, for in December 1664, the proceedings against her were suspended and some of her own and her husband's property, including the books taken by the Holy Office, was returned to her. Don Bernardo had died in prison on September 16, 1664, before his case was settled. Some years later, in April 1671, a sentence absolving him was pronounced by the

Inquisitors, and his remains were transferred to the convent of Santo Domingo in Mexico City for ecclesiastical burial.

Diego de Peñalosa, the successor of López de Mendizábal as governor of New Mexico, was an adventurer who had an eventful career in various parts of the New World and later in London and Paris. A native of Lima, he spent his youth in that city and in La Paz, where his family had property holdings and enjoyed a certain local prestige. He was tutored by one of his uncles who was in holy orders, and later studied "grammar and rhetoric" with the Jesuits in Lima. His public career began as regidor of La Paz, and when only eighteen years of age he served as *procurador* of that city in litigation before the audiencia of Charcas. Later on, while serving as *alcalde provincial* of the Santa Hermandad in the La Paz area, serious complaints were filed against him, and he was summoned before the viceroy in Lima. To escape arrest he took refuge in the Augustinian college, and a short time later his friends put him on board a vessel for Panama. From there he traveled to Nicaragua and spent some time with the bishop, who was his uncle. From Nicaragua he went to Mexico, where he held office as an alcalde mayor, and in 1660 he was appointed to the governorship of New Mexico.

His chief aim as head of the provincial government was personal profit and gain, and in pursuing this end he did not hesitate to employ fraud or misuse the authority of his office. He took advantage of his position as judge of residencia to acquire a large amount of property belonging to López, and when he learned that the latter was about to be arrested on orders from the Holy Office, he seized more of his belongings. Father Posada, as agent of the Holy Office, demanded return of López's property, but Peñalosa refused to comply and hurriedly sent off a large part of it for sale in Parral. The prelate acted with dispatch and had the goods embargoed at Parral before they could be sold. This action aroused Peñalosa to bitter anger and hostility against the prelate, which resulted in strained relations during the spring and summer of 1663. In the autumn the situation was aggravated by the fact that Peñalosa gave orders for the seizure of a colonist who had taken refuge in ecclesiastical sanctuary. Posada made repeated demands for the return of the prisoner, and was ready to impose excommunication if the governor failed to comply. Peñalosa now resorted to violent measures, arrested the prelate, and prepared to expel him from the province. But he finally backed down and negotiated a peaceful settlement of the issue.

During these hectic months he had also aroused considerable resentment in other ways. He made extravagant statements concerning the nature and extent of his authority as governor, and allegedly made scurrilous remarks about the prelate and the tribunal of the Holy Office. Friar and colonist alike were scandalized by a certain levity which characterized his conversation on religious topics, by his coarseness of speech, and the brazen manner in which he flaunted certain phases of his personal conduct. Realizing that his position had become untenable and desirous of disposing of such property of López as still remained in his hands, he left for New Spain early in 1664, before his successor arrived.

Reports of Peñalosa's activities had already reached the Holy Office, and these were supplemented by a mass of testimony later submitted by Father Posada. An order for Peñalosa's arrest was issued by the Inquisition on June 16, 1665, and the next day he entered the jail of the tribunal. His property was placed under embargo, and detailed inventories were made of the furniture, clothing, arms, and other personal effects found in his residence in Mexico City. The lists include many books on a wide range of subjects. Although some of these may have been purchased after his return to Mexico City, it may be assumed that he had many of them with him in New Mexico. Some of the volumes had formerly belonged to López de Mendizábal, and the list probably contained others that he had taken on various occasions when he seized López's property. In any case he had a larger library than López. In addition to the property listed in the inventories, he made a statement concerning things which he had given as security to various persons in Mexico City. One item says that a certain Diego de Rojas held "many books and other things."

Like López and his wife, Peñalosa had in his possession a fairly large number of strictly devotional works, some of which he undoubtedly had taken from them, but the remainder of his library was more varied and extensive. The collection includes moral and political philosophy and satire, a miscellaneous collection of historical works, some books on theology and law, a treatise on horsemanship, Nebrija's grammar and vocabulary, an *Estilo de cartas*, an *Arte poética*, and Gracián's treatise on rhetoric, plus one pastoral and one picaresque novel and a volume of comedias.

The lists indicate an especially strong interest in politico-moral philosophy. We have already mentioned the possibility that his copy of Saavedra Fajardo's *Empresas políticas*, which was dedicated to Prince Baltasar Carlos and dealt with the education and obligations of a prince, had originally belonged to López de Mendizábal. Whether it was acquired in this way or in more legitimate fashion, it fits in with one of the largest single sections of Peñalosa's library. He owned almost all of the works of the Aragonese Jesuit Father

Baltasar Gracián, including the *Héroe*, the *Discreto*, the *Oráculo manual y arte de prudencia*, the *Político*, and his masterpiece, the *Criticón*, all of which exalt the virtues of the outstanding individual at the expense of the common herd. The cruel satire of Francisco de Quevedo, two of whose books are listed, is also impregnated with scorn of the vulgar. Less important works belonging to the same general category are Alonso Núñez de Castro's *Séneca impugnado de Séneca* and Antonio López de Vega's *Heráclito y Demócrito de nuestro siglo*, which is in the form of dialogues between a courtier and a philosopher. One of the two books by Juan de Zabaleta, *El día de fiesta*, consists of satirical sketches of life in Madrid, and his *Errores celebrados* contains maxims, witty sayings, etc. There is also a translation from the Italian called *Letras humanas*.

The historical works he owned fall into two groups. His career as a public official in the Indies explains his ownership of such items as Juan de Torquemada's *Monarquía Indiana*, Bernardo de Vargas Machuca's *Milicia Indiana*, and less general works such as a chronicle of Mechoacán and Gaspar de Villagrá's *Historia de la Nueva México*. In addition to these, he had a volume called *Viaje del infante cardenal don Fernando de Austria* by Diego de Aedo y Gallart and a translation of Count Mayolino Bisaccioni's *Guerre civile d'Inghilterra*. Apparently he was much interested in the latter, for it was among the books he asked for while he was a prisoner in the jail of the Holy Office, describing it as "the imprisonment and death of the King of England at the hands of the Parliament." Perhaps he was vain enough to draw some comparison with his own situation.

Both Peñalosa and López dabbled in literary composition. Most of it, according to the documentary sources, was in the form of poetical satire against the clergy. Unfortunately, none of these efforts are preserved in the records of their trials, and there is no way of judging how talented they were in this direction, but we may assume that Peñalosa made use of his treatises on poetry and rhetoric and similar works.

Apparently Peñalosa had done enough reading on ecclesiastical subjects and canon law to feel that he was qualified to argue with the local clergy on points of doctrine and ceremonial, as well as to insist upon having his own way in matters involving civil and ecclesiastical jurisdiction. He aroused great resentment on both counts. In a petition to Peñalosa's successor, Governor Juan Durán de Miranda, Father Posada said that the former governor's procedure could not be excused on the ground of ignorance since he had acquired sufficient knowledge and experience in judicial posts of responsibility to know better. Another indignant friar, Bernardo López de

Cobarrubias, testifying against Peñalosa at the convent of Santo Domingo in January 1664, spoke his mind in no uncertain fashion:

> Item, the declarant asks this Holy Tribunal to take from the said Don Diego de Peñalosa all the books he has, both moral and expositive, because he is too much inclined to censure the priest's manner of saying the mass, whether it is good or bad, and whether he performs the ceremonies well or badly. . . . And let him be asked how he understands matters of morality having to do with cases of conscience, because he sets himself up as a synodalist desirous of examining the priests, his purpose being to mock and scoff at their persons and at what they know or do not know.

In another connection, with regard to some rather dubious documents found among Peñalosa's papers, the Inquisitors took pains to set him straight on the subject of forbidden reading:

> They also told him that he was not to read papers or books that did not carry the approval of the Holy Mother Church, the place where they were written or printed, the name of the printer or scribe, the author's name, and authorization..

From time to time during his imprisonment Peñalosa requested permission to have certain books. These petitions were usually unsuccessful, and it is possible that part of the reason lies in the foregoing. Shortly after he was admitted to the jail he asked for the *Horas del oficio de Nuestra Señora* and Saavedra Fajardo's *Empresas políticas*. This request was denied, and a little over a week later he tried again, asking for the *Sermons* of Manuel de Nájera, with no greater success. About a year later, in July 1666, a second request for the *Empresas* was ignored. In September 1667, no action was taken on a note to the tribunal in which he asked to be allowed to have the *Heráclito y Demócrito* and the "imprisonment and death of the King of England" already referred to, but about three months later the rather pathetic appeal for "a book to read" was finally granted and the tribunal said that he might have a "spiritual book."

The sentence of the court was pronounced on February 3, 1668. He was subjected to a heavy fine, perpetual ineligibility for military and political office, and banishment from New Spain and the West Indies. On the following day he took part in an *auto de fe* and made formal abjuration of his errors. Toward the end of the year he set sail from Veracruz, apparently for Spain, but several months later he turned up in England where he tried to obtain support for an attack on the Spanish Indies. Failing in his efforts, he moved on to Paris where he continued his intrigues against the Spanish Crown. He died in France in 1687.

In addition to books privately owned, the provincial governors had the use of volumes kept in the library or archive of the Casa Real in Santa Fe. By virtue of their office, the governors served as superior judges in civil and criminal cases affecting the secular jurisdiction, and it was necessary to have on hand legal and administrative treatises for reference in the conduct of judicial business. As already noted, some of the works cited by Vidania in his defense of Rosas may have been in the archive of the Casa Real. In 1663, during the dispute over violation of ecclesiastical sanctuary, Peñalosa wrote a letter to Father Posada in which he cited various authorities. One was the *Summa Sylvestrina* of Silvestro Mazzolini, also cited by Vidania in 1640. In his testimony before the Holy Office, Peñalosa also mentioned Hevia Bolaños's *Curia philipica*, Solórzano Pereira's *Política Indiana*, and a treatise on procedure by Gabriel de Monterroso y Alvarado, all of which had apparently been at his disposal in Santa Fe.[25]

The documentary sources at present available record few references to books owned by soldiers and colonists. The lists of personal effects of members of the Oñate expedition reveal that Captain Alonso de Quesada had "seven books on secular and religious subjects," and that Juan del Caso Baraona, an enlisted soldier, owned "five medical books by recognized authorities."[26] A document of 1636, giving an inventory of the property of a certain Francisco Gómez de Torres, deceased, lists a "volume of devotional papers."[27] Francisco de Anaya Almazán, who served as secretary of government and war for several governors, was the owner of a copy of the *Curia philipica*.[28] Such, in brief, is the record for the period prior to 1660.

In 1662, four New Mexico soldiers—Cristóbal de Anaya Almazán (son of Francisco), Diego Romero, Nicolás de Aguilar, and Francisco Gómez Robledo—were arrested by the commissary of the Holy Office and sent to Mexico City for trial.[29] The lists of personal effects in their possession at the time of their entry into the jail of the Inquisition show that the first three had one or more books. As might be expected, they were all of religious character, such as catechisms and books of prayers and devotions. It is interesting to note that Nicolás de Aguilar, who had three books, including a copy of the

Gospels, later told the Inquisitors "that he could not read or write, that only now was he learning his letters."[30]

The trial proceedings indicate that in some circles in New Mexico there had been considerable debate on doctrinal matters, especially with regard to the spiritual relationship contracted by the priest, the baptized, and the sponsors as a result of the sacrament of baptism. The principal charge against Anaya was that he had denied the teachings of the Church on this point, and both Romero and Gómez were accused of similar views, although the major charges against them were of another character. In testimony before the tribunal both Anaya and Romero admitted that they had expressed erroneous views concerning spiritual relationships but alleged that their ideas had been derived from certain books (authors and titles not given). Romero, for example, told the court that he had had no deliberate intention of opposing the teachings of the Church but had "misunderstood" what he had read on the subject. His excuse probably had some validity, for according to his own testimony "he could read and write but very little and badly."[31] But the Inquisitors had little patience with these excuses, as is evidenced in their denunciation of Anaya for "going about on his own authority, introducing himself as a learned doctor, and engaging in disputes on matters that were not for him to decide."[32] The sentence of the court in Anaya's case called for public abjuration of his errors before his fellow citizens in New Mexico. Romero, who was found guilty on other charges as well as the one discussed above, was banished from the province.

Despite the punishment meted out to these offenders, the colonists continued to engage in dispute on doctrinal matters and to read theological books which they were ill prepared to interpret or understand. In 1669 Fray Juan Bernal, commissary of the Holy Office, wrote to the Inquisitors as follows:

> I consider it an extremely undesirable thing that certain laymen of this kingdom should have in their houses *Summas de Theologia Moral*, because they do not understand what they read in the Summas or grasp the meaning as they should because of the manner in which the summarists express it by question and interrogatory, which these readers take for affirmation. . . . Fray Diego Parraga has told me that it was a shame that certain secular persons of this province had Summas, because, being ignorant people, they wanted to be taken for men of knowledge, learned and well read, saying in their ignorance things offensive to pious ears, which they justify by the Summas, and the reason is that they do not understand them.[33]

The interest in theological questions, illustrated by these remarks and by the proceedings against Anaya and Romero, is not surprising. New Mexico was a mission province, in which the conversion and indoctrination of the Indians was supposed to be the most important objective of governmental policy and administration, and it was inevitable that religious matters should have formed an important topic of discussion in all circles. The friars, inspired by zeal to teach the Indians and give them an understanding of basic religious truths and dogmas, naturally kept a watchful eye on the colonists, and challenged ideas and practices that might undermine the loyalty of the Indians to the new ways. Conscious of the supreme importance of their mission, they were also quick to defend the privileges and immunities of ecclesiastical status and the jurisdictional authority of the Church. On the other hand, the missionary program frequently ran counter to the interests of the governors and colonists, giving rise to the unseemly disputes and controversies which characterized the history of the province during this period. Thus it was unavoidable that the colonists should display considerable interest in all manner of religious questions. Not content to accept the pronouncements of the friars on such subjects, they tried to form their own judgments on the basis of such books and tracts as were available. Unfortunately, they lacked the specialized training and education necessary for the proper interpretation of the books they read.

Bernal's remarks, quoted above, constitute an interesting commentary on the general situation in New Mexico, but they have even wider significance as an indication of the kind of books regarded as especially dangerous by the tribunal of the Holy Office. The Inquisitors, charged with the duty of keeping watch over books that circulated in the colonies, were chiefly concerned about works of a doctrinal character which might be misconstrued by the unlearned and inspire unorthodox views. In denouncing the misuse of the *Summas de theologia* in New Mexico, Bernal gave expression to this basic attitude toward books and their readers, a point which is also illustrated by the nature of the books doña Teresa de Aguilera gave up when the edict against prohibited reading was published in Santa Fe in 1662.

Notes

This essay originally appeared as "Books in New Mexico, 1598–1680," *New Mexico Historical Review* 17 (July 1942): 226–70. © 1942 by the Historical Society of New Mexico and the University of New Mexico Board of Regents. All rights reserved. Reprinted by permission. Minor stylistic changes have been made to the essay for the current publication, and, where possible, full names and other identifying information for the writers and works mentioned in the essay have been added for the convenience of present-day readers.

1. Francisco Rodríguez Marín, *El "Quijote" y Don Quijote en América* (Madrid: Librería Hernando, 1911); Francisco Fernández del Castillo, ed., *Libros y libreros en el siglo XVI* (Mexico City: Archivo General de la Nación, 1914); Edmundo O'Gorman, ed., "Bibliotecas y librerías coloniales, 1585–1694," *Boletín del Archivo General de la Nación* 10 (1939): 661–1006; Irving A. Leonard, *Romances of Chivalry in the Spanish Indies with Some* Registros *of Shipments of Books to the Spanish Colonies* (Berkeley: University of California Press, 1933); Irving A. Leonard, "A Shipment of 'Comedias' to the Indies," *Hispanic Review* 2:1 (1934): 39–50; Irving A. Leonard, "Notes on Lope de Vega's Works in the Spanish Indies," *Hispanic Review* 6:4 (1938): 277–93; Irving A. Leonard, "Don Quijote and the Book Trade in Lima, 1606," *Hispanic Review* 8:4 (1940): 285–304; Irving A. Leonard, "Los libros en el inventario de bienes de don Pedro de Peralta de Barnuevo," *Boletín Bibliográfico . . . de la Universidad Mayor de San Marcos de Lima* 14 (1941): 1–7; Irving A. Leonard, "Best Sellers of the Lima Book Trade, 1588," *Hispanic American Historical Review* 22 (1942): 5–33; Otis H. Green and Irving A. Leonard, "On the Mexican Booktrade in 1600: A Chapter in Cultural History," *Hispanic Review* 9 (1941): 1–40; and José Torre Revello, *El libro, la imprenta y el periodismo en América durante la dominación española* (Buenos Aires: J. Peuser, 1940).

2. [Note from the editor] I have removed a short paragraph, immediately following, in which the authors discuss the appendix included at the end of their article. Upon the advice of external reviewers, the appendix is not reproduced here. I urge the interested reader to consult the original *New Mexico Historical Review* publication for details. Throughout this chapter, I have also removed from the text all references to the catalog of books in the appendix.

3. The record of Benavides's investigation is found in Archivo General de la Nación, Mexico City (cited hereafter as AGM), Inquisición, vol. 356. For a secondary account of the investigation and the causes which prompted it, see France V. Scholes, "The First Decade of the Inquisition in New Mexico," *New Mexico Historical Review* 10 (1935): 195–241; and France V. Scholes, *Church and State in New Mexico, 1610–1650* (Albuquerque: University of New Mexico Press, 1937), chapter 3.

4. Vidania's opinions and letters are found in AGM, Inquisición, vol. 595. For an extensive account of Rosas's controversy with the friars, see Scholes, *Church and State*, chapters 5, 6.

5. Fray Bartolomé Romero to the commissary general of New Spain, October 4, 1641. Archivo General de Indias, Seville (cited hereafter as AGI), Patronato, leg. 244, exp. 7.

6. Porphyry's *Isagoge*, or *Introduction to the Categories of Aristotle*, was translated into Latin by Boethius and had great influence upon the development of scholasticism. Among the works of Father Pedro de Fonseca, a famous Portuguese Jesuit theologian of the sixteenth century, whose philosophical writings were widely

disseminated and reached many editions, is a treatise called *In Isagogem Porphyrii*. Domingo de Soto also wrote a treatise *In Porphyrii Isagogen Aristotelis* (Venice, 1552).

7. Possibly Father Gregorio de Valencia, a prominent Jesuit theologian of the second half of the sixteenth century. He was sent to Germany to teach theology and to work against the influence of Martin Luther, and later summoned to Rome by Pope Clement VIII. He died in Naples in 1603. He was the author of both controversial and scholastic works.

8. Probably Diego Covarrubias y Leiva (1512–1577), the eminent Spanish theologian and jurist, professor of canon law and author of books on a wide range of subjects.

9. AGI, Patronato, leg. 244, exp. 7.

10. AGM, Inquisición, vol. 629, exp. 2.

11. This petition, dated July 1660, is found in AGM, Papeles de Bienes Nacionales, leg. 1214, exp. 6.

12. AGM, Inquisición, vol. 507.

13. AGM, Inquisición, vols. 507, 587.

14. AGI, Guadalajara, leg. 139. Passage translated in J. M. Espinosa, *First Expedition of Vargas into New Mexico, 1692* (Albuquerque: University of New Mexico Press, 1940), 199–203.

15. "Relación verdadera q. el pe predicador fr. Fran.co Perez guerta de to, orden de S.t fran.co guardian del convento de galisteo hiço al R.mo Comiss. Gen.¹ de la dha. orden de la nueba esp.a" 1617? AGM, Inquisición, vol. 316.

16. AGM, Inquisición, vol. 595.

17. See Scholes, *Church and State*, chapter 2.

18. Ibid., chapter 3.

19. AGM, Inquisición, vol. 356.

20. AGM, Tierras, vol. 3286.

21. For a lengthy account of the administrations of López de Mendizábal and Peñalosa, see France V. Scholes, *Troublous Times in New Mexico, 1659–1670* (Albuquerque: University of New Mexico Press, 1942), chapters 2–10.

22. Record of the property embargoed to satisfy Manso's claims appears in AGM, Tierras, vols. 8268, 3286.

23. The lists of goods, including books, embargoed by Posada after the arrest of López and his wife appear in AGM, Tierras, vol. 3283.

24. The trial proceedings of López are found in AGM, Inquisición, vols. 587, 593, and 594; the *proceso* against doña Teresa is in vol. 596.

25. AGM, Inquisición, vol. 507.

26. AGI, Mexico City, leg. 25. Apparently Juan del Caso had more than an ordinary layman's interest in medicine, for he also had various kinds of medications and a few surgical instruments. He may have been a barber-surgeon.

27. Biblioteca Nacional, Mexico City, leg. 1, doc. 8.

28. Trial proceedings in the case of Cristóbal de Anaya Almazán, AGM, Inquisición, vol. 586.

29. See Scholes, *Troublous Times*, chapter 8.

30. AGM, Inquisición, vol. 512.

31. AGM, Inquisición, vol. 586.

32. Scholes, *Troublous Times*, 190.

33. AGM, Inquisición, vol. 588, exp. 8.

Contributors

Adams, Eleanor B. Initially trained as a literary scholar, Eleanor B. Adams is recognized for her historical studies, many of them written in conjunction with France V. Scholes and other scholars. An expert paleographer, Ms. Adams often contributed transcriptions and translations for other researchers. She was the author of numerous academic articles and of *A Bio-Bibliography of Franciscan Authors in Colonial Central America* (1953). Ms. Adams died in 1996.

Chávez, Helen Fabela. Born in Brawley, California, Helen Fabela began working in the fields at the age of seven in the Imperial Valley, and later in the San Joaquin Valley. At age fifteen, when her father died, she quit high school to work at a grocery store and then full-time in the fields to support her mother and six siblings. In 1948, after a three-year courtship that included jitterbug dancing, she married César E. Chávez and raised their eight children. She supported her husband in many ways in his organizing efforts in the Community Service Organization (CSO) and while he was cofounding the National Farm Workers Association (NFWA). In addition to her acts of civil disobedience, for which she was arrested, less publicized were her daily handwritten CSO reports and her teaching literacy to migrant workers during voter registration drives. Although reluctant at first, she managed the United Farm Workers (UFW) Credit Union for more than twenty years, which offered a rare opportunity for farm workers to finance a better quality of life.

Cortés, Alma Ester. Alma Cortés grew up in Austin, Texas. She moved to New Brunswick, New Jersey, to attend Rutgers University. Alma also lived briefly in New York while she finished her master's degree in early childhood education at Bank Street College of Education. In June 2006, Alma moved to Los Angeles, where she currently resides. She is the director of an infant/ toddler development center on the UCLA campus. Alma is also a lecturer for the UCLA Applied Developmental Program (ADP), a psychology minor at UCLA.

Cota-Cárdenas, Margarita. Born eight miles north of the Mexicali/Calexico border in California, Margarita Cota-Cárdenas's family was of Mexican origin, and her first language was Spanish. They moved to the San Joaquin Valley in central California to work in agriculture. She finished elementary and high school in Newman, California. Margarita began writing in English in high school, and she continued throughout her college years. She has lived in Arizona since 1970, when she moved to Tucson with her two young children. She became involved in Chicano community issues and literature while studying for her PhD at the University of Arizona. While taking a Chicano literature class taught by the poet and author Miguel Mendez, she was inspired to begin to write about her own family's history. In 1975, the police shooting of a young Chicano under questionable circumstances was the catalyst for Margarita, outraged, to write a short story about the incident. This was the beginning of her first novel, *Puppet*, which is written mostly in Spanish. In 1976, while at the University of Arizona, she also was cofounder and editor with Eliana Rivero of Scorpion Press. This pioneer Chicana feminist press published the anthology *Siete Poetas* in 1978. Margarita is the author of *Noches despertando in conciencias* (Tucson: Scorpion Press, 1977); *Puppet* (Austin: Relámpago Press, 1985); *Marchitas de Mayo: Sones pa'l Pueblo* (Austin: Relámpago Press, 1989), *Sanctuaries of the Heart/Santuarios del corazon* (Tucson: University of Arizona Press, 2005), and *La gente de los girasoles* (Merced, CA: AlternaCtive PublicaCtions, 2010) among other publications. Margarita taught Mexican and Chicano literature and culture at Arizona State University from 1981 to 2002, when she retired as professor emerita. She is still writing poetry and novels about Chicano/Chicana reality. She says, "My stuff is not for the faint of heart; so check it out!"

Cumpián, Carlos J. Shortly after his first birthday, Carlos J. Cumpián's Korean War–veteran father moved the family from San Antonio, Texas, to Sacramento, California. When Cumpián was four, his family moved to rural San Jose, California, where his mom taught him to read. Back in Texas by age seven, Cumpián, his three sisters, three brothers, and parents lived with his Tejano maternal grandparents in Carrizo Springs, with his paternal grandparents in Crystal City, and then in their own home in the lower Rio Grande valley city of Harlingen. After the area experienced an economic slump, his family moved back to San Antonio. Soon, Carlos's father found better employment opportunities in Chicago, where he resettled the family. Since his late teens, Carlos has lived in Chicago, with the exception of a brief residence in Carbondale, Illinois. Never forgetting his roots, he has made nearly annual visits to his *tierra natal.* Cumpián has been an educator in language arts for Chicago high school students for fifteen years. He has served as adjunct professor for Columbia College and the University of Illinois at Chicago. Aside from formal classroom service, he instructs youth and adults in creative writing and poetry workshops in various venues across the Midwest. Cumpián is married to Chicago poet and professional editor Cynthia Gallaher-Cumpián. He is the author of *Coyote Sun, Latino Rainbow, Armadillo Charm,* and *14 Abriles: Poems.*

Daniel, Minerva. A proud farm worker's daughter from the Central Valley of California, Minerva Daniel enjoys weaving in details of life experiences into her writing. Minerva is a former contributor to the *Modesto Bee* Community Writer's Group.

De la Cruz, Vito. Both Yaqui and Chicano, Vito de la Cruz is a graduate of Yale University and the University of California Boalt Hall School of Law. Vito grew up in the lower Rio Grande valley in a migrant farm worker family and has lived in Texas, Connecticut, Massachusetts, California, Nevada, and Washington. Presently, Vito practices law with Tamaki Law in Yakima, Washington, focusing on representing injured people. De la Cruz has been a guest columnist for the *Reno Gazette Journal, Ahora* (Reno's Spanish-language newspaper), the *Huffington Post,* and *Red, Brown, and Blue.*

Díaz, Cuauhtémoc B. A native of Tangamandapio, Michoacán, Mexico, Cuauhtémoc Díaz has lived in various parts of Mexico and the United States. When he was eleven years old, he left Mexico to join his older sister, who was living in the San Fernando Valley, California, at the time. He later returned to Mexico to finish his elementary and middle school education. Later, Cuauhtémoc moved to Kansas City, Missouri, where he lived with his godfather for a year. Díaz graduated from the Universidad del Valle de Atemajac

(UNIVA) in Guadalajara, Mexico. He obtained a bachelor's degree in journalism (communications). Cuauhtémoc returned to the United States after he graduated and lived and worked in Manteca, California; Longmont, Colorado; the San Fernando Valley; and Merced, California, where he has lived now for more than twenty years. When he lived in the San Fernando Valley, he worked for the American Cancer Society and was one of the first persons from the San Fernando Valley Chapter to get certified as a medical interpreter. Upon moving to Merced, Cuauhtémoc worked for the Merced City School District through the Bilingual Community Liaison program. Cuauhtémoc has always been an active member of the community and was a founder of the 3 Peques Tour Company, which provided assistance to families who lived in the Merced area and traveled to Mexico to visit their families each year. He now owns and runs a family business in Merced and continues to volunteer as an interpreter and translator for the community. Cuauhtémoc is a cancer survivor and is happily married, with three sons and four grandchildren.

Flores, Argelia. Argelia was raised in Seville, a small rural community in Tulare County in California's San Joaquin Valley. Her parents raised nine children on their earnings as farm workers. During the summer and on weekends, once old enough to help, the children also worked in the fields. Argelia and her siblings were always encouraged by their parents to study and do well in school. Although her father and mother were only able themselves to complete second and sixth grade, respectively, they understood and valued the opportunities an education would provide. Argelia obtained her bachelor of arts from the University of California, Santa Cruz, and has worked at various jobs. Her current responsibilities are as a health educator with the California Health Collaborative and as a program assistant with United Way of Tulare County. Reading is one of the best ways to explore, learn, and imagine; thankfully, Argelia can do this in two languages. Since 1992, Argelia has aimed to read a book a week.

Flores-Manges, Irma. Born in Laredo, Texas, on the border between Mexico and the United States, Irma Flores-Manges writes: "I lived in San Antonio until I was eight. My mom took me and my sister back to Laredo after our father died. We did not have much money but we had family. I was raised in a large extended family all living within a couple of blocks of each other. The support system in the family was phenomenal. I went to Catholic schools

Our Lady of Guadalupe and Ursuline Academy, graduating in 1971. I moved to Austin to go to the University of Texas, receiving a degree in anthropology in 1974. I got married and lived in Biloxi, Mississippi, for a year. I moved to Alamogordo, New Mexico, for five years, which was beautiful with all the mountains and desert. I loved living in New Mexico and I go back whenever I can because it is a special and enriching place for me. I went back to Austin, Texas, and received a degree in library science in 1983. I have been a librarian for the Austin Public Library for thirty years. I am the branch manager of the Cepeda Branch Library. I live in Austin with my mom, Andrea Flores, and son, Joshua Manges. I have two daughters, Kristina and Aisha Manges, and four grandchildren, Aryanna, Christopher, Christian, and Israel Aparicio. Other important people in my life are my nieces, Sandra and Kendra Chavera, and my nephew, Ryan Lozano. My mom is the most influential woman in my life, always giving to everyone she knows and praying for everyone. I would not have become the woman I am today without her strong influence in my life. I owe everything to her. I love you Mom."

Flores-Paniagua, Veronica. A longtime journalist, Veronica Flores-Paniagua began her career in Brownsville, Texas, covering education for the *Brownsville Herald*. Most of her work has been in Texas, reporting for her hometown newspaper, the *Corpus Christi Caller-Times*, and also working as a reporter for the *San Antonio Light* and later the *San Antonio Express-News*, where she also was city editor and metro columnist. In Houston, Flores-Paniagua was an assistant national editor and city editor for the *Houston Chronicle*. Her career has taken her to Stanford University in California, where she was a John S. Knight Journalism Fellow, and Chicago, where she was a reporter for the *Chicago Sun-Times*. In 2011, Flores-Paniagua went to work for the nonprofit small-business lender, Accion Texas, as vice president of communications. She was called back to journalism in early 2013 and now is outlook editor for the *Houston Chronicle*. Flores-Paniagua received her bachelor's degree in journalism from the University of Houston.

Gutiérrez, Shonnon. In her own words, Shonnon Renae Gutiérrez is "a cup-half-full Chicana that sees the world with love and compassion." Born and raised in Los Angeles County, she continues to reside in southern California. Shonnon spent many years of her childhood living in the affluent Agoura Hills area, where her mother cleaned beautiful homes. At the age of thirteen, her family moved to Mexicali, Mexico, where she was later left behind to fend for herself for over a year. Having lived and thrived in various circumstances, including living in a single room with her parents and three siblings, on her own in a foreign county, as head of household at the age of fifteen, and as a single parent, Shonnon Gutiérrez is a survivor. An avid reader, Ms. Gutiérrez is self-educated and returned to formal education in the fall of 2013. She is a great storyteller and is working on documenting many of her childhood memories.

Hanna, Monica. Born in Los Angeles to parents from Mexico and Egypt, Monica Hanna was instilled with the importance of literacy and education from a young age. She completed an undergraduate degree in English at the University of California, Berkeley; during her time as an undergraduate she also spent a year studying in Bologna, Italy. After earning her BA, she taught high school in Houston for two years before completing her graduate course-work in New York. She earned her PhD in comparative literature from the Graduate Center of the City University of New York, where she studied the literatures of the Americas and Europe in English, Spanish, and Italian. She wrote "In the Stacks" during the process of writing her dissertation. She has taught at CUNY, Mount Holyoke College, and the U.S. Naval Academy. She is now an assistant professor of Chicana and Chicano studies at California State University, Fullerton, where she teaches literature and writing courses. Her research focuses on literary representations of national and transna-tional histories.

Hernandez-Jason, Beth. A PhD candidate in world cultures at the University of California, Merced, Beth Hernandez-Jason is currently completing her dis-sertation on the work of John Rechy, situating his work within the literary traditions of U.S., GLBTQ, and Chicano literature by using a reader-response and reception theory approach. Her reviews have appeared in *MELUS*, *Az-tlán*, *Ventana Abierta*, and *Camino Real*, and her article comparing the work of María Amparo Ruiz de Burton with Harriet Beecher Stowe's *Uncle Tom's Cabin* recently appeared in the eighth volume of the Recovering the U.S. His-panic Literary Heritage series. Hernandez-Jason was born and raised in the San Joaquin Valley and lived most of her life in Fresno, California. She also attended school in Wales for two years, where she received an international baccalaureate, and then went to college in Newberg, Oregon. Her father is of Mexican American descent, and her mother is a Wisconsin native of French German heritage.

Kelson, Maria. Writing under her former name, María Meléndez, Maria Kelson has published three poetry titles: *How Long She'll Last in This World* and *Flexible Bones*, both with University of Arizona Press, and a chapbook, *Base Pairs*, with Swan Scythe Press. She is currently working on a mystery novel set in the redwood country of Humboldt County, California. She was born in Tucson, Arizona, and spent her childhood in the East Bay area of northern California. After graduating with a bachelor's degree from Colorado State University in Fort Collins, she lived with her husband and their family in Wyoming, South Carolina, Indiana, and Utah, with a five-year layover in Davis, California, where she received a master's degree in English and creative writing from the University of California, Davis. Her various professional positions have included English as a Second Language instructor, writer-in-residence at the UC Davis Arboretum, poet-teacher with California Poets in the Schools and Colorado Humanities' Writers in the Schools, creative writing faculty member and fellow with the Center for Women's Intercultural Leadership at Saint Mary's College in Notre Dame, Indiana, lecturer in creative writing and literature at Utah State University, editor of *Pilgrimage* magazine, and independent editorial consultant. Since 2009 she has lived in Pueblo, Colorado, where she teaches at Pueblo Community College. Her poetry collections have been finalists for the PEN Center USA Award, the National Latino Book Award, and the Colorado Book Award. Her essays have appeared in *Sojourns*, *Ms.* magazine, and elsewhere.

Macías, Anthony. An associate professor in the Department of Ethnic Studies at the University of California, Riverside, Anthony Macías is the author of the book *Mexican American Mojo: Popular Music, Dance, and Urban Culture in Los Angeles, 1935–1968*. He has published articles in *Boom: A Journal of California*, the *Jewish Role in American Life Annual Review*, the *Journal of African American History*, *Aztlán: A Journal of Chicano Studies*, and *American Quarterly*. His current research project analyzes the cultural politics of Chicanos and Chicanas, race, and representation in American cinema, television, and popular music vis-à-vis the U.S. national character, racial imaginary, and body politic. He has consulted for exhibits by Hollywood Bowl Museum, the California Ethnic and Multicultural Archives at the University of California, Santa Barbara, the Seattle Experience Music Project Museum, and the Japanese American National Museum. He was born and raised in Sacramento, California, received his BA in history from the University of

California, Berkeley, and also lived in Ann Arbor, where he received his MA and PhD in American Culture from the University of Michigan. Macías's work has taken him as far abroad as Mexico City, Costa Rica, the Netherlands, and Spain's Basque country.

Márquez, María Teresa. A professor emerita at the University of New Mexico University Libraries, María Teresa Márquez was responsible for the acquisition of materials for Chicano/Chicana studies and assisted scholars and students at the Center for Southwest Research with their research projects. Márquez earned degrees from the University of Texas at El Paso, California State University, Fullerton, the University of Illinois, and the University of New Mexico. Her literary interest is the Chicano/a mystery novel. She is originally from El Paso and now lives in Albuquerque, New Mexico.

Martín-Rodríguez, Manuel M. Born in Seville (Spain), where he obtained a Licenciatura en Filología Hispánica, Martín-Rodríguez relocated to the United States in 1985 to continue his studies and research on Chicano/a literature. His graduate education was completed with an MA from the University of Houston (1987) and a PhD from the University of California, Santa Barbara (1990). Martín-Rodríguez has lived in Connecticut, Michigan, and Wisconsin, in addition to Texas and California. At present, he is professor of literature at the University of California, Merced, where he is one of the founding faculty. He has published numerous articles in academic venues as well as the books *Rolando Hinojosa y su "cronicón" chicano: Una novela del lector* (1993), *La voz urgente: Antología de literatura chicana en español* (1995), *Life in Search of Readers: Reading (in) Chicano/a Literature* (2003), *Gaspar de Villagrá: Legista, soldado y poeta* (2009), and a scholarly edition of Gaspar de Villagrá's *Historia de la nueva Mexico* (2010).

Martínez, Eliud. A professor emeritus of creative writing and comparative literature at the University of California, Riverside, Eliud Martínez, PhD, is the author of the novel *Voice-Haunted Journey* (1990) and of the scholarly book *The Art of Mariano Azuela*. He is also the editor of *American Identities: California Stories of Multiple Ancestries* (2008). He has published other essays and short stories as well. Born in Pflugerville, Texas, and raised in Austin, he has lived and traveled in Mexico, the United States, France, Spain, Italy, Greece, Switzerland, Germany, and Holland. He has lived in Chicago, New York City, Buffalo, Athens, Ohio (where he did graduate work), and

Riverside, California, where he has resided since 1972. He is married to the former Elisse Natalie Weintraub of Buffalo and has two grown daughters, five grandchildren, and one grandchild on the way.

Meléndez, A. Gabriel. Professor and chair of the Department of American Studies at the University of New Mexico, A. Gabriel Meléndez grew up in the Mora valley, a largely Hispanic area of northern New Mexico. His family moved to Albuquerque in the early 1960s, and Meléndez attended public schools there and went on to do his university studies at the University of New Mexico. He holds a PhD in Latin American literature from the Department of Modern and Classical Languages (University of New Mexico, 1984). After obtaining his doctorate, Meléndez taught at the University of Utah in Salt Lake City and at Mills College in Oakland, California, prior to returning to Albuquerque to complete a Rockefeller Humanities Fellowship Residency at the University of New Mexico in 1991. He joined the faculty in American studies in 1994. A literary, social, and cultural critic, Meléndez has research interests in critical regionalism and cultural representation in Chicano-Latino film, autobiography, and ethnocritical theory. His first book, *So All Is Not Lost: The Poetics of Print in Nuevomexicano Communities, 1836–1958* (Albuquerque: University of New Mexico Press, 1997) was reprinted with the title *Spanish-Language Newspapers in New Mexico, 1836–1958* (Tucson: University of Arizona Press, 2005). He is the coeditor of *The Multicultural Southwest: A Reader* (Tucson: University of Arizona Press, 2001), *Recovering the U.S. Hispanic Literary Heritage*, vol. 6 (Houston, TX: Arte Público Press, 2006), and *Santa Fe Nativa: A Collection of Nuevomexicano Writing* (Albuquerque: University of New Mexico Press, 2010). His other works include *Reflexiones del Corazón* (Albuquerque: Tamarind Institute, 1993), a portfolio of images and texts produced with Miguel Gandert and María Baca for the Tamarind Institute; *The Biography of Casimiro Barela* (Albuquerque: University of New Mexico Press, 2003); and *The Writings of Eusebio Chacón* (Albuquerque: University of New Mexico Press, 2012). Professor Meléndez's most recent book, *Hidden Chicano Cinema: Film Dramas in the Borderlands* (New Brunswick, NJ: Rutgers University Press, 2013), presents a scholarly account of a series of film or "specular moments" in borderlands history that are replete with drama, intrigue, and the politics of cultural representations, elements that are as much the result of specific cinematic practices as they are of a set of sociocultural encounters peculiar to the Southwest. Also in 2013, Meléndez published *The Legend of Ponciano Gutiérrez and the Mountain*

Thieves (Albuquerque: University of New Mexico Press, 2013), an illustrated book for young readers. Meléndez is on the board of directors of the Recovering the U.S. Hispanic Literary Heritage project, serves on the editorial board of *Aztlán: A Journal of Chicano Studies*, and is a general editor for the Pasó por Aquí Series on the Nuevomexicano Literary Heritage at the University of New Mexico Press. He is also a contributing member to the National Digital Newspaper Program Advisory Committee based at the Zimmerman Library at the University of New Mexico.

Morton, Carlos. With billing in more than one hundred theatrical productions in the United States and abroad, Carlos Morton's professional credits include the San Francisco Mime Troupe, the New York Shakespeare Festival, the Denver Center Theatre, La Compañía Nacional de México, the Puerto Rican Traveling Theatre, and the Arizona Theatre Company. He is the author of *The Many Deaths of Danny Rosales and Other Plays* (1983), *Johnny Tenorio and Other Plays* (1992), *The Fickle Finger of Lady Death* (1996), *Rancho Hollywood y otras obras del teatro chicano* (1999), *Dreaming on a Sunday in the Alameda* (2004), and *Children of the Sun: Scenes for Latino Youth* (2008). A former Mina Shaughnessy scholar and Fulbright lecturer to Mexico and Poland, Morton holds an MFA in drama from the University of California, San Diego, and a PhD in theater from the University of Texas. Morton has lived on the border between Mexico and the United States since 1981, teaching at universities in Texas, California, and Mexico. He is married to the former Azalea Marin and has three sons: Seth, Miguel Angel, and Xuncu. He is professor of Theater and Dance at the University of California, Santa Barbara.

Ortega, Veronica. A visual artist in the Inland Empire, Califaztlan, Veronica Ortega (Hernández) promotes art and culture through local events and carries a Chicana-themed clothing line. Born in Glendale, Arizona, her family spoke English and Spanish. Veronica attended a Head Start program and skipped to the first grade. Moving to California, she attended three different schools in San Jose and later finished school in Perris, Riverside County. As a student, Veronica was inspired by the Movimiento Estudiantil Chicano de Aztlán (MEChA) and the Chicano Movement to pursue a college education. She earned a degree from the University of California, Riverside, in Chicano studies and sociology, being the first in her family to attend college. She has a background in cultural programming, having worked in UC Riverside's

Chicano student programs. She also serves as a mentor to students at Moreno Valley Puente and the North High School Law Academy. Veronica continues to be inspired by familia, artists, and activists, and by small moments in life.

Rodríguez, Ever. Born and raised in Mexico City, Ever Rodríguez has lived in California since the early 1990s. He writes prose and poetry, fiction and nonfiction. His education includes a BA in Spanish literature and an MA in library and information science. He is a writer and translator for San Francisco's oldest bilingual newspaper, *El Tecolote*, and he collaborates with other nonprofit and activist organizations in the San Francisco Bay area. He works with the Latin American collections at Stanford University Libraries.

Rodríguez, Lupe. Born in Monterrey, Nuevo León, Lupe Rodríguez moved to California at the age of two, where her parents had decided to try to provide a better future for her and her siblings. Lupe is the oldest of seven children, and she took on the role of a mother for her brothers and sisters while her parents worked in the fields. She also worked in the fields and packing houses during her summer vacations. Lupe attended elementary, middle, and high school in Orosi, California, and became an instructional aide for the Cutler-Orosi Unified School District after finishing high school. Lupe now lives in Dinuba, California, having retired two years ago. She occasionally fills in as a substitute teacher at the school district where she used to teach full-time, and she enjoys helping out at school events as a volunteer. Rodríguez was diagnosed with breast cancer in 2012 and has been through several surgeries; she is a cancer survivor. She enjoys watching Spanish and English soap operas, or novelas, and enjoys her free time with home decorating.

Sánchez, Shanti Alexandra. A native of Los Angeles, Shanti was twenty-four years old at the time of this writing. In her own words: "I come from a hardworking, yet loving family whose roots are from Mexico. Because my parents have taught me to value education, I have always strived to excel in my studies. From elementary to my second year of high school, I was in a private school. Unfortunately, my mother could no longer pay my tuition because my dad had suffered a stroke and could no longer help with household expenses. Hence, my mom had to assume all responsibilities of the home and family. I was transferred to a public school, where I learned of my potential as a Latina. I was not going to apply to the university, but my counselor, Alex

Paredes, convinced me. I was admitted to the University of California, Merced, in 2007, and I graduated with my bachelor of arts in psychology with a minor in Spanish in 2010. For a year, I worked with Hope Street Family Center, helping families and their children to combat the discrepancy of communication between them and the Los Angeles school district. There, I realized I could help my community more if I had a better education, therefore I went back to school. I am currently in my second year of the master's program in clinical counseling at the California School of Professional Psychology at Alliant International University, located in San Francisco. With a license in counseling, I hope to be able to help people with minimal resources to excel. My goal in life is to obtain a doctorate in social work and establish a program to help Latino families overcome the oppression that we live in today."

Scholes, France V. A professor of history at the University of New Mexico, the institution he joined in 1925 after his studies at Harvard University, France Vinton Scholes's professional service also included membership in the Division of Historical Research at the Carnegie Institution of Washington. An authority on the Franciscan missionaries, with extensive archival research experience, Scholes published numerous studies on colonial New Mexican history as well as on the Mayas from Yucatán and Guatemala. Scholes died in 1979 at the age of eighty-two.

Tafolla, Carmen. The first poet laureate of the city of San Antonio, Carmen Tafolla was born and raised on the west-side barrios of that city. Tafolla holds three degrees (BA, MA, and PhD) from the University of Texas at Austin. She has taught at a number of institutions throughout the Southwest and was director of the Mexican American Studies Center at Texas Lutheran College. Tafolla has published five books of poetry, eight children's picture books, seven television screenplays, one nonfiction volume, and a collection of short stories. She has received numerous awards, including the Tomás Rivera Mexican American Children's Book Award in 2010 for *What Can You Do with a Paleta?*

Valero, Carolina. Born in Visalia, California, Carolina Valero was raised in Guadalajara, Jalisco, Mexico. She lived in Mexico for seven years, and, at the age of twelve, she returned to the United States with her father and two brothers to live in Dinuba, California. In 2005, Carolina enrolled in the

University of California, Merced, where she graduated with a bachelor's degree in literature and cultures. In 2009, Carolina returned to Dinuba and began instructing Zumba fitness at local gymnasiums and health clubs. She is also part of the Cinco de Mayo Pageant Committee in Dinuba, where she volunteers her time helping young ladies in the community by guiding them to obtain a higher education and succeed in life. Carolina now resides in Fresno and is planning to apply for graduate school for the fall of 2014.

Vázquez, Fernando. Born in Los Angeles in 1944, Fernando was raised on a cattle ranch near Visalia, California, in the southern San Joaquin Valley, where he graduated from Fresno State College after serving as an infantry officer in the U.S. Army. He later attended the University of California, Berkeley, on an NIMH Fellowship in social psychology. During this period he also participated in *charreadas, jineteando yeguas y toros,* and riding bulls and broncs in college rodeo competitions. Fernando directed a bilingual education program in a suburb of Denver and rode with the local charros, performing *el paso de la muerte.* After returning home and serving as an administrator for the Department of Corrections, he was appointed to the Board of Prison Terms as a deputy commissioner; this duty culminated in retirement after thirty-two years of service to the State of California. During this time, he also rode in the Rose Parade for six years with the charros. His children now grown to adulthood, Fernando trains horses and riders for competitive mounted shooting, including assisting police mounted units in acclimating their horses to gunfire.

Vázquez, Lucía D. Growing up in the small central valley town of Goshen, California, located on Highway 99, Lucía Vázquez was exposed at a young age to the farm worker movement, in which her family was very active. During her youth, she spent many summer days in supermarket parking lots explaining the grape boycott. Ms. Vázquez is passionate about reading and has organized several projects to promote reading, including Latina book clubs, to increase the number of quality Latina books available in school libraries. She received her MA from the University of California, Merced. Her thesis, "Chicas' Lit: Today's Young Adult Latina Literature" (2009), is a thorough analysis of that expanding body of literature. She serves as a trustee on the Visalia Unified School District Board of Education (2011–2015). Currently, Ms. Vázquez works as a community organizer in a small Kern County community for the Dolores Huerta Foundation.

Index

Because they are already catalogued there, this index contains no references to books in the private libraries analyzed in the last three chapters.